FABLES of the NOVEL

FABLES of the NOVEL
FRENCH FICTION SINCE 1990

Warren Motte

DALKEY ARCHIVE PRESS

Portions of this book have appeared in earlier form in the *French Review, Neophilologus, Studies in Twentieth Century Literature, World Literature Today,* and *A French Forum: Mélanges de littérature française offerts à Raymond C. et Virginia A. La Charité.* I thank the editors for permission to use that material here. All translations are mine, unless otherwise noted. I have sought advice—and upon occasion solace—from many friends and colleagues. Among them, I would especially like to thank Jean Alter and Gerald Prince.

Cover art copyright © 1999 by Andrzej Michael Karwacki at 1217studios.com

Library of Congress Cataloging-in-Publication Data:

Motte, Warren F.
    Fables of the novel : French fiction since 1990 / Warren Motte.— 1. ed.
        p. cm.
    ISBN 1-56478-284-0 (cloth : alk. paper) — ISBN 1-56478-283-2 (paper : alk. paper)
    1. French fiction—20th century—History and criticism. I. Title.

PQ671 .M66 2003
843'.91409—dc21

                                                                        2002073507

Partially funded by a grant from the Illinois Arts Council, a state agency.

Dalkey Archive Press books are published by the Center for Book Culture, a nonprofit organization with offices in Chicago and Normal, Illinois.

www.centerforbookculture.org

Printed on permanent/durable acid-free paper and bound in the United States of America.

For Nicholas and Nathaniel Motte

CONTENTS

Introduction

Readers familiar with the contemporary novel in France are currently witnessing, I believe, the most astonishing reinvigoration of French narrative prose since the "new novel" of the 1950s. In the last few years, bold, innovative, and richly compelling models of the novel as literary form have been proposed by a variety of young writers. Those models severely question—and in some cases eschew outright—traditional strategies of character, plot, theme, and message. The term "postexotic" has been used to describe some of this work, for a common denominator seems to be the rejection of the exceptional and the extraordinary in favor of a focus on the ordinary and on the banality of everyday life. The protagonists of these novels are for the most part diffident creatures, recumbent and essentially passive folk who grapple unequally with the vexations that quotidian existence imposes upon them. Narrative style has been flattened, as if these authors wished to suggest that in the novel (like in everyday life, as opposed to "history"), it is difficult to assign pertinence to any given event. The role of the reader has shifted, too, in significant ways, for these new novels demand new strategies of reading and interpretation. In short, what has come about is a significant recasting of the French novel's horizon of possibility.

Allow me to be clear about the *kind* of novel that concerns me here. I confess that I am not particularly interested in mainstream fiction, though I read a great deal of it in both dimensions of my readerly life, that is to say, both as a professional reader and as a general, or amateur reader. Let's name some names, just by way of example. Writers such as Michel Host, Patrick Grainville, Didier Decoin, Lucien Bodard, Frédérique Tristan, Dominique Fernandez,

Yves Navarre, Yann Queffélec, Jean Vautrin, Eric Orsenna, Pierre Combescot, Pascale Roze, and Didier van Cauwelaert are all accomplished, worthy novelists; nevertheless I find their works too bland, like eating fried eggs without salt. There is no accounting for taste, of course; and I am willing to believe that my own taste is idiosyncratic and laden with quirks of various sorts. Yet it is not merely a matter of taste. The figures I mentioned are also, every one, Prix Goncourt laureates—and I admit that that is why I mentioned them, rather than many others one might think of. It seems clear to me that the literary *mundillo* in France generally recognizes and supports novels that are "safe," novels that uphold received convention, rather than questioning or (still less) subverting it. That is not to say that no "risky" writing is ever recognized in an institutional manner. One thinks for instance of the Goncourts awarded to Marguerite Duras for *L'Amant (The Lover)* and to Jean Echenoz for *Je m'en vais (I'm Gone).* But when such an event does occur, one may perhaps be excused for inferring that the champagne ran a bit too freely during the deliberation luncheon.

For my part, I am interested in the avant-garde because I am firmly persuaded that the avant-garde is where the novel as a literary form changes shape and moves along in new directions. Of course, the avant-garde continually remakes itself, too. In the 1960s, the novelistic avant-garde was fierce, deliberately radical, and, to many readers, forbidding. Think, for instance, of Marc Saporta's *Composition no. 1,* the novel whose pages came unbound and were to be shuffled like a deck of cards before each reading; or Maurice Roche's *Compact / Circus / Codex* trilogy; or the works of Pierre Guyotat and Jean-Pierre Faye; or even the early novels of Philippe Sollers, before he became such a drone. In the last twenty years or so, however, the novelistic avant-garde has assumed yet a new shape. It has become what might be called the avant-garde with a human face, an avant-garde that seems to welcome its readers with open arms, while still insisting on innovation. I believe that this new current was inaugurated in the novels of Raymond Queneau, and confirmed in those of Georges Perec. Clearly and demonstrably experimentalist in character, relying on systems of formal constraint that are in some cases impossibly arcane, those texts are nonetheless novels that can also be read luxuriously, "flat out on one's bed," as Perec himself put it (*Penser / Classer* [Think/Classify] 10).

From roughly 1980 onward, novels displaying both a mixture of experimentalist features and a high degree of narrativity[1] began to appear in
greater numbers. As was the case in the 1950s with the "new novel," the Editions de Minuit positioned itself in the thick of this trend, promoting innovative fiction tirelessly and with considerable editorial courage. Minuit offered a
home to a variety of young writers who launched their careers in the 1980s,
people like Marie Redonnet, Jean-Philippe Toussaint, Jean Echenoz, Eric
Chevillard, Christian Gailly, Eugène Savitzkaya, Marie NDiaye, François Bon,
Antoine Volodine, Annie Zadek, Bernard-Marie Koltès, Jeanne Hyvrard,
Christian Oster, and Patrick Deville. And indeed yet another generation of
innovative Minuit writers appeared in the 1990s, figures such as Hélène Lenoir,
Jacques Serena, Emmanuel Adely, Philippe Raulet, Isabelle Lévesque, Jean-
Michel Béquié, Eric Laurrent, Yann Apperry, Yves Ravey, Caroline Lamarche,
and Jean-Pierre Chanod, all of whom seem poised to lay claims for distinction
in the novelistic avant-garde. Other publishing houses have offered shelter
and succor to experimentalists, too, most notably perhaps POL, whose cata-
logue includes Danielle Mémoire, Emmanuelle Bayamack-Tam, Marie
Darrieussecq, Emmanuel Carrère, Eric Villeneuve, Iegor Gran, and Marc Le
Bot. Lydie Salvayre, Marie Desbiolles, and Patrick Roegiers have been associated with Le Seuil; Annie Ernaux, Emmanuèle Bernheim, and François-
Xavier Molia with Gallimard[2]; Linda Lê with Christian Bourgois; Olivier
Targowla with Maurice Nadeau; and still other avant-gardists such as Jacques
Jouet, Marcel Bénabou, Alina Reyes, Richard Morgiève, and Hervé Le Tellier
have moved from house to house without finding a permanent home. Each of
those writers has suggested new ways of conceiving the novel as a cultural
form, in a refreshing variety of manners. Their writing is recursive in character; but that recursiveness does not occlude the fundamental vocation of the
novel, storytelling. Quite to the contrary, their storytelling is enriched thereby.

Undoubtedly, the notion of the specular text, the book-as-chronicle-of-
its-own-elaboration, has been a key feature of contemporary French literature, at least since André Gide's *Les Faux-monnayeurs* (1925; *The Counterfeiters*). In recent years, that topos has become in a sense the imposed figure of
"serious" writing, in the absence of which no text can aspire to distinction.
Indeed, one frequently hears the argument that the increasing tendency of the

novel to examine its own nature is a sure sign of that form's dotage and imminent demise. I have learned much, over many years, from works such as Lucien
Dällenbach's *Le Récit spéculaire (The Mirror in the Text)* and Linda Hutcheon's
Narcissistic Narrative. Most importantly, perhaps, I have learned that self-con-
sciousness is an aspect of narrative which may be more or less pronounced in
a given time or a given place, but which in any case is constantly and readily
available to storytellers, and is lustily exploited by the canniest among them.[3] I
find Hutcheon's description of the metafictional dimension of narrative as
"process made visible" (6) very apposite; and I agree with her when she suggests that when fiction puts its own premises on display, one of the important
consequences is a transformation of the reader's role into one that is more
articulative, creative, and indeed collaborative—for one of the most intriguing things the reader may find in metafiction is the offer of a vastly more
ample franchise in the literary contract.[4]

Let me put a few more cards on the table, by way of explaining some of
the choices I have made in this book. I have said that I am interested both in
specular technique and in stories. The kind of writing that intrigues me the
most deeply is the sort in which those two things find their closest and most
felicitous mutual complementarity. Each of the novels I deal with here seems
to me to present—among the many other different things they may offer—a
fable of the novel, a tale about the fate of that form, its problematic status, its
limits, its possibilities. If I have decided to deal with novels published since
1990, it is largely because I am persuaded that the specific fabulist tendency
which I want to focus upon has become widespread all of a sudden, in a variety of shapes and avatars. Obviously, it is a risky business to speak critically
about the "extreme contemporary." Living authors, in their infinite perver-
sity, may invalidate commentaries brought to bear on their mid-career work,
well after the fact. One may deplore that eventuality, but one has to live with
it. Equally obviously, one cannot hope to deal in detail with each and every
novel that has appeared since 1990. In this book, I have chosen a set of ten texts
that I consider to be exemplary of the major tendencies of the novel (a choice
which is based on my readings of many, many other novels from that period),
and which in their aggregate represent a reasonable sampling of the recent
French novelistic avant-garde. Devoting a chapter to each, I will try to suggest

the particular questions that each novel poses with regard to the tradition of the French novel as a whole, and the manner in which these texts can be seen to contribute to an identifiable trend in the evolution of that genre in contemporary French literature.

Among the ten novelists I have decided to speak about here, J. M. G. Le Clézio is perhaps the least experimentalist and the most "canonical." Not coincidentally, he is also the one who has been at his trade the longest, having begun writing in the early 1960s. If I have chosen to deal with him in this book, it is because his writing seems to me to center upon the notion of *distance* in the novel in very interesting ways, staging the novel itself as a genre that has drifted ever further from the center of things. In the case of *Onitsha* (1991), that fable of the novel is told through the story of a young boy who finds himself on the cusp of adolescence in an unfamiliar world. As Le Clézio tells the tale of his character's nascent literary apprenticeship, it becomes clear that the boy's search for a role to play in the world is figural of that of the novel itself—this novel, certainly, but also that of the novel as a cultural form. In *La Nébuleuse du crabe* (1993; *The Crab Nebula*) Eric Chevillard offers us a protagonist who is a man without qualities. Or rather, "Crab" has qualities in abundance, so legion and so mutually contradictory that he cannot claim any of them as truly his own. Like the contemporary novel, Crab is astonishingly proteiform. Alienated and abysmally unadapted, his existence is threatened most direly by silence; and thus he speaks continually. But to whom? Linda Lê speaks to us quite deliberately from the margins. Her books testify to a will to put literary language on trial, and in each she meditates in some fashion or another upon the difference between the mother tongue and the acquired language. *Calomnies* (1993; *Slander*), as its title suggests, is a slanderous text. In dialogical counterpoint, Lê will ask us to reflect upon the uses and abuses of novelistic language, and upon the ways in which the novel may engage the world: the world of personal experience, the political and social world, and the world of letters.

In *Coup de foudre* (1995; Love at First Sight) Eric Laurrent offers for our inspection and edification "Chester," a thoroughly ridiculous man. Chester is a schlemiel in the noblest sense, a beautiful loser who triumphs through nullity, turning the very act of losing into a form of art. Exploiting his character's eccentricity for comic effect, Laurent comments too, obliquely but nonetheless pungently, on the increasing eccentricity of the novel with regard to other means of cultural expression. He wagers heavily thereupon, representing that eccentricity in a highly exaggerative, parodic manner, and turning it to ludic effect, carnivalizing the novel's efforts to regain the paradise it seems to have lost, in an attempt to turn the novel's very otherness into a real (if undoubtedly tenuous and provisional) strategic advantage. The fictional conceit that serves as the motor of Jacques Jouet's *La Montagne R* (1996; *Mountain R*) is simple enough: the leaders of a fictional (but transparently French) "Republic" undertake to construct a 1500-meter mountain near the capital as a monument to national prestige. Telling the story of the ways in which the project ineluctably fails, Jouet invites us to think about the conditions of possibility of monuments, be they physical or imaginary. Speculating closely on the curious mutual affinities of mountains and novels, he asks us also to consider whether, if it is no longer possible to build national monuments, the same might be true of literary monuments. Marie NDiaye's *La Sorcière* (1996; The Witch) is a tale about a witch whose powers, lamentably feeble as they may be when compared to others of her sorority, nevertheless suffice to make the other people in her world revile and shun her. The fantastic elements of NDiaye's tale are played out against the backdrop of the most unrelieved banality imaginable, as "Lucie" struggles to come to terms with the arcane rituals of the suburban quotidian. Among Lucie's gifts, the most salient is perhaps her gift for fabulization—and it is just that gift which NDiaye herself puts on display in this novel. There are many kinds of fables here: fables of the individual, fables of family, fables of society and its discontents; fables of gender and sexuality, fables of alterity and alienation; fables of the natural and fables of the supernatural; fables of the writer and fables of the reader. Interweaving those fables and coaxing them into a dynamic of reciprocal complementarity, Marie NDiaye gradually conjures up an apparition of the novel itself as a kind of sorcery.

Jean Echenoz's *Un An* (1997; A Year) is very broadly governed by the principle of incertitude, both on the level of the told and on the level of the telling. Presenting the story of a young woman who becomes homeless, the novel follows her as she wanders through the remarkably merciless landscape of contemporary French society. Yet as she wanders, so does her tale; and so too, necessarily, does the reader. Echenoz asks his reader to negotiate a narrative path where conventional points of reference are very largely lacking, following a diegetical trajectory that seems to be aleatory and directionless. Yet there is a demonstrable logic here, for Echenoz suggests that his protagonist's wanderings are figural of the way the novel as literary form wanders on our cultural topography, seeking an insertion that is no longer taken for granted. Just as constructive individual identity is very much at the mercy of capricious social forces, so too is that social construct which we call the novel—and the fate of both, in the current order of things, is extraordinarily precarious. Christian Oster touches upon similar themes in *Le Pique-nique* (1997; The Picnic), a story about people who become lost. Characters become lost in his novel, certainly; but so too, Oster suggests, do the writer and the reader. Playing ironically among those benighted figures, Oster encourages us to entertain the possibility that both writers and readers may turn to certain kinds of literature precisely in order to lose themselves, pleasurably, within the (relatively) safe confines of fiction. Considered as a whole, Jean-Philippe Toussaint's writings may usefully be viewed as an epic of the trivial; and in *La Télévision* (1997) he focuses his considerable wit upon one of the most eloquent contemporary expressions of triviality, television. The hero of his novel—if that is the right word for such a weak-kneed individual—is an art historian who has taken a sabbatical year in order to write a book on Titian. Yet instead of writing, he spends his time watching television. Whether staring into the richly furnished but largely meaningless panorama of his television screen, or gazing in his constitutionally otiose fashion into the emptiness of his computer monitor, the protagonist ponders a series of troubling questions. Why is writing so difficult, and watching television so easy? Why is he drawn to the latter when, as an academic and a card-carrying intellectual, he should be drawn to the former? What outcome can one hope for when the novel and television go head-to-head in the bloody arena of cultural competition?

If I have chosen to close my book with a discussion of Lydie Salvayre's *La Conférence de Cintegabelle* (1999; The Cintegabelle Lecture), it is at least in part because that text seems to me to anticipate the critical act more presciently than any of the other texts I've dealt with, calling that act into question, parrying it before the fact, and indeed coercing it in interesting ways. Constructing her novel around a lecturer who has very little to say, and absolutely no clue as to how he might say it, Salvayre's tale has quite a bit to say about speech and speeches—and most particularly about the kind of speech we call literary criticism. Salvayre intends to amuse us thereby, certainly, but she also intends to make us reflect constructively upon how we read novels. She slyly offers us a text that reads like the negative image of a novel, where most of the conventional gestures of the *romanesque* have been inverted. Salvayre wishes us to read her novel *against* the novel, as it were, in order better to call into question the set of traditions, conventions, and protocols which govern that genre as it is practiced today. In just that perspective, the hobby horse that her lecturer sinks his spurs into most vigorously is the notion that "conversation," once preeminent among the arts in France, has become lamentably corrupted in our time. In an ironically one-sided dialogue, he will attempt to enlist his fellow citizens of Cintegabelle in a vast national program to rehabilitate conversation; but his inept maunderings on the subject will serve merely to confirm in their minds beyond any possibility of doubt that conversation is in fact stone-dead. The conversation that Salvayre initiates with us, however, may enjoy a quite different fate. The fable of the novel that she proposes here is intended to ramify (and one of the beauties of narrative is that it does tend toward ramification) well beyond the boundaries of her own text. There, it will encounter other fables of the novel and enter into a dialogue—or a polylogue, more accurately—with them. In my view, Salvayre's fable does just that; and along with the other fables I have mentioned here, as well as many more that I haven't, it participates in a conversation as lively, as incisive, as bold, and as thoughtful as any that I can imagine.

NOTES

[1] I borrow the term "narrativity" from Gerald Prince, who defines it in the following way: "The set of properties characterizing narrative and distinguishing it from nonnarrative; the formal and contextual features making a narrative more or less narrative, as it were. The degree of narrativity of a given narrative depends partly on the extent to which that narrative fulfills a receiver's desire by representing oriented temporal wholes (prospectively from beginning to end and retrospectively

from end to beginning), involving a conflict, consisting of discrete, specific, and positive situations and events, and meaningful in terms of a human(ized) project and world" (*Dictionary of Narratology* 64).

[2] Caveat lector: F.-X. Molia is my wife's first cousin, and I hope that I won't be accused of nepotism if I suggest that his *Fourbi* (Stuff) is a stunning, abundantly promising first novel.

[3] Dällenbach invokes the *Quixote* in his brief for the venerable character of narrative specularity: "If Cervantes's novel represents for them [the Romantics] 'a system of elementary romantic poetry,' it is first because it contains a philosophy and a critique of the novel; second because its second part reflects the first part and the reflexions in the first part; and finally because by putting the evolution of the genre into perspective in its critique of novels of chivalry and of its own inserted novellas, the text suggests that it is itself only one moment in the infinite history of the unfolding of poetic forms" (*The Mirror in the Text* 177). Hutcheon, for her part, turns toward Ovid: "Self-informing narrative does not signal a lack of sensitivity or of humanitarian (or human) concern on the part of the novelist. Nor is it a mark of crisis, of the asphyxiation of fiction by an overworked critical intellect, or by an excessive curiosity about writers, or by the novelist's loss of faith in his work, or by cubism, film or any of the other possibilities suggested by its detractors. If self-awareness is a sign of the genre's disintegration, then the novel began its decline at birth, as the ironic reading of the Ovid in the Introduction suggested" (*Narcissistic Narrative* 18).

[4] See Hutcheon 20 and 144: "What narcissistic narrative does do in flaunting, in baring its fictional and linguistic systems to the reader's view, is to transform the process of making, of *poiesis,* into part of the shared pleasure of reading"; "The act of reading becomes a creative, interpretative one that partakes of the experience of writing itself. These fictions are about their own processes, as experienced and created by the reader's responses."

I

∾

J. M. G. Le Clézio's
Elsewhere

For many critics, J. M. G. Le Clézio's principal virtue as a writer is his ability to construct a novelistic landscape that is dramatically different from the real world of his readers, a deeply evocative, seductive "elsewhere" to which we travel on the virtual journey of his fiction.[1] Such a technique is of course one of the privileged gestures of narrative, at least since Homer; yet in Le Clézio's texts it assumes a richly personal specificity which may be read, I think, as his authorial signature. I should like to examine that effect, focusing upon what I consider to be the most exemplary of Le Clézio's recent novels, *Onitsha* (1991).

Like many of Le Clézio's writings, *Onitsha* is a novel of apprenticeship. It tells the story of a young boy named Fintan who leaves France for Africa with his mother, in order to join a father whom he has not seen for many years. The very first words of the novel inscribe the theme of the journey and announce that it will occupy the foreground of the tale: "The *Surabaya,* an aging three-hundred-ton ship of the Holland Africa Line, had just left the dirty waters of the Gironde estuary, bound for the west coast of Africa, and Fintan looked at his mother as if it were for the first time" (13, 3).[2] Fintan's reluctance to embark upon that journey—"I don't want to leave I don't want to go there," he protests (16, 6)—may be interpreted as a move in the strategy Le Clézio deploys in order to enlist his reader in the imaginary voyage of the novel. For Fintan's remark is figural of the reader's own natural hesitation to leave the familiar behind and strike out for the unknown. It serves to situate the reader in solidarity with the principal character of the novel, and to suggest that, just as Fintan's journey becomes inevitable once he embarks upon the *Surabaya,* so too our journey becomes inevitable once we begin to read.

During the ocean voyage, which occupies the first of the novel's four parts, Fintan will refer to his destination as "there" [*là-bas*]. It is an apparently simple term, and yet the fact that it recurs in Fintan's discourse with such insistence leads one to believe that it is less innocent than it might seem. It is useful to remember, too, that the term *là-bas* comes equipped with certain literary connotations in the modern French tradition, and a broad allusive field fashioned in the first instance by Baudelaire and Mallarmé. Baudelaire's "L'Invitation au voyage," much like *Onitsha,* describes an initiatory ocean journey toward a radical "other," a place that is utterly different from the world we know: "My child, my sister / Think of the sweetness / Of going there to live together!" And Mallarmé's "Brise marine" likewise prescribes an ocean journey into the unknown as antidote to the mortal ennui which afflicts the poet: "The flesh is sad, alas! and I've read all the books. / To flee! To flee there!"

Clearly, Le Clézio appeals to that tradition in the first part of *Onitsha.* Under his pen, the term "there" is powerfully intertextual, an overdetermined signifier that serves to designate a place defined, for the moment, only by its alterity. Throughout his novel, Le Clézio will play on the idea of alterity, shaping it and nuancing it within the structure of the text in order to propose it as his principal theme. As he contructs that theme, it may dawn upon the reader that the meditations Le Clézio brings to bear can be interpreted on another level as well. There, the struggle is not that of a young boy coming to terms with an environment he finds utterly unfamiliar, but rather that of the novel itself as a literary form, seeking to furnish a place for itself in the suddenly unfamiliar landscape of our contemporary culture.

Gradually elaborating his novelistic vision of Africa, Le Clézio relies on a discourse of opposition: seen through European eyes, Africa is a place where everything, from social conventions to the most trivial protocols of daily life, is *different.* In refining that difference, Le Clézio exploits the notion of the exotic massively,[3] invoking it as both a natural and a cultural term. On the one hand, Africa is vast, tropical, abundant, and opulent, a perfect example of Mallarmé's "exotic nature."[4] As a landscape, it is everything that Metropolitan France is not. On the other hand, its cultural conventions, as they are described in *Onitsha,* seem bizarre, "foreign," and strangely encoded to Fintan—and, by extension once again, to Le Clézio's readers.

The most powerful technique that Le Clézio uses to project his vision of the exotic upon the reader is involved with his naming practice. In the economy of fiction, as Roland Barthes has pointed out, the proper name is "the prince of signifiers."[5] Proper names, whether anthroponyms or toponyms, are always semiotically motivated in fiction, unlike in real life; they speak volumes about the people or places they designate. Le Clézio's novel is no exception to this rule, and in fact his onomastic strategy is announced in the very title of the book. For most of Le Clézio's readers, the word "Onitsha" is a floating signifier, waiting to be invested with meaning. As such, it is the first cipher in the hermeneutic code of the text,[6] for it serves to pique the reader's curiosity. Clearly, the word is a "foreign" one whose resonances, to a French ear at least, are exotic. Even if the reader happens to know that "Onitsha" is the name of an actual city in Nigeria, the evocative force of the word is undiminished, within the same connotational field. In other words, the title of the book itself serves to announce the theme of the journey toward the unknown; and it will serve throughout the novel as the principal locus of "otherness." To ensure that his reader will recognize this, Le Clézio stages the word "Onitsha" very deliberately: "It was a magical name. A magnetic name. There was no resisting it. [...] It was a very beautiful, very mysterious name, like a forest, like the meandering of a river" (46, 33).

The word itself has an incantatory power, Le Clézio suggests; in Fintan's mind it conjures up a world of mystery and strangeness. For Fintan, it is the primary term in a catalogue of other "magical names" that he hears during his voyage.[7] The reader is encouraged to interpret it in the same way. Moreover, granted the elaborate way Le Clézio weaves the word "Onitsha" into the associative texture of the novel, we recall each time we encounter it that it is also the title of the text. That is, it serves as a sort of shifter, urging us to read doubly, not only on the level of the novel's intrigue, but also on the metaliterary level, reminding us incessantly that the novel is not only the story, but also the *fable* of the story. And if Le Clézio intimates so often that the word "Onitsha" casts a sort of spell upon Fintan, he obviously hopes that the novel of the same name will have an analogous effect upon its reader.

On the ship carrying him to Africa, Fintan succumbs willingly to the power of the place name: "Names went the rounds of the dinner tables: Saint-Louis, Dakar. There were other names Fintan loved to hear: Langue de Barbarie and Gorée, names soft and terrible at the same time" (31, 19). Indeed, the mere enunciation of those exotic names sends him into a dreamlike state, a kind of trance. Uttered one after another, as in a litany or an incantation, they make Fintan dream of strange worlds: "They were headed for Takoradi, Lomé, Cotonou; they were headed for Conakry, Sherbro, Lavannah, Edina, Manna, Sinou, Accra, Bonny, Calabar" (36, 24). In short, for Fintan at least, those names are the initiators of fiction, projecting his imagination into realms of rich—and hitherto unsuspected—narrative possibility. In similar fashion, Le Clézio intends that these names should open a narrative vista for his readers, a horizon upon which his novel will take shape.

Just as the toponyms in *Onitsha* evoke the unfamiliar, the "foreign," so too do the anthroponyms. Fintan's own name, for instance, is a very strange one. Indisputably, it is not a French name; and indeed a French reader would find it difficult to identify its origin. Perhaps it sounds Celtic. But in any case, granted its opacity in the referential code of the text, it marks the character who bears it as a strange person. And indeed all of the other major figures in the novel bear the same stamp of alterity, imprinted upon them in the first instance by their names. Fintan's mother, for example, is named Maria Luisa, for she is Italian by birth; his father is an Englishman named Geoffrey Allen; the ship's officer who takes Fintan and his mother under his protection during the ocean voyage is a Dutchman named Heylings. When Fintan and his mother arrive in Onitsha, the reader is bombarded with a variety of native names that seem equally strange to a French ear: Marima, who keeps house for Geoffrey Allen (and after whom Fintan's sister, conceived in Onitsha, will be named); Okawho, a servant in another European household; Bony, a fisherman's son who befriends Fintan; Oya, a young woman upon whom Fintan and Bony spy as she bathes in the river. Among the European community, there is Sabine Rodes, a shadowy acquaintance of Geoffrey's. Rodes is marked by the fact that his first name is that of a woman, rather than a man. Yet Le Clézio suggests that his alterity is more profound still, and Fintan's father warns him away from Rodes, insisting precisely upon the strangeness of his name, appealing to a logic that the reader understands, even if Fintan himself does not: "He said, 'Rodes is not a very good name, it is not a name like ours. Do you understand?' Fintan didn't understand a thing" (100, 81).

In one way or another, then, all of the principal characters in *Onitsha* are designated as "other"—if to varying degree—by virtue of the fact that their names fall outside the referential field of French language and culture. And there is another curious phenomenon at work here, for in fact there is no character who bears an ordinary, easily identifiable French name. It is as if the referential field defined by the language of the novel had no sure guarantor, no center. Personal identity (which the proper name normally serves to reify, after all) is consequently unstable and problematic in *Onitsha*. This is exacerbated by the fact that the central figures of the novel are plurinymous. Heylings calls Fintan "Junge," for instance. Fintan himself refers to his mother not as "Maman" or even "Maria Luisa," but rather as "Maou." Fintan cannot bring himself to call Geoffrey Allen "Father," and his mother refers to her husband sometimes by his first name, sometimes by his family name. Bony's name is likewise unstable: "His real name was Josip, or Josef, but because he was tall and thin they called him Bony" (69, 54). One suspects early on that this plurinymity is a very deliberate effect, and that it is deeply intricated in the thematics of the novel, a suspicion that is amply confirmed by the final words of *Onitsha,* where Fintan learns of Sabine Rodes's real identity, some twenty years after he first encountered him: "The letter went on to say that his real name was Roderick Matthews, and that he was an Officer of the British Empire" (251, 206).

Le Clézio's use of onomastics to elaborate a discourse of alterity is part of a broader strategy through which he questions language itself. His novel constantly puts "foreign" languages into play against the backdrop of the referential language, French. When Fintan gets to Onitsha, he is fascinated by the languages he hears there. He listens with delight to the native voices, which suggest vast new linguistic possibilities to him: "They called out the name of the rain: 'Ozoo! Ozoo!' [. . .] Fintan listened to the voices, the shouts of the children, calling, 'Waa! Waa!'" (62-63, 48-49). His mother shares his fascination, and in fact sets out to learn Marima's language: "Maou learned the words in her language. *Ulo,* house. *Mmiri,* water. *Umu,* children. *Aja,* dog. *Odeleude,* it's soft. *Je nuo,* drink. *Ofee,* I like it. *So!* Speak! *Tekateka,* time is passing. . . . She wrote the words down in her poetry notebook, then read them aloud, and Marima burst out laughing" (149, 122). But there are other new languages, too, such as English, the language of the colonial rulers. That is Fintan's father's native tongue, of course; curiously however, Fintan turns toward Bony rather than Geoffrey Allen for advanced instruction in English—and in another language as well: "He knew all kinds of curses and swearwords in English; he taught Fintan what 'cunt' meant and other things whose meaning he did not know. He could also speak in sign language. Fintan quickly learned to speak the same language" (69, 54).

Throughout *Onitsha,* Le Clézio interrogates the notion of the "mother tongue." For the vast majority of his readers, that language is French; yet for Fintan, things are not quite as simple, because *his* mother's native language is Italian. Maou speaks French with an accent, with "foreign" inflections that appeal strongly to Fintan's ear: "Fintan listened to the melody of Maou's voice. He liked her Italian accent, its music" (21, 10). Often, Fintan asks Maou to speak to him in Italian: "Speak to me in your language," he says (119, 98). And when she does, the music which Fintan hears in that language becomes literal, for Maou sings to him in Italian: "Maou rocked to and fro in her rattan chair, singing *filastrocche, ninnenanne,* softly at first, then more loudly. It was strange [*étrange*] to hear these songs and the gentle sound of the Italian language mingling with the sounds of the water, the way it used to be in Saint-Martin" (155, 128). Whereas for most of us the idea of the "mother tongue" is essential and largely unproblematic, subtending much of the way we view the world of experience, Le Clézio carefully points out how slippery that notion may be. For Fintan, his mother's tongue is *étrange,* that is, "strange" or "foreign"; and yet he takes great joy and comfort in it.

Not everyone in Onitsha shares his linguistic relativism. When Fintan's family attends a party at the home of the British Resident, for instance, Maou happens to call out to Fintan in Italian, with socially catastrophic results:

> Maou had called to Fintan in Italian. Mrs. Rally came over and said, in her timid little voice, "Excuse me, but what *sort* of language are you speaking?" Later, Geoffroy reproached Maou. Lowering his voice to show that he was not shouting—perhaps also because he knew full well he was wrong—he said: "I

do not wish you to speak to Fintan in Italian, particularly at the Resident's house." Maou replied: "And yet you used to like it, once." Perhaps it was from that day on that everything changed. (156, 128)

Within the narrative economy of the novel, that event is crucial because it marks a point where Geoffrey Allen begins to distance himself from his wife and his son. Thematically, it is crucial, too, for it is emblematic of the way in which, according to Le Clézio, we are determined by language. In the eyes of the British colonial community, Maou is marked as "other" by the fact that she speaks Italian, and the members of that community will shun her because of that. Though other reasons for excluding her are invoked (she is too "familiar" with the natives, she is unwilling to embrace the colonial ethic, she is "unconventional," and so forth), her original sin is linguistic in character: her language is not the language of power. The "ceremony of punishment," as Michel Foucault puts it (49), must be enacted upon Maou; she must be marginalized in order to preserve the disciplined society of Onitsha.

The novel which bears that name, however, takes a rather different stance on the issue of language and power. Just as Le Clézio problematizes the idea of the "mother tongue," so too does he suggest that language's capacity to establish and preserve power is not absolute. *Onitsha* presents its reader with a linguistic polyphony in which a variety of languages—and theories of language—vex each other, question each other. The French of Le Clézio's novel is deliberately unstable, constantly interrupted by other languages, Italian, English, African languages, pidgin. In the place called "Onitsha," Le Clézio asks us, what is a "native language" and what is a "foreign language"? Is autochtony a question of birth or of power? What makes for an exile? When Maou is banished from colonial society, it merely serves to confirm a marginality which marked her from the beginning of the story. Born into an Italian family, uneducated and dirt-poor, Maou was already a marginal figure, even in Metropolitan France. The fact that she was an orphan was indeed one of the reasons Geoffrey Allen had been attracted to her: "Perhaps it was for that reason that Geoffroy had chosen her, because she was alone, because, unlike him, she had no family to renounce" (84, 68). Yet she is not alone in the margins of Onitsha's society, whether "native" or "colonial." Oya, the young woman whose sexuality fascinates Fintan and Bony, is an outcast among the natives: "It was said she was a prostitute from Lagos and that she had been in prison" (93, 75). Sabine Rodes is feared and shunned by the other Europeans: "He was without doubt the most despised man in Onitsha's little European community" (99, 79). More broadly still, Le Clezio describes the radical alienation of both the native community and the European community, pointing out an essential truth about colonial regimes: in such a society, nobody is truly "at home." Through the evocation of issues such as this, as in his onomastic strategy, the lesson that Le Clézio wishes to convey is that there is no *center* here, no fixed, reliable point from which the question of marginality may be adjudicated.

In that sense, *Onitsha* is a book about exile, in which that condition is taken to be universal. The principal vehicle of that discourse is Fintan himself. Like his mother, he is described from the beginning as a marginal being. He is a male, yet he grew up in a feminine universe, ruled by his grandmother and his aunts as much as by his mother. He is a young boy, and thus he sees the adult world from outside. He is French, but his mother is Italian and his father is English. In Onitsha, he is not enfranchised in European circles; yet neither is he admitted into the society of Bony and the other African boys. When he returns to Europe near the end of the novel, he is sent to an English boarding school. There, too, he becomes a pariah; and it is interesting to note that his alienation is linguistic in origin. Quite simply, the English boys exclude Fintan because he doesn't speak their language:

> When he arrived at the school, Fintan spoke pidgin, inadvertently. He said, "He don go nawnaw, he tok say," he said "Di book bilong mi." That made them laugh, and the house master thought he was doing it on purpose to create a stir. He ordered Fintan to stand against the wall for two hours with his arms spread. That too, he had to forget, those words jumping and dancing in his mouth. [. . .] He could not read their expressions, he did not understand what they wanted. He was like a deaf-mute, watchful, always on guard. (234, 191-92)

Fintan's keenest insight—and the crux of this novel of apprenticeship— comes as he gradually recognizes his existential status as an "outsider," and learns to deal with it productively. It has been pointed out, by critics such as Sander Gilman, Edward Said, and Gayatri Chakravorty Spivak, for example, that the outsider, while painfully excluded from society, nonetheless occupies a position which offers certain real advantages in terms of perspective.[8] Speaking of the alienation of the intellectual in society, Said argues that point eloquently: "So while it is true to say that exile is the condition that characterizes the intellectual as someone who stands as a marginal figure outside the comforts of privilege, power, being-at-homeness (so to speak), it is also very important to stress that that condition carries with it certain rewards and, yes, even privileges" (*Representations of the Intellectual* 53). Fintan's situation in *Onitsha* is a similar one: though he cannot speak the language of power to power, his very exclusion from power, coupled with his sharp recognition that his marginalization emanates from a highly dubious "center," enables him to survive. He will engage in what Ross Chambers has called "oppositional behavior," that is, he will exploit small faults, or flaws, in the system of power, in order to disturb that system (*Room for Maneuver* xi). In the same manner, Le Clézio's text implicitly questions the manner in which literature's cultural status has gradually but ineluctably shifted from the central to the marginal, and offers a program for turning that very marginal status to the novel's advantage.

According to Le Clézio, one of the areas in which power's hegemony may be seen to be less than total is in its cultural practices, and most conspicuously, in literature. When all else fails and his marginality threatens to submerge him, Fintan takes refuge in stories. He inherits his taste for literature from his mother. Maou is a reader, Le Clézio tells us; she turns constantly toward literature in order to palliate her solitude and her sadness. Alone with her infant son in France during the war, with Geoffrey in Africa and unable to join them, Maou reads *Gone with the Wind* (82, 67); depressed and ill with fever in Onitsha, she reads Joyce Cary's *The Witch* (108, 88). Geoffrey, too, is a reader, and he sees in literature a radiant image of everything his life might have been, had things turned out differently. His library in Onitsha contains various kinds of books—anthropological studies by Margaret Mead, Sigfried Nadel, and E. A. Wallis Budge; novels by Cary and Rudyard Kipling; travel narratives by Percy Amaury Talbot, C. K. Meek, and Sinclair Gordon (110,

89-90). As different as they may seem, however, Geoffrey's books share a common theme: like *Onitsha* itself, they are all devoted, in one way or another, to the evocation of an exotic "other." And Geoffrey is powerfully seduced by that "other." He spends days poring over the Egyptian Book of the Dead, for example, losing himself in it, until the world it offers him comes to seem more real than the far less attractive world surrounding him in Onitsha. In a sense, then, Maou and Geoffrey are ideal readers: they enter into the textual contract wholly and unreservedly, fulfilling the role assigned to them as readers to the very letter. Clearly, Le Clézio hopes that we will approach his novel in much the same manner.

Fintan's devotion to literature is still more profound. Like many children, he is introduced to literature by his mother: as far back as he can remember, Maou had told him stories, recited nursery rhymes and poetry to him. During moments of particular stress, he continues to ask her to do that, even now that he knows how to read on his own. During the ocean journey, for instance, he asks Maou to recite some "verses" to him, and she responds with a poem in Italian, which soothes him (29, 17-18); once they get to Onitsha, he continues to ask her for the same sort of consolation, and she recites Italian nursery rhymes to him (113, 93; 208, 170). In each case, Le Clézio produces these texts in Italian in the pages of his novel, perhaps to suggest that, for Fintan, the "mother tongue" is literature itself. For it is through his mother's voice that Fintan accedes to the world of fiction and dream. Indeed, the text itself is less important to Fintan than the voice that reads it, for the voice has a power to shape the text—any text—to its own ends. As Maou reads aloud to him from a book called *The Child's Guide to Knowledge,* for instance, Fintan perceives a strange and wonderful world *through* the simple, prosaic words of the text: "Fintan liked to dream of all these extraordinary things—kings, marvels, fabulous peoples" (204, 166). Once again, Fintan's experience is staged as emblematic, for Le Clézio intends that we should approach literature in the same way, and that through our reading of *Onitsha* we should be offered a vision of the marvelous "other" similar to Fintan's own.

If Le Clézio proposes reading as a means of ingress into that "other," he also intimates that writing may lead one there. In Fintan's case, just as his mother's example had guided him in his apprenticeship as a reader, so too does her writerly activity inspire him. For Maou writes incessantly, and writing, like reading, offers her a way of coming to terms with her alienation. Her writing is not sophisticated or polished, but on the contrary naive (in the mathematical sense of that word) and happily unaware of literary convention; it is process rather than product. Moreover, Le Clézio carefully describes Maou as being free of specific linguistic constraints when she writes, as if writing itself, *écriture,* were somehow beyond the various languages that she is obliged to juggle, with more or less success, in her daily life: "Was she writing stories, or letters—she wasn't really sure. Words. She began, not knowing which direction she would take—French, Italian, sometimes even English, it made no difference" (26, 15). Writing represents for Maou everything that her daily experience refuses her: integration, serenity, expression, and the access, through dream, to a virtual, and better, world: "To write, listening to the rustle of water against the hull, as if one were travelling up an endless river. [. . .] To write was to dream. Out there, once they reached Onitsha, everything would be different, everything would be easy" (26-27, 15-16).

Her example is a determinative one for Fintan. Watching her write, he is awakened to the possibilities that writing offers a person, even one as besieged as his mother. After returning to Europe, Maou gradually ceases to write. When she moves to the South of France, leaving Fintan in boarding school in England, she gives him her old notebooks. Two decades after the events in Onitsha, Fintan looks back upon Maou's writings from that period, seeing in them a powerful, enduring legacy:

> She no longer writes in the afternoon in her school notebooks those long poems that resemble letters. When Maou and Geoffroy left for the south of France with Marima, over fifteen years ago, Maou gave all her notebooks to Fintan in a big envelope. On the envelope she had written the *ninnenanne* Fintan liked so much, the one about Befana and l'Uomo Nero, the one about the Stura bridge. Fintan read all the notebooks, one after the other, for a year. After all this time there are still pages he knows by heart. (246-47, 201)

Maou no longer writes now; but Fintan does. Following his mother's example, Fintan had begun to write long ago, during the ocean voyage from France to Africa. Even at that initiatory moment, Fintan senses that writing may provide him with the same kind of solace that Maou finds in it. Troubled by the attentions that an Englishman named Gerald Simpson is paying to Maou on the *Surabaya,* and dreading the encounter with his father which awaits him at the end of his journey, Fintan sits down to write a story: "It was good to write this story, locked in the cabin, so quiet, with the glow of the night light and the heat of the sun rising above the hull of the motionless ship" (49, 35). His story is the tale of a young woman who goes to Africa for the first time and discovers a strange new world. Clearly, he is writing his own story, scripting it as he wishes it to unfold, using fiction—much like the marvelous new African words he hears during the voyage—as incantation. And he will continue to work on his story throughout his time in Onitsha,[9] embroidering upon his fictional world in an effort to come to terms with the experiential world he encounters there.

Fintan entitles his story "A Long Journey." The fact that this is also the title of the first part of Le Clézio's novel, during which we see Fintan begin to write, suggests in a very compelling manner the theory of literature that *Onitsha* proposes to its reader. For literature is essentially reciprocal, Le Clézio argues: its reciprocities are played out creatively and infinitely in any literary exchange, between writer and writer, for example, or between writer and reader. Fintan's "long journey" is emblazoned in specular fashion within Le Clézio's "long journey." Yet from our perspective as readers, the relations of container and contained are not quite that clear, for in fact we read the one *as* we read the other. Thus do stories speak to each other, Le Clézio implies, easily traversing boundaries that in real life may appear to be hermetic. The uses of literature, too, are distributed reciprocally among the partners in literary exchange; and they also may be turned toward a questioning of the boundaries that surround us. A character in a novel may choose to write a story in which he invokes an exotic, foreign world, as a means of coming to terms with his own sense of being an "outsider." A novelist may offer an imaginary journey to his reader in order to encourage him or her to consider what alterity means and how it works in our lives. A reader may see the literary construction of the "other" for what it is, and begin to consider otherness as, precisely, a construct.

That is the range of reflection which *Onitsha* presents most eloquently, I think. At the end of the novel we once again see Fintan writing, this time as an adult. He is composing a letter to his younger sister, Marima, trying to tell her about Onitsha. It is a world that she has never seen, starkly different from her own. Yet Fintan feels that it is crucial that Marima should imagine that world— if only through his description of it, and thus tentatively. For he is deeply persuaded that, however distant and foreign it may be in Marima's eyes, Onitsha is somehow hers, too. We leave him there, struggling to build another world from words, much like Le Clézio himself, writing *away*.

NOTES

[1] See for example Didier Pobel 79-80: "J. M. G. Le Clézio's strength seems, certainly, to reside in large part in his aptitude to enlist us, without exoticism, as indissociable companions in *A Long Journey*. [...] To read Le Clézio is to be sheltered and strangled simultaneously, during *A Long Journey* in the immobility of the gaze, during which we never cease to subjugate ourselves, never cease to surpass ourselves, never cease to renew ourselves."

[2] Here and throughout, I have used Alison Anderson's translation. The first page numbers refer to the original, the second to the translation.

[3] Here, I demur at Didier Pobel's assertion that Le Clézio's manner of enlisting his readers in a "voyage" excludes exoticism. Quite to the contrary, Le Clézio positions his text explicitly in a literary tradition which uses the "exotic" as one of its central terms. That practice distinguishes him, moreover, from many of his contemporaries (Jean Echenoz, Marie Redonnet, Jean-Philippe Toussaint, and Emmanuèle Bernheim come to mind) whose writings evoke ordinary, quotidian, "endotic" worlds.

[4] See "Brise marine": "Steamer rocking your masts / Weigh anchor for an exotic nature."

[5] See Barthes, "Analyse" 34: "A proper name must always be questioned carefully, for the proper name is, in a manner of speaking, the prince of signifiers; its connotations are rich, social, and symbolic."

[6] In *S/Z,* Barthes defines that term in the following manner: "The inventory of the hermeneutic code will consist in distinguishing the different (formal) terms according to which an enigma stages itself, declares itself, formulates itself, then hesitates and finally reveals itself" (26).

[7] See for example 20, 9: "A string of dark islands hung from the horizon.

'Look, Madeira, Funchal.' Magical names"; and 24, 13: "He said magical words: 'Tenerife, Gran Canaria, Lanzarote.'"

[8] See Gilman 17: "I am not neutral, I am not distanced, for being an outsider does not mean to be cool and clinical; it must mean to burn with those fires which define you as the outsider"; Said, *Culture and Imperialism* xxvii: "Yet when I say 'exile' I do not mean something sad or deprived. On the contrary belonging, as it were, to both sides of the imperial divide enables you to understand them more easily"; and Spivak's response to the assertion that her critical attitudes reflect the fact that she is an "outsider": "I have thought about that question. Even after nineteen years in this country, fifteen of them spent in full-time teaching, I believe the answer is yes. But then, where is the inside? To define an inside is a decision, I believe I said that night, and the critical method I am describing would question the ethico-political strategic exclusions that would define a certain set of characteristics as an 'inside' at a certain time. 'The text itself,' 'the poem as such,' 'intrinsic criticism,' are such strategic definitions. I have spoken in support of such a way of reading that would continue to break down these distinctions, never once and for all, and *actively* interpret 'inside' and 'outside' as texts for involvement as well as change" (102).

[9] See for instance 56, 42; 95, 77; 106, 86.

II

⚯

ERIC CHEVILLARD'S
CRAB

The fictional worlds that Eric Chevillard constructs are exceedingly quirky ones, governed by curious logics, animated by outlandish events, and peopled by very strange characters indeed. They would seem to have very little to do with our own world, were it not for those astonishing moments when worlds collide. Born in 1964, Chevillard has to date produced eleven novels at the Editions de Minuit, beginning with *Mourir m'enrhume* (Dying Makes Me Sick) in 1987. The world of Chevillard's that intrigues me the most is a distant one, a nebula in fact, the one that he presents in *La Nébuleuse du crabe (The Crab Nebula)*, which appeared in 1993 and was awarded the Prix Fénéon. Appropriately enough, the world of this novel is a cloudy one; but nonetheless it is, I feel, extremely seductive. I would like to navigate my way through it here in order to suggest the ways in which it comments upon one of the more nebulous phenomena of our own world, the contemporary novel.

The protagonist of Chevillard's novel—I hesitate to call him a "hero," for reasons that will shortly become apparent—is a man named "Crab."[1] Chevillard presents him in the first lines of the text, and also obligingly warns his reader that Crab is a man of many parts: "Given a choice between deafness and blindness, Crab would lose his hearing on the spot, without a moment's hesitation. Yet he values music far more than painting. And this is not Crab's only contradiction, as we shall see" (7, 1).[2] Certain details that Chevillard furnishes may tempt us to believe that Crab is a hero in the conventional mode: in one of the many conflicting accounts of his birth, we are told that he was abandoned and taken in by a she-wolf; we learn that he has traveled widely, on the Ganges, the Mekong, and the Limpopo for example; and he is the proud owner of a vast desert (103, 103; 67, 64-65; 71, 69). He is clearly a man of extremes—and his extremities testify to that: he was born with webbed feet; he awakes one morning to find that his legs and left hand have disappeared; and his penis, when erect, measures a heroic 8,848 meters, just like Mount Everest (102, 101; 43, 39; 82, 81). Yet it shortly becomes clear that Crab is a man of very little wit. He believes, for instance, that women's right ears are actually their vaginas (and vice versa), which allows him to enjoy a rare voyeuristic pleasure in society; and two eminent specialists, Dr. Parkinson and Dr. Alzheimer, concur in their diagnosis of Crab as "a broken-down old geezer" (79, 76-77; 115, 116). In short, despite certain distinctions, Crab is a man very largely without qualities, as Chevillard points out:

> There's no point in keeping it a secret any longer: all his life, Crab was a wholly insignificant individual devoid of charm or personality, whose elementary vocabulary still included far too many words and expressions for his inane thoughts, so that he often spoke completely at cross-purposes and made himself ridiculous. Fortunately for him, no one paid the slightest attention to what he said. (85-86, 84)

Granted that, what could possibly make Crab deserving of our interest? For my part, I believe that Crab performs a kind of passion play of the contemporary novel and the vicissitudes with which it grapples in our culture. Chevillard stages that play in a deliberately exaggerated manner, using as his chief props irony, humor, and self-deprecation. Like the contemporary novel, Crab is astonishingly proteiform.[3] Just when one expects him to stand on his own feet, he decides that henceforth he will walk on his hands; and the guests at Crab's christening discover to their chagrin that what is actually being celebrated is his funeral (10, 3; 40, 36). Among his many forms, however, he cannot claim any one of them as his own; that is, there is no reliable, immediately recognizable *shape* to him, no common denominator in his infinite and vertiginous mutability. He is a very strange individual, and his alterity strikes the people he comes in contact with immediately and irrevocably, just as the strangeness of certain kinds of avant-garde writing undoubtedly strikes people weaned on well-made narratives in popular literature, film, and television.

Faced with a horizon of possibility that seems to be ever more constricted by the day, Crab's field of reference becomes reduced: he speaks principally of himself, reflecting on the myriad vexations of his existence and on his responsibility to render an account of the ineffable. He has everything to say, but no language in which to say it—or only a paltry simulacrum of language, one in which every word is merely a dismal specter of the words that used to be available, but are now impossibly out of reach. Moreover, and most crucially, he wonders if anyone is listening.

Chevillard wonders that right along with Crab, of course; and he encourages us to ponder that question, too. On every page of *La Nébuleuse du crabe,* we are implicitly asked if we are still reading, and, if so, why? Chevillard gradually elaborates a portrait of the artist in this novel, but it is an extremely wry one, fraught with irony and propelled by double-edged paradoxes. Certainly Crab functions as a figure of the writer, and Chevillard exploits that parodic analogy gleefully throughout the novel.[4] Yet he also holds Crab up to his reader like a funhouse mirror, intending that we should recognize ourselves in him—if only in a hopelessly misshapen, ridiculous form. Crab is a freak, obviously enough, but so is the writer perhaps, when compared to normal folk; and so, too, is the reader of experimental fiction, or at least that reader freakish enough to accept the wager that Chevillard tenders here.

Clearly, *La Nébuleuse du crabe* is not for everybody: it is a perverse book that addresses itself to a perverse imagination. Crab himself is a man divorced from the society of his fellows since birth. He was born in a prison, Chevillard tells us, where his mother was incarcerated (for reasons that remain unclear to Crab, appropriately enough). When his mother had served her sentence, she was set free; yet the authorities tell Crab that he must remain:

> Crab bristled; for what reason and by what right had they kept him locked away here since his birth? But the warden answered that there had been a considerable decline in the number of misdeeds and murders in the area since Crab's birth and throughout the whole of his vile existence between those walls, a drop so precipitous it could not be put down to mere coincidence. In vain Crab reminded him that he had not yet been born when those crimes were committed—it's no easy thing to provide proof of or eyewitnesses to your non-existence. He was advised to reconsider his defense strategy. He pleaded guilty

and justice was done; he was sentenced to life imprisonment amid heartfelt applause. The crowd left the courtroom wearing smiles of satisfaction. There was a palpable sense of relief in the air. People like that Crab fellow were made for a life behind bars. (45, 41)

As curious as this passage may seem to us initially, Chevillard is playing on a familiar topos, one that has been amply explored in contemporary literature, at least since Kafka, the theme of the individual who is inculpated for crimes of which he or she is not aware and who is obliged to struggle in a carceral system where one is guilty from the outset. It is important to recognize, then, that the world to which Chevillard is alluding is a *novelistic* one, and that he is relying on his reader's recognition of that fact. Chevillard's game is double here. On the one hand, feeling that such a theme, in its maturity, is now ripe for parody, Chevillard exploits it for ludic effect. On the other hand, he is suggesting yet again that his protagonist is a man who is radically and dramatically different from others—so much so that the only solution to the danger he poses to society is to lock him up. Read on the metaliterary level, as I believe it should be, the passage may be seen to suggest that this novel, too, is unlike others, and that it puts its own alterity on display with considerable ostentation, turning its "otherness" this way and that, all the while mocking that very gesture and thereby prompting us to question it.

Crab's most salient characteristic, as Olivier Bessard-Banquy has pointed out, is the fact that he is utterly unadapted ("Chevillard écrivain" 899). Admittedly, the social landscape of our world may seem at times impossibly labyrinthine, yet Crab has the talent to transform the simplest of social interactions into catastrophe: "Crab paged through his appointment book and replied that no, alas, to his deep regret, he could not make it to the party; he had made other plans for that night: to stay home all alone and have a really shitty time" (54, 52). On those rare occasions where he ventures deliberately, and with the best of wills, into the social world, the results are dismal at best. Having decided to introduce two of his friends, "Onan" and "Narcisse," to each other, Crab finds to his dismay that they have nothing whatever to say, either to the other or to him, and he struggles manfully to fill the discursive void (80, 78).

If he finds himself alienated from others, he also discovers that he doesn't really know himself. A scene early in the novel where Crab gazes into the mirror illustrates that point neatly: "There was one decisive day in Crab's life, an obligatory reference: a morning when everything seemed alien to him. Looking in the mirror, on reflection, he realized that he himself was the anomaly" (9, 3). He is painfully conscious of his unconsciousness; he senses obscurely that in order to *be,* he must become aware of his being; yet that vital prospect recedes ever more maddeningly, even as he advances toward it:

> You wouldn't think it to look at him, but Crab is doing his best to become a man, a real one. A man in every sense of the word. A complete man.
>
> Alas, he has only a vague and fragmentary conception of the nature of this important personage; his half-amused, half-appalled contemplation of his own body—by turns burning with desire, racked by hunger, blue with cold—tells him precious little in the end; each of those states is only one discrete aspect of a single subject as observed from a given point of view. What he wants is to grasp the full complexity of man with just one look. But man is never fully himself, not even when desire, cold, and hunger lay claim to him all at once. (41, 37)

Crab is indeed a man of many parts, as I argued earlier, and therein lies the rub. His parts don't fit, they fail to signify collectively as "man," he is composed as an aggregate, rather than as a whole. Once again, Chevillard is troping wryly on a literary commonplace, the mirror scene where a character fails to recognize his or her own reflected image. Yet something else is going on here, too, for Crab is in fact trying to *read* his body—and his lectoral efforts founder on his parts. If Crab is essentially fragmented as a man, so too is *La Nébuleuse du crabe* essentially fragmented as a novel. Composed of fifty-two brief chapters, each one largely anecdotal, with very little obvious narrative logic prevailing among them, *La Nébuleuse du crabe* puts the notion of the novel on trial and challenges its reader to find coherence. In other words, Chevillard's account of Crab's reading of his body is intended to foreground and parody the dilemma that faces us as we attempt to make sense of this text. Just like Crab, our reading is necessarily and insistently interrupted. We may find that the interstices between the parts of this text loom larger than the parts themselves; we may fall into the cracks of this novel; we may even decide that this piece of writing is so disjunctive that it is ultimately undeserving of the term "novel." Yet I would like to argue that Chevillard elaborates this strategy of interruption precisely in order to make us reflect upon narrative coherence as a notion, and to point out the fragility of that notion's foundations, even in the most well-made stories. Upon close examination, he suggests, the "parts" of any fictional world tend toward disjunction—and the closer that examination becomes, the more pronounced that phenomenon appears. In short, what we have in this passage, and in others like it throughout *La Nébuleuse du crabe,* is a simultaneous presentation of theme as technique, and technique as theme.

Another novelistic commonplace that Chevillard appropriates and turns to his own purposes is the idea that human existence is mocked and rendered absurd by death. Here again Chevillard inflates that topos to grotesque proportions and parodies it, inviting us to reflect upon it as a naked literary cliché. Like many fictional heroes, Crab is haunted by death. The contemplation of his own mortality inspires dread and trembling in his timid soul—all the more so, granted that death is the very first line in his curriculum vitae. Chevillard tells us that Crab was born dead; that his godmother declared that he died a day or two before his birth; and that, "Nipped in the bud, Crab will die on the vine" (36, 31-32; 52, 48). Chevillard's novel proposes to recount the life of Crab; yet Crab is a stillborn hero, and once one relates that event, there is very little left to say. Or perhaps on the contrary, once one has gotten that fundamental fact of Crab's existence out of the way, everything else becomes possible. For Crab is a death artist, constantly and beautifully dying in the past, the present, and the future, in every way imaginable: "Crab was supposed to die of cancer. The doctors gave him two months. Then he was run over by a bus. The best laid plans . . ." (48, 44). Like that of many distinguished figures in our cultural history, Crab's greatness is recognized only after his death; and that very recognition will breathe dramatic new life into him: "Crab died absolutely alone, down and out, in the bleakest poverty. Many years have passed; his name has become glorious, and his circumstances have improved considerably" (121, 121-22). Phoenix-like, Crab triumphs over death; he rises again from the worst calamities imaginable; he is patently a man to contend with. Yet Crab is not besotted with his own immortality, far from it: he saws off the branch upon which he is seated in order to build himself a coffin; he contemplates suicide and dreams of brandishing his own head on the end of a pikestaff; he never forgets any of the cemeteries in which he has been buried (64, 61; 110, 111; 117, 118).

It is neither cancer nor an errant bus that threatens most gravely to put an end to Crab's days, but rather that most pernicious pestilence of modernity, ennui: "He was forced to take to his bed. Summoned once again, the doctors could only confirm their futile diagnosis. Crab was dying of boredom. All their learning was in vain" (53, 50). For here is a man who lives through dying, yet who finds his life mortally stultifying. Crab is a seeker, to his credit: he searches for meaning in a world from which meaning has been evacuated; he looks under every rock beside the dubious path he follows for some semblance of coherence; he struggles to *be* in a life where simply being—stripped of the trappings with which we commonly adorn it—is the only given. He is left with not much at all, perhaps only speech: "So he speaks, he says anything at all, something and its opposite, that the elephant should dress in buckskin, and he is dismissed as delirious when in fact he is fighting for his life" (15, 9). In a similar manner, Chevillard launches his career as a novelist at a time when many people argue that the novel as a cultural medium has exhausted its possibilities. Yet even at the bleakest of times, Chevillard suggests, there is always more to say. And one might even take as one's subject the very idea of the novel's exhaustion, turning that gloomy discourse against itself in an effort to prove that the reports of the novel's demise (to paraphrase Mark Twain) are premature.[5] If such a project were carried out with enough resourcefulness, enough deftness, and enough wit, the resurrection of the novel might well rival that of Crab himself.

If, like Crab, one finds that the only tool that remains is speech, so be it. Alas, the social dimension of speech defeats him utterly. He never knows what to say to those people who address him; he wishes he could reply to them wittily and immediately, but he can imagine his replies only long after the moment has passed. In order to palliate his conversational deficiency, Crab decides to write his replies down in advance and, thus armored, he presumes that he will be largely equal to any discursive situation he may encounter (88, 87-88). Or at least when the people he meets are men, for Crab realizes to his shame that he is absolutely incapable of understanding the language that women speak (74, 72). The sad fact of the matter is that speech as a vehicle of interpersonal communication holds no prospect of salvation for Crab. What he practices—and what he relies upon to persuade himself that he exists—is speech as speech, that is, as an exercise in solipsistic subjectivity intended merely to furnish, however meagerly, the void that surrounds him. I use the word "exercise" advisedly because Crab practices speech like other, less-embattled people might practice sit-ups, or weightlifting, or jogging. He speaks to stay in shape, in some form of human shape. He is continually in danger of falling out of shape, moreover. His tongue feels waxy to him upon occasion; he has the distinct impression that it is hardening ever more, and will eventually leave him incapable of speech, at the end of a long and ineluctable process of petrification: "In order to slow the process, Crab is forced to talk continuously, even if it means saying nothing of interest" (15, 9). Crab has nothing to say, but the notion of saying nothing is intolerable to him because he senses that speech is his only solid claim to humanity.[6] He must speak, then, even if what he utters is fundamentally vacuous.

Wagering boldly on the very vacuity of his character's speech, Chevillard poses an ironic question: is Crab's language so very different from much of the language that we hear around us on a daily basis?[7] What relations prevail, moreover, between the language that Crab speaks and the metalanguage that Chevillard is uttering in *La Nébuleuse du crabe*? Crab's speech, like the novel itself, is fragmented, discontinuous, and insistently iterative: "Inevitably, there are some dull patches in his discourse, slow spots, irksome repetitions" (15, 9). Those effects are played out on two levels, as we listen both to Crab and to Chevillard, as we follow both the story and the tale of the story. Speech gives us shape, Chevillard argues, just as Crab relies upon his speech to shape him. If that shape turns out to be rather different from the one we have until now held as ideal, it may be because that ideal is largely bankrupt. That, of course, has been the principal message of the avant-garde since its inception; and it is a message that Chevillard articulates, in different ways, on every page of his novel.

Speaking endlessly and apparently without direction, Crab stays one step ahead of silence. It is not that he has never experienced silence. On the contrary, Crab has inhabited silence in the past, and has reflected upon it usefully:

His long practice of solitary meditation has taught him, if nothing else, to distinguish the many forms of silence, which meet with only an unchanging and obtuse insensitivity in the untrained ear. There is, then—among others—a string silence, a wind silence, a percussion silence, no more alike than the instruments thus classified, but on occasion their sonorities meld into a symphonic silence in which slow, stately movements, or martial ones, alternate with sprightly little phrases and silly arabesques, playing on a variety of motifs and rhythms in order to fully express the complexity of the situation, whatever that situation may be. (27-28, 22)

Where ordinary folk hear nothing, Crab hears *something*. And not just any something, either: for him, silence is infinitely orchestral. His own speech textualizes the music he perceives. His words, saying nothing much, engage those unvoiced melodies felicitously, producing a song that is limpid in its simplicity, compelling in its harmonies, and potently evocative of the emptiness of his existence—even if he alone hears that song.

Crab's perception, I think, is that of the artist, that romantic figure who conjures something out of nothing. Let me be more precise. Crab sees the world artistically; he finds patterns of sheer beauty in the magma of the quotidian, and he is capable of organizing those patterns in his imagination in aesthetically satisfying ways. It would be legitimate to call him an artist, if only he were capable of mobilizing his vision in order to create art—but that is precisely where Crab comes up short. Let's call him a virtual artist, then. Chevillard tells us that Crab has tried his hand in a variety of creative media. He distinguished himself particularly, for example, in photography, by virtue of the keenness of his eye, his sense of light, and his extraordinary powers of observation. Crab would have been recognized as the greatest photographer of his time, Chevillard notes, if he had had the luxury of a camera; but he died, we are told, in 1821, one year before Nicéphore Niepce's invention (86-87, 86). A photographer without a camera: that's Crab in a nutshell.

In a similar manner, Crab throws himself body and soul into painting, but with neither canvas, nor paint, nor brush (18, 13). He dreams of becoming a jazz trumpet player, but without a trumpet (31, 25). What he attempts, in other words, is to create something out of nothing—and utterly without means.

Chevillard offers his account of Crab's vain efforts as a ludic commentary on his own efforts in *La Nébuleuse du crabe,* for he presents his novel (in one of its aspects at least) as a story about nothing, whose hero is a nobody with very little to say. That is, Chevillard is not dealing here with great deeds performed by noble figures; nor is he carrying a mirror alongside a road. He is inviting us to ponder, rather, what Mallarmé called "the empty paper which whiteness forbids," and asking us what one may *do* with it. Were one an artist, one might decide to sketch a swallow. But one swallow is not enough for Crab: what he wants to do is to sketch all of the swallows in the world (23, 18). Crab must have it all, or he will have nothing. His aesthetic imagination is an absolutist one;[8] and, as fertile and full of promise as it may seem to him, it will necessarily founder upon the rocks of practice. When Crab turns to the piano, he feels that he is destined for a great career: "Once again that sudden frenzy gets hold of Crab, propelling him toward the piano where once again he realizes that while the virtuosity in his fingers allows him to lift the lacquered lid of the keyboard with genuine brio, the concert abruptly ends there" (25, 20). In each instance, Crab's creative efforts stall at that crucial moment when everything is possible, but nothing is accomplished.

Crab's career as an inventor is scarcely more rewarding. "Crab is the inventor of the bleak picture machine [*la machine à broyer du noir,* literally, 'the machine for grinding blackness']," Chevillard remarks, "A wonderfully ingenious and efficient machine, easily mastered after a few weeks' practice. Crab has every reason to be proud of it. Nevertheless, the National Institute of Industrial Property refuses to give him a patent, remarking that his invention is no different from an ordinary typewriter" (21-22, 17). Clearly—and characteristically—Crab is both ahead of his time and hopelessly outdated. The ironic relations between Crab's situation and that of Chevillard, moreover, are suggested here with particular poignancy. A writer, too, grinds away at blackness, braying that color laboriously in order to distribute it creatively upon the whiteness of the page. Chevillard raises an interesting question here too, one that is fundamental to his writerly project as a whole: can one invent something that already exists, be it a machine or a literary form like the novel?

Among all of his forays into artistic creation, the efforts that Crab devotes to writing are the most sustained. He does not lack for material, Chevillard notes. Humiliated, neglected, and trod upon throughout all of his days, "Crab had enough material to write all night" (58, 56). Like Mallarmé's blocked poet, Crab works in darkness, striving to blacken the page in front of him. He writes in order to pass the time, so that the passage of time may be rendered bearable. Crab's writing traces his own passage through time, in a black chronicle of his existence. Curiously, he comes to feel that he is leaving too many traces behind him, and that somebody might be stalking him. In an effort to stay one step ahead of whoever might be pursuing him, he writes ever more frenetically, even unto exhaustion:

> Crab leaves sentences behind him, a frail wake testifying to his recent passage, but he is no longer there, he is long gone, and their curious meanders, their multiple detours are simply the path of his zigzag flight, revealing his effort— thus far unrewarded—to break the thread that he unwinds behind him as he advances, no matter what he does, no matter where he goes, his struggle to finally break free of that trail of ink, thanks to which he would be pursued and apprehended were he not fortunately much quicker than his reader; but fatigue will rear its head one day, he will slow down, his reader will fall upon him. He is advised to stop writing and lay low for a while; the trail will soon fade. Of course. Crab would only have to give up moving. But since writing is his only means of motion, the slightest shadow of a gesture would set the blood-thirsty pack on his tail again. (60, 57-58)

Crab's dilemma poses important questions about the practice of writing, and most particularly about the writing of the self. Does one write one's story in order to reveal oneself, or on the contrary the better to hide from scrutiny?[9] Moreover, how does the writing of existence inflect upon that existence? Are existing and the telling of existence mutually irreconcilable? Must one choose definitively, as Sartre's Roquentin famously believed, between one and the other?[10] Does writing offer the Ariadne's Thread that will allow the subject to find his or her way out of the labyrinth of the self, or rather does it serve merely to ensnare the writer in ever more intricate knots? Like many other moments in *La Nébuleuse du crabe,* but perhaps more obviously and powerfully than most, this passage calls our attention to writing as writing, rather than as a representation of something else. That is, as Crab frets about the traces his writing leaves behind him as he advances, Chevillard invites us to consider the gesture of writing in its most material aspect, the way it traces a path upon the page, zigzagging from left to right, then back to the left, and from top to bottom, then back to the top. He also asks us to consider what it means to walk such a path, both for the writer and for the reader. The former looks ahead, choosing whether to zig or to zag, blazing a trail toward some destination that is more or less well defined depending upon the case; yet he or she also—and simultaneously—looks behind, always wondering if somebody is following, and if so, how closely. The latter forges onward, guided by signposts that may be in certain instances perfectly reliable or in others utterly misleading, occasionally taking false turns and retracing his or her steps, hoping to arrive finally at some terminus where the sense of this peregrination will finally become clear.

In other terms, what Chevillard offers for our inspection in this passage is the *spectacle* of literature in both its production and its reception. Characteristically, his tone is playful and self-deprecating: Crab's lucubrations are absurd ones, and the portrait of the artist that we see in him is carnivalized in the extreme. Nonetheless, through those ludic effects, Chevillard's more serious purposes become apparent. He is asking us to watch him write, and to watch ourselves reading. That very situation is made literally—if wryly—manifest in the text on one occasion, as if to dispel any lingering doubts we may have had about what Chevillard is really up to here; and it is played out quite explicitly as spectacle:

> Crab is writing the following little text in the public library, with no other intention than to offer his lovely table mate the spectacle of a poet in action— thus from time to time he sits with his pencil suspended between heaven and earth, between the eternal and the abyss, and allows himself a long moment of idle meditation, but then suddenly, as if inspired, obeying some incontrovertible order from on high, he bends over his notebook and writes out this very sentence, feverishly, with the slightest of smiles on his lips, a smile of quiet satisfaction, which soon becomes a skeptical pout, and then an ugly grimace of disgust, and Crab fiercely scratches out the last few words and recopies them verbatim, feverishly, with the slightest of smiles on his lips, a smile of quiet satisfaction, all the while miming the ardor of a fresh, brow-furrowing inspi-

ration, and then he lifts his pencil again, he runs an agitated hand through his hair, he favors the world around him with a vague glance, noticing as he does so that his spectacular act has indeed impressed his table mate, since she has her nose buried in a thick book on Italian Renaissance painting, trying to make an impression herself, obviously, you can see it in the way she turns the pages, the way she lingers over every reproduction with feigned emotion, takes hurried notes, quickly checks her watch, thrusts her pen and her notebook into her bag, puts on her coat, leaves the book lying open on the table, and runs toward the exit. But Crab doesn't care, he has effortlessly filled up his page thanks to her, his workday is done. (61-62, 59)

Crab puts eveything he has into his "spectacular act." The decor is perfect: where better to stage the drama of literature than in a public library? His spectator is a beautiful, coyly attentive one, he senses, just waiting to be seduced by the sight of an artist manfully honing his craft. If his efforts are less than wholly successful, well, you can't win them all. It's the art that's important, not the life. And undoubtedly more sensitive souls do exist, somewhere out there, ones less callous, less deeply cynical than the young woman in the library, ones who will not remain indifferent to the vital process of creation put thus enthrallingly on display.

We are such souls, Chevillard insinuates. We will not refuse to be moved by such a scene, nor will we be deaf to such an appeal. Gentle Readers from first word to last, we are lovingly bludgeoned by apostrophe, both overt and covert, throughout *La Nébuleuse du crabe*. "Open your eyes wide," Chevillard exhorts us as Crab delivers yet another virtuoso scene in this drama, "Are you convinced? Or do you want him to repeat the experiment?" (17, 11). Chevillard greets us warmly at the door and sits us down front row center. Everything proceeds as if Crab were playing a command performance for us alone— which in a real sense, of course, he is. So too is Chevillard himself, I believe, both through and against his protagonist, using Crab both as mask and as foil in this novel where writing itself is played out as theater.

As Crab plays out yet another scene, Chevillard intends that we should watch him in rapt attention. Having finally sat down to write his masterpiece, Crab has hit upon a method of composition that will enable him to produce a truly remarkable book, "involving, in this first stage, the combination of every word listed in the dictionary, in every possible permutation" (90, 89). The manuscript that results from that process is as high as a mountain, and it contains in its pages, well, everything that has ever been written—and also everything that might one day be written: "Crab had a wealth of material at his disposal, containing every book that has ever been or ever will be" (91, 90). Let us not forget that this is the man who wished to draw all the swallows in the world. His literary goal is likewise absolute; but he will not stop at the foot of the mountain. Taking that vertiginous manuscript, Crab will make strategic, considered deletions until all that is left is a hundred pages of text. Like Praxiteles chipping away from a block of marble everything that is not "Phyrne," Crab will sculpt from the *prima materia* of an impossible lexicon the perfect book, the one that was there, potentially at least, all along: "that was how Crab wrote his book—and he doesn't believe it would be possible to go about it any other way" (92, 91).

Crab's project calls literature itself sharply into question, both parodically and in a more sober tone, too. In one perspective, his creative methods are not far removed from those of the monkeys banging away on their typewriters who one day produce the entire text of *Hamlet.* There is an idiocy to his creative vision that is somehow strongly appealing, also. It appeals most strongly, perhaps, to the notion of the artist as *vates,* as an inspired, noble idiot, a notion that subtends much of our thinking about creation, even when the creator we identify appears to us as the very antithesis of the idiot. Is Crab's conception of the book so very different from that of Mallarmé, of Joyce, of Queneau? Seen through the eyes of a beautiful dreamer like Crab, isn't the greatest *chef-d'oeuvre* merely a disordered dictionary, as Cocteau once suggested? Literature is combinatoric in character, we will easily admit, and the lexicon is finite; granted that, what prevents any writer from finding that combination of words which will be hailed, universally and resoundingly, as the book of books?

Yet that book, once written, would clearly announce the end of all books; and perhaps such an eventuality appeals somehow to Crab.[11] In his own case, having finished the book of his life, he feels it unnecessary—and indeed in a sense ethically impossible for him—to live any further: "Crab will lie low at home from now on, now that he has finally finished his memoirs. Does nothing. Never moves. Lips sealed. Eyes closed. Has an absent air about him. Nothing must ever happen to him again. Never again. The least little event would spoil everything. Even death. It's all in the book lying before him, his life in its entirety. Nothing to add. Finished" (122, 124). His struggles are over, he feels, precisely by virtue of the fact that he has accounted for them, each and every one, in words. He has brought himself finally into being, but in doing so has left himself no more room to *be*.

I wonder if Eric Chevillard is not telling a similar story about the novel in *La Nébuleuse du crabe*. Like Crab himself, this text is continually turning back upon itself, biting its own tail, in an effort to consume its own body and thus disappear. Gestures of that sort are legion in this novel, and the first of them occurs on the very first page: "We should expect nothing more from Crab. There is no point in urging him to prove less erratic or more logical in his choices. Crab is ungraspable, not evasive or deceptive but blurry, as if his congenital myopia had little by little clouded his contours" (7, 1). It is a very curious way to introduce a character, and to inaugurate his story. If we can "expect nothing more from Crab," what is the point of pushing onward? If he is truly "ungraspable," "blurry," if his profile is "cloudy," how can we hope to come to terms with him? Perhaps here already Chevillard is suggesting that we should direct our attention elsewhere. For it shortly becomes clear that Crab serves in this text as a stalking-horse for a sustained meditation on literary form, a meditation in which each characteristic attributed to Crab may be read as a commentary on *La Nébuleuse du crabe* itself—and, more broadly, on the status and potential of the novel as a cultural practice.

Like Crab, this novel is "ungraspable," "blurry," and "cloudy": in a word, *nebulous*. Our expectation of "more" is a legitimate one only insofar as we are willing to displace our semiotic desire and to reconfigure in a creative manner what we mean by "more." Chevillard argues that our traditional conception of the "more" offered by the novel is no longer valid and that this novel will not provide satisfaction to us if we read it in a conventional fashion. We must look elsewhere, he suggests; and consequently the early pages of *La Nébuleuse du crabe* present a portrait of a man who is searching for something as yet unidentified, just like us. "His course of conduct is never easy to follow," Chevillard says of Crab (8, 1), and his remark may be taken as a general warning that our standard reading protocols will not be of much avail here. As

Crab looks for meaning and direction in his life, finding little or none, the
questions he asks are just the ones this novel asks of itself: "Suddenly he no
longer understood what he was about, what he was doing there, and especially what he was supposed to do in order not to disappoint, in order to perform his function, what function, and how to proceed, and where to begin, to
begin what?" (9-10, 3). They recapitulate, too, the kinds of questions the reader,
stumbling through the first pages of *La Nébuleuse du crabe,* might well ask.
Importantly, they also echo the kinds of questions a novelist like Chevillard
asks of himself as he sets out to write a novel.

In that web of analogy, he argues, lies the "more" that this kind of literature offers, both to the writer and to the reader. Through a finely crafted
pattern of paradox, outright contradiction, and irony, this novel erects narrative possibilities one after the other only to subvert them, hovering always on
the threshold of becoming in order to suggest that the fundamental desire of
writer and reader is focused on the possibility that a work of literature might
become. In that sense, Chevillard's creative vision, like that of Crab, is an absolutist one, for it is animated by the faith that something new will emerge from
a process of deliberate and radical eschewal of convention.[12] Chevillard argues
that his readers are full partners in such a process and that there are close,
highly articulative relations prevailing between the writer's quest and that of
the reader. Those relations become most apparent precisely in those moments
where the story threatens to consume itself.

Such moments abound in *La Nébuleuse du crabe,* of course, and I have
already pointed out more than a few of them. As a final gesture, I would like
to return briefly to the moment when Crab has finished writing his memoirs.
He feels that nothing is left to be said at that point, and that nothing remains
to him other than to withdraw, in good crustacean fashion, into his shell; and
we too may feel that we can "expect nothing more from Crab" at that point,
just as we were warned, duplicitously enough, at the novel's beginning. Yet
just as we are led to believe that Crab's story is over ("Nothing to add. Finished."), Chevillard tells us on the contrary that there is "more,"[13] and the
novel edges obliquely in fits and starts, crablike, toward its point of closure:

> At the end of the performance, the curtain did not fall—stuck in the flies no
> doubt—and since the audience expected the show to go on, Crab had no choice

but to keep it up. He hesitated a moment; they thought he'd forgotten his lines, and the indulgent crowd gave him an ovation. Crab bowed and resolved to perform the whole play again from the beginning. There were a few cat-calls at first, of course, but the more enlightened members of the crowd understood that this was a daring metaphor for the eternal return, or even a fierce satire of our serial existences, and urged silence upon the carping dullards. The second performance was applauded far more warmly than the first. But the curtain still did not fall. (122-23, 125)

Still the crowd is not satisfied and obliges Crab to continue. He improvises, he sings, he recites poetry, he tells tales, he discourses on ethics and philosophy, he even gazes moodily upon Yorick's skull, and still the curtain fails to fall:

> And then Crab sank into silence, slowly, inexorably, vertically, he sank in and eventually disappeared from the gaze of the audience. There was some confusion among the spectators, a moment of uncertainty, of incomprehension, but they quickly settled on the only credible hypothesis: a trapdoor had opened beneath Crab's feet—of course, there was a trapdoor concealed in the stage—and, by common agreement, this symbolic burial of the character, replacing the fall of the curtain or the sudden blackout that traditionally signifies the end of a show, was in itself worth the price of admission; with one blow it erased the long days of boredom that had preceded it. *(Applause.)* (124, 126)

That is where *La Nébuleuse du crabe* ends, in a discourse that questions the notion of closure, then turns back upon that very question and puts it, too, on trial. One has been conditioned in everything which precedes to expect nothing less vexing than that. What intrigues me particularly here is the manner in which the *play* of the novel, implicit throughout *La Nébuleuse du crabe,* suddenly becomes overtly and unmistakably explicit. For Crab is quite literally on stage here, and with him the novel itself. So are we, for that matter, if we can recognize ourselves in the guise of a public that is never sated, utterly tyrannical in its demands, and always clamoring for "more." We won't settle for a simple repetition of what has preceded; we won't be lulled by song, poetry, or tale; having suffered through "the long days of boredom," we require something much more spectacular than a curtain. Crab's performance, in other words, can end with nothing less than spectacle—and the same is true of Chevillard's performance in *La Nébuleuse du crabe*. Their exit astonishes us. Even if we are quick to suspect the trick through which it was achieved, we are nonetheless delighted by it. In the course of this droll performance, we have been at times confused, befuddled, mocked, and ill-used; but we may now leave the theater thinking—for the moment at least—that we have witnessed something new.

NOTES

[1] Crab returns in *Un Fantôme* (1995; A Ghost), but I shall restrict myself here to a discussion of *La Nébuleuse du crabe*. In "The Ghosts of Eric Chevillard," Jordan Stump provides an excellent analysis of the way Chevillard recycles his character, and also outlines the mutual affinities prevailing among all of Chevillard's protagonists in his first seven novels.

[2] Here and throughout, I have used Jordan Stump and Eleanor Hardin's translation. The first page numbers refer to the original, the second to the translation.

[3] See Olivier Bessard-Banquy's remarks about Palafox's "continual metamorphoses" in Chevillard's third novel ("Chevillard écrivain" 894).

[4] See for instance Bessard-Banquy, who calls Crab "the emblematic character of the writer" ("Eric Chevillard: Un écrivain à découvrir" 48).

[5] See for instance John Barth's remarks in his famous essay, "The Literature of Exhaustion": "Suppose you're a writer by vocation—a 'print-oriented bastard,' as the McLuhanites call us—and you feel, for example, that the novel, if not narrative literature generally, if not the printed word altogether, has by this hour of the world just about shot its bolt, as Leslie Fiedler and others maintain. I'm inclined to agree, with reservations and hedges. Literary forms certainly have histories and historical contingencies, and it may well be that the novel's time as a major art form is up, as the 'times' of classical tragedy, Italian and German grand opera, or the sonnet-sequence came to be. No necessary cause for alarm in this at all, except perhaps to certain novelists, and one way to handle such a feeling might be to write a novel about it" (*The Friday Book* 71-72).

[6] See Stump and Hardin vii: "For Crab's nature—his life itself—hangs by a slender thread: language. And language, thank goodness, expresses both the

impossible and the possible with the same blithe dexterity; moreover, if left to its own devices, it drifts merrily and ineluctably down a never-ending stream of associations and enumerations. It is this unstoppability and this freedom that determine the shape of Crab's experience."

[7] In that perspective, see Bessard-Banquy: "Lost in the forest of mass literature, smack in the middle of a happy epoch of permanent televised chatter, drunk with the refrains of egregious politspeak, Chevillard's books, like much of contemporary French literature, express a distrust of language which manifests itself most particularly when he has nothing to say" ("Eric Chevillard: Un écrivain à découvrir" 48).

[8] See Bessard-Banquy's remarks about the narrator of Chevillard's *Préhistoire:* "His vision, like that of all of Chevillard's heroes, is a kind of ordinary madness of the Absolute" ("Une Littérature du trou noir" 977).

[9] See Georges Perec's remarks in one of his most autobiographical texts, *W ou le souvenir d'enfance (W or The Memory of Childhood):* "Once again, the traps of writing were set. Once again, I was like a child playing hide-and-seek and who doesn't know what he fears or desires the most: to remain hidden or to be found" (14).

[10] See *La Nausée (Nausea):* "Here is what I thought: for the most banal event to become an adventure, it suffices and it is necessary to begin to *tell* it. [. . .] But one must choose: to live or to tell" (61-62).

[11] See Stump 827: "Crab [. . .] attempts to write a book so utterly perfect as to obviate the need for speech, thereby ushering in—once again—a new era of unbroken silence."

[12] See Pierre Jourde 204: "In the same gesture, Eric Chevillard's oeuvre performs a universal destruction and postulates a total writing, a writing of the absolute."

[13] See Jean-Louis Hippolyte 31: "Each of Chevillard's texts emblematizes a process of entropic unraveling of the world that ultimately exhausts itself, along with the text. Each text tries however to survive itself, and to go past its own heat-death, its own demise. This constitutes the crux of what most postexotic narratives are about: how to tell a story that must not end?"

III

∾

Linda Lê's
Language

Born in Dalat, Vietnam in 1963, Linda Lê has lived in France since the age of fourteen. She focused on literature during her university studies and worked on a doctoral thesis dealing with Henri Frédéric Amiel's *Journal intime* before turning to creative writing (Yeager 257). Her record as a writer is noteworthy in several respects. Since she inaugurated her career in 1987 with *Un si tendre vampire* (Such a Tender Vampire), she has published eleven novels and collections of short stories.[1] Her books testify to a deep fascination with language, and a strong will to renovate that particular language which we call literature. They question literature closely, and put many of its conventions on trial, adumbrating in this fashion new directions for narrative fiction. In a word, Linda Lê's writings are experimentalist. Though each of her texts presents aspects that are deserving of critical comment, I will speak here about her novel *Calomnies* (1993; *Slander*), because I feel that it is her richest, most intriguing text to date, and also because it has a great deal to suggest about the nature of writing and the status of the novel in our time.

Jack Yeager has argued that *Calomnies* is Lê's most autobiographical book; yet he acknowledges that the correspondences between this fiction and Lê's life are precarious at best.[2] For my part, I would like to put the question of autobiography largely in abeyance in my discussion of this novel. I am motivated to do so by a variety of reasons. First, I confess that it is partly a matter of prejudice: quite simply stated, I am not very interested in authors' lives. More objectively (and undoubtedly more importantly) we have very little hard information about *this* author's life. Finally, I believe that there are other themes, concerns, and discourses in this novel that are more compelling—more fully articulated and exploited by Lê herself, and more rewarding for my local purposes here, that is, in a consideration of the ways in which the contemporary novel examines itself as a cultural form.

Allow me to describe briefly certain aspects of organization and setting in *Calomnies*. The novel is strongly dialogical in its structure, with two narrative voices speaking in alternating chapters. Those voices belong to an uncle and his niece. Both currently live in France, and both emigrated from a country that is never precisely identified, though the context makes it clear that it was located somewhere in the former French Indochina. The uncle emigrated against his will: having fallen in love with one of his sisters, he was committed to an insane asylum by his family. Returning for a visit, he found that his sister had hanged herself, and his family had him committed yet again, but this time in France—and in one of its most desolate regions, the Corrèze. At the moment when the novel begins, the uncle has lived in France for fifteen years, having spent ten years in the asylum and five years working quietly in a local library after his release. The niece was very young when the family sent her uncle away, and she herself arrived in France somewhat later. Now, she is wondering about her family history, and most particularly about the issue of her paternity, for her mother has told her that her biological father was not the man whom she had always called "Father," but rather a "Stranger" (22,13),[3] a military man with whom her mother had had an affair. Hoping to find the truth of the matter, the niece writes a letter to her uncle (whom she has not seen since he was sent away), asking him for his version of the story; and it is with this gesture of *correspondence* that the novel begins.

The prospect of a profound correspondence between these two individuals is a fragile one, for both of them have been significantly damaged by experience, if in different ways. It will play itself out linguistically, moreover, through the mediation of the written word, because the uncle and the niece never actually meet, and what the niece is asking of him is a written account of her family history. The vehicle of that account will be the French language, just like the niece's letter to her uncle, since both the uncle and the niece are now more familiar with French than with their mother tongue. The alternation of their voices throughout the novel, while the uncle ponders what he might write to her and the niece waits for his reply, sets up another kind of correspondence. That correspondence has a tensive character to it, for the questions the niece has asked her uncle in her letter are impossible ones, and they are intended to elicit answers from the uncle that are equally impossible. In this sense *Calomnies* is a high-wire act stretching from one of the very edges of French society to another, and bridging the center vertiginously upon a language strained to the breaking point.

Both the uncle and the niece are marginal figures with regard to main-stream French society, and both of them recognize their marginality with re-markable lucidity.[4] In the first instance, it is their ethnicity that marks them as different, as foreign. Yet in both of their cases, ethnicity is only the most obvi-ous outward sign of their difference, and a variety of other considerations mark them still more indelibly with the brand of alterity. The uncle, of course, was designated as insane and sent to live with other insane people, hermeti-cally sealed off from mainstream society in the sort of community that Erving Goffman has termed a "total institution."[5] Even within that community of outcasts, however, the uncle finds himself marginalized by the other inmates:

> Ten years locked up in this colony of half-wits, ten years spent side by side with psychos, spastics, dodderers, lobotomy cases, geniuses who bungled their vocation. Ten years among the albinos, waxen faces that come alive only to insult me, to call me Monkey-Face during their rare moments of lucidity. (9, 1)

When at last he is discharged into society and goes to work in the public library, he discovers that only his name has changed rather than his status with regard to the people around him: "Before I was called Monkey-Face. Now they call me the Chinamad" [*Chinetoqué*] (17, 8). "Chinamad" is a port-manteau word, cruelly but neatly conflating the epithets "Chinaman" and "mad," grafting together in that manner the two handiest signs of the uncle's alterity. As harsh as they may be, moreover, "Monkey-Face" and "Chinamad" are the only names that the uncle can call his own in the economy of this story, for he is otherwise anonymous, as is his niece. Linda Lê does not provide a name for either the uncle or the niece; the closest she comes to naming either of them is when she suggests that the niece has an "international given name" (161, 134). The tactic is a highly deliberate one: a name is after all the first guarantor of identity within a group, and to be nameless is to be very largely unidentified—as a person, that is, instead of as a social "case."

The survival tactics that the uncle deploys devolve precisely on his identification as a social case, and they shift subtly as his situation shifts. While he was in the asylum, he played the role that had been scripted for him: "I played the madman so I wouldn't go mad" (26, 17). It is an example of what Ross Chambers has called "oppositional behavior,"[6] and it allows the uncle some small leeway within a regime that is otherwise utterly constraining. Upon his discharge from the asylum, the uncle chooses to lead, insofar as possible, a subterranean existence: "I owe it to normal people, happy people, not to offend them with my presence" (116, 97). Camouflage or clandestinity: the options available to the uncle are meager, unattractive ones at best; and both tactics will serve only to attenuate his pariah status and make it livable, rather than to reverse it and allow him to find integration in society—for that, in his view at least, is clearly impossible.

The niece's marginality is perhaps more subtle than that of her uncle, but it is no less real, and she struggles mightily under the burden that it places on her. Like her uncle, she is an uprooted figure: she feels no solid, affective attachment to the country from which she has emigrated; nor does she feel reliably anchored in France. She is alienated from her family and has severed most of her ties with her mother and her other relatives. Her feeling of alterity goes well beyond questions of nation and family, however. As Jack Yeager has pointed out, the niece is a "psychological nomad" (260). She senses that she is very much adrift, and wherever she may find herself, she feels that she is a stranger, a foreigner. That feeling is made explicit in the words of a song that runs through the niece's head:

> I'm a stranger here,
> I'm a stranger everywhere,
> I would go home, but
> I'm a stranger there. (32, 22)[7]

Words are important to the niece, for she is a writer. She believes moreover that the career she has chosen—if indeed it is a matter of "choice"— marks her still further as being unlike other people. She views writing itself as a kind of affliction, and, in her moments of despair, a shameful sort of afflic tion, much like her uncle's madness. The men she has known are all involved in some fashion in the literary establishment, and the niece feels that each of them has tried to appropriate her and mold her in his own image. There are for example her former lovers "Weidman" and "Bellemort," both of them writers. There is her editor, the nefarious "Counselor," who imperiously tries to get her to write the book that *he* has conceived for her. Her friend "Ricin," a publisher, is perhaps an exception among the males that she knows; yet even he speaks to her from a point of centrality and power with regard to which she feels very foreign indeed.

In her letter to her uncle, she tells him that he is the only member of the family with whom she wishes to have any sort of ties (12, 3). They have not seen each other, nor have they had any other sort of contact, since the uncle was sent to France, when the niece was a very young girl. Consequently, the niece's remark seems strange to the uncle, and he wonders about the thinking that motivated it: "Her goal escapes me. What drives her to amass peculiarities, to warp her destiny, to strive for defects, only defects?" (127, 106). Perhaps this is an exercise in self-flagellation, or a misplaced *nostalgie de la boue,* or rather an effort on the niece's part to read her own alienation through the more literal text of her uncle's story. Upon reflection, however, the uncle will admit that certain analogies are to be found between his own existence and that of his niece, and that certain fundamental circumstances link them. Chief among these is the feeling of dislocation: "We are from Nowhere, *she* and I" (173, 143).

Yet the uncle may not be entirely correct in that assessment, because in point of fact they are both from *some* place. As ill-defined as that place may otherwise be, it is clearly—just like France—one which defines and maintains its center through a systematic relegation of undesirable elements to the margins of society. That broad social dynamic finds its exact representation (and its confirmation) within the family dynamic. The uncle recalls that in the old country one of the elders of the family, who was thought to be insane, was incarcerated in the family house. From time to time, he would escape, never getting out of the yard, however. A relative who owned a zoo provided a neat solution to the problem: a cage was brought to the house, and they locked the elder up in it. When the family acted, they decided to save appearances through a convenient fiction: they let it be known that the elder had died, and even held a public funeral for him, complete with empty coffin. Yet he continued to live in his cage for many years thereafter, until he died. From that little parable, and from his own experience with the family as well, the uncle draws a cruel lesson:

> Every generation sacrifices one of its own so that the others can lead their lives sheltered from the threat of madness. Every generation designates the one who will be the acknowledged madman. The others make a show of their extreme prudence, conform to what they believe to be the rules of normal life, save face. The man with the knife has been sacrificed. He's the one who passes for crazy in the eyes of the world. The one who takes all the stigma upon himself, who clears the others of the suspicion of being deranged. (25, 15-16)

Among the family members of his own generation, the arbiter of normalcy seems to have been the uncle's sister, the mother of his niece, a figure whom the niece herself refers to as "Madamother" [Madamère]. Alas, she felt herself to be the only truly normal person in the family, and had suggested just that to her daughter upon one occasion: "Madamother said, It was my destiny to be surrounded by pariahs" (23, 13). She cited as examples the elder in his cage and the uncle in his asylum, but also her own husband, "the man without a cent" as she called him (23, 13), whose sin was his inability to provide for Madamother's material needs. Her husband's lack of success as a provider is what drove Madamother to have an affair with the foreign military man who is the niece's true father—or so Madamother claimed. The husband was also a "dreamer," apparently (13). It is a word that is uttered by Madamother with extreme distaste and scorn, but it may have been one of the qualities that endeared him so to his presumptive daughter. For the niece loved her father deeply, and the uncle recalls that she demonstrated her love for him constantly, in spite of the fact that the rest of the family mocked and shunned the man. The uncle also remarks that the husband loved the little girl, even though he realized that he was not her father (53, 42).

As Tolstoy pointed out, unhappy families are the only ones that really interest us as readers. In *Calomnies,* the uncle correctly reads unhappy family history as the text that accounts for what both he and his niece have become;

and importantly, it is a text that generates other stories, the story of his own "madness" and the story of his niece's decision to become a writer. "I have dedicated ten years of my life to madness," he muses, "she will dedicate as many to writing. We are, *she* and I, the runts of the litter in this family of crazies. We were the only ones to escape, to flee from the family; instead of being saved, we turned out to be incapable of leading a normal life" (19, 9). In other terms, they have "escaped," they have "fled," but only into a kind of existential no-man's-land, where both of them will live in exile.

The notion of exile is an important one in *Calomnies*. Linda Lê scrutinizes that notion in its political sense on several occasions, but she is perhaps more interested still in what it means to be an exile in the metaphysical sense. Criticizing the niece's slavish devotion to her former lovers, Weidman and Bellemort, Ricin tells her: "In love, you have always behaved like a woman in exile who hopes to fulfill all the necessary conditions in order to apply for the position of model immigrant" (71, 58). It is easy to argue that the niece's exile from her homeland has necessarily colored her way of relating to other people and her manner of being in the world. Yet I think the question is more intricate than that. For one thing, her story suggests that her feeling of alterity was inculcated in her before she emigrated. For another, it may be that she sees in her exilic status a way of establishing her own independence, despite the considerable costs that such a move entails. It is in a similar perspective that Jack Yeager has noted an anomaly in Linda Lê's own writing: "Vietnamese writers of earlier generations who wrote in French implicitly expressed the hope of fitting in, whereas Lê's texts convey a desire to remain at the margins" (262).

Like Linda Lê, the niece may recognize one of the more insidious moves that power may perform with regard to those who are relatively disempowered: power may appropriate the powerless in certain instances, and promote them in a carefully staged fashion—"Vietnamese writers," "Francophone writers," "women writers"—in order precisely to put the full pageant of power on public display.[8] The niece may feel that the best defense against such a move is mobility itself, even if such a choice condemns one to a life in the margins of things. Edward Said has remarked that exile is not necessarily an unmitigated evil, particularly for the intellectual, on the condition that he or she can turn what it offers to advantage: "Exile for the intellectual in this metaphysical sense is restlessness, movement, constantly being unsettled, and unsettling others" (*Representations of the Intellectual* 53).[9] Even as she complains of her feeling of dislocation, the niece relies heavily on her mobility in order to deflect the constraints that power seeks to place upon her. I feel, too, that Linda Lê relies on a similar strategy, for her novel is a very mobile piece of work, constantly shifting voice and perspective, sketching out quick swerves in theme and topos, never quite settling where one might expect it to.

Such a strategy is evident on many levels in *Calomnies,* and it is often most apparent in passages where the word *métèque* occurs. That word plays an important role in the lexical economy of the novel, and it is used four times in all.[10] It is also a very slippery word in French, one that is highly charged with ideological prejudice, and one whose meaning is never precisely clear. According to the the the *Dictionnaire historique de la langue française, métèque* comes into French from the classical Greek *metoikos* which, in Athens, designated a foreigner living in the city and enjoying certain privileges, without holding citizenship. Formed from *meta* and *oikos* ("home," "homeland"), it signified properly "who changes residence." Initially introduced in France by scholars of Greek history, it came into more common use in the late nineteenth century, deployed in a xenophobic discourse of "national defense" against "cosmopolitan" elements in French society (Rey 1235). In terms of its current usage, the *Larousse* defines it simply as a pejorative word denoting a "foreigner residing in a country" (Dubois 571), while the *Robert* nuances it somewhat further, adding some ethnic precision but also rehearsing uncritically some of the racist discourse in which the word is habitually couched: "Mediterranean foreigner residing in France whose physical traits and manners are very unpleasant" (Rey and Rey-Debove 1191). There is no precise equivalent of the word in English. *Harrap's New Shorter French and English Dictionary* gives "foreigner," "alien," "dago," and "wop" (Mansion M: 21); *Harrap's French-English Dictionary of Slang and Colloquialisms* adds "wog" to "dago" and "wop" (Marks 143). Esther Allen, in her otherwise excellent translation of *Calomnies,* has left the word in the original, glossing it with the epithets "swarthy foreigner," "dirty foreigner," and "dirty barbarian."[11]

Clearly, both the uncle and the niece have felt the lash of the word *métèque,* and both have had to come to terms with it. Neither is "Mediterranean," of course, but they are both "foreigners," and by virtue of their ethnic origin they may seem to certain kinds of people in France to have a "very unpleasant" physical appearance (it will be recalled, for example, that the other inmates of the asylum refer to the uncle as "Monkey-Face"). Linda Lê's use of the word puts both of those considerations into play in a broad semantic field that marks the person to whom it is directed as an "outsider," someone who is once and for all excluded from society. Even when the authorities praise his work, the uncle remarks that their encomium is carefully qualified and relativized, for they read him through the ideological lens of the *métèque*. He performs his job in the library very well indeed, and—will wonders never cease?—he even reads some of the books in that library: "The librarian holds me up as an example. The madman, the loathesome, swarthy foreigner, the *métèque,* who set himself to reading books. Culture saves . . ." (10, 2).

The uncle understands that others read his niece first and foremost as a *métèque,* and that such a reading necessarily colors whatever further impressions people may have of her. Yet he recognizes too that his niece's *métèque* status is more complex and conflicted than his own: "To the pride of being a *métèque,* a swarthy foreigner, writing in a language that is not her own, she wants to add the suspicion of illegitimacy, her semicertainty that she is of mixed blood" (127, 106). In other words, not only is she a *métèque* in the eyes of others, she also feels herself to be a *métèque* in her own blood. For that blood is *mixed:* her biological father was a "foreigner" in her country of origin. And if the niece was a lovechild, she was nonetheless very badly loved. The foreigner left the country soon after her birth; he sent her occasional presents during the first seven years of her life, then, afterward, nothing. "You are the daughter of no one," muses the uncle, "the forgotten offspring of a runaway lover" (158, 131).

The uncle perceptively identifies pride as an element of the way the niece views her status, the pride of writing in French from the position of an outsider. It is interesting to note, moreover, that in both of these iterations of the word *métèque* that I have quoted, the issue of otherness is deliberately intricated with literature: in the uncle's case, with the fact that he reads literature; in the niece's, with the fact that she writes literature. Language is perhaps the crucible in which the *métèque* is most closely tested; certainly that is true in *Calomnies*. Learning to speak a language, learning to write a language, learning to turn that language to one's most pressing needs may enable a person to establish a livable place for himself or herself in the interstices of power. When the niece complains to her friend Ricin about the influence her editor, the "Counselor," is trying to exercise over her, Ricin gives her a piece of advice: "Keep to yourself. Keep on being a *métèque,* a swarthy barbarian. Cultivate the margins, work the edges" (33, 23).

The niece will take that advice to heart, as difficult in practice as it may be. Beyond that, I believe that it is also legitimate to read in that passage the outline of a broad case that Linda Lê makes for alterity in her novel. In a fine example of "oppositional behavior," she takes the word *métèque* and scrutinizes it, examining the prejudice that subtends it and the xenophobic ideology that enables it, laying it bare and then reappropriating it for her own uses. She turns the word against itself and makes it signify anew, on her own terms— much like the Black Pride movement in America in the 1960s reappropriated the racist epithet "black," or, more recently, the way Queer Theorists have reappropriated the word "queer." She recognizes that the notion of ethnic homogeneity is a myth, a pernicious and dangerous myth, but a myth nonetheless. As Edward Said put it in *Culture and Imperialism,* "No one today is purely *one* thing" (336); and in that same work he calls for the progressive intellectual to adopt a "contrapuntal perspective" (32) in order better to understand and describe phenomena of power and exclusion.

It seems to me that *Calomnies* can usefully be described as a novel written in counterpoint. That effect is most obvious in the alternation of voice in its chapter structure. Yet both of the voices are in themselves largely contrapuntal in tone as well. The uncle turns his niece's request to him this way and that; he moves back and forth between a feeling of solidarity with her and a sense of their irrecuperable difference; his voice is at times cajoling and at others stridently critical. In a similar manner, the niece shifts her perspective fluidly, focusing here on her family history and there on her career as a writer and its vexations; longing on the one hand for inclusion and basking on the other hand in her solitude; struggling to live and laboring to write her life. In very large part, contrapuntal effects such as these account for the extraordinary mobility of *Calomnies* that I alluded to earlier. They are founded upon

Linda Lê's desire to reflect on language (most particularly literary language) in new ways; and upon her will to represent an account of that reflection in the fictional world of her novel.

In his reading of *Calomnies,* Jack Yeager argues that "The problematic of language lies at the heart of all colonial and post-colonial narrative texts in French" (260). That assertion is a valid one, I believe. Yet here is another contrapuntal effect to consider: in certain of its aspects, *Calomnies* presents itself as a postcolonial work; in others, however, that stance is considerably attenuated in order to situate the idea of alterity on broader, more metaphysical ground. Lê examines language exhaustively, and in a variety of manners. Pursuing the contrapuntal strategy that characterizes her style in the novel as a whole, some of her approaches to the problem invoke issues of colonialism and power, while others largely elide that question to focus more generally on the ways a writer— any writer—struggles with the written word.

As the uncle ponders the difficulties of his own linguistic apprenticeship in French, he reflects also upon his niece's relation to that language:

> I had to learn French among madmen. Meanwhile, French has become her only language, her tool, her *weapon.* The weapon she uses against her family, against the Country. Thanks to that weapon, she will always be alone. She's a *métèque,* a dirty foreigner, who writes in French. For her, the French language is what madness has been for me: a way of escaping the family, of safeguarding her solitude, her mental integrity. (12, 4)

The analogy that he draws between his madness and his niece's writing is an intriguing one. It suggests that if both madness and writing enable the subject to construct his or her identity apart from the script that has been given to them by the group to recite, they both inevitably mark the subject as being outside the pale. There is another kind of symmetry at work in that analogy, too. The uncle learns to speak French in order to survive in the asylum, in order to script his "madness" and make it livable. Later, under the benevolent tutelage of a figure called "the Monk," he will learn to read French literature, and most particularly poetry (86, 70). The niece writes in the first instance in order to make some sense of the madness from which she has sought to escape, as if the only way to free herself of that madness were to *represent* it, as faithfully as possible, in words.

Linda Lê problematizes and enriches her discourse on language through a meditation on the relations of the "mother tongue" and the "second language." The niece writes the letter to her uncle in French, as I mentioned; and the uncle's "report" will be written in that language too. As the uncle explains, their relations with their mother tongue are now so distant and eroded as to make communication in French imperative for them: "The letter and the report are written in French. She no longer knows her native language. For fifteen years I haven't spoken that language" (172, 143). Yet the mother tongue still holds some power for the niece, and in fact it precipitated her decision to write to her uncle. The niece was sitting in a public park one day when a man she didn't know addressed her in her mother tongue. She encountered him several times thereafter and learned that he was a shoemaker in her neighborhood. Each time they met, she would deflect his importunities, but she gradually came to realize that she could no longer leave the question of her paternity unresolved, and thus she wrote the letter to her uncle (19-20, 10). Later, the niece begins to understand that the issue of her family history is deeply imbricated in the problem of language, and more precisely, in her own history of linguistic emigration. Her change of skin is less definitive than she might have thought, for the mother tongue still has some considerable power over her. The shoemaker treats her as a "compatriot," appealing her to recognize in effect their shared history. When she complains about this to her friend Ricin, he urges the niece to resist the shoemaker, or else sacrifice all the independence she has so laboriously constructed for herself: "If you fall into the trap he's setting for you, he'll make you into a guilty doll, he'll force you to go back to the Country, to relearn your native language, he'll put it in your head that you've betrayed the Country, that you must write in your own language" (70, 57).

In *Calomnies,* the question of the mother tongue is thus bound up in feelings of guilt and treachery. Renouncing a mother tongue (and whether that "renunciation" be deliberate or circumstantial is largely moot here) is not a simple gesture, and no matter how one may try to repress that language, it will always return. Moreover, it is an "unnatural" gesture—for what is more "natural" than one's mother tongue? Writing in a second language is in this perspective an act against nature. Yet the difficulties one may encounter can be rationalized by virtue of that consideration: the new idiom is a different kind of language, learned "artificially" rather than "naturally," and one doesn't expect it to come easily. The niece is surprised, thus, to realize that many of the conflictive feelings she feels toward her mother tongue vex her relations with the French language, too. Perhaps the explanation lies in the ideological grid through which she has sifted the question of mother tongue versus acquired language. As Jacques Derrida puts it in *Le Monolinguisme de l'autre (The Monolingualism of the Other)*, a meditation upon his own relationship with his mother tongue, "The language called 'maternal' is neither purely natural, nor particular, nor inhabitable" (112). Derrida questions the idea that one "possesses" the language that one calls one's own: "But who possesses it, in fact? And who is possessed by it? Is it ever in possession, language, a possession possessing or possessed? Possessed or possessing properly, like one's own thing? What about this being-at-home in a language toward which we never cease to return?" (35-36). Those kinds of interrogations are all the more troubling for the niece because, having deliberately assumed the mantle of the *métèque,* having forgotten her first language and struggling constantly with her second, she really has no language that she can call her own.

It remains to her thus to elaborate a new kind of language; and that, more than anything else, is what *Calomnies* is about. Appropriately enough, the niece inaugurates her project in a *literal* manner, for her first gesture is the letter she sends to her uncle. The effect of that letter upon the uncle is dramatic, since it transforms him from a reader into a writer: "It's been five days since the letter arrived and for five days I've had a headache. I don't read anymore. I scribble. [...] I'm writing a report. On *her* life. On my life. A report on betrayal. How I was betrayed by my own. How she betrayed them in turn. As if she were avenging me" (12, 3). That transformation is all the more profound, granted the important role that reading has played in the uncle's existence, ever since the "Monk" taught him to read French in the asylum. The uncle views reading as something that allowed him to withstand his experience in the asylum, and indeed eventually enabled him to escape from it. In the distinctly less carceral world of the public library where he has worked for the last five years, the uncle has continued to read, in order simply to survive:

"I've done my share of cultural spadework too, of course. Five years in a public library, reading everything that passed through my hands. Culture, I told myself, culture at all costs—the idea was to get my head back together" (9-10, 1). Clearly, the library has been a place of refuge for the uncle, a kind of halfway house between the radical alienation of the asylum and the intimidating regime of mainstream society. It is a place where he can exercise a modest degree of freedom and attend to those of his needs which he feels to be most important:

> Still, I feel pretty good in this library. [. . .] In between shelving, I can stroll around, do nothing, smoke a cigarette in the hall. I'd rather retreat to the far end of the library, find a hiding place, and read. I never read a book all the way through. I choose every kind of book. I go from novels to journalism to historical narratives to diaries. The main thing is to have a parade of words moving under my eyes. (10, 1-2)

Against the backdrop of the library—that is, by metonymy, against the backdrop of the entire literary canon—Linda Lê stages a reflection on literature and its uses in *Calomnies*. That reflection is organized contrapuntally, moreover: sometimes she couches it in irony, sometimes she speaks more frankly; sometimes she focuses upon the uncle, sometimes upon the niece; sometimes she asks what it is to read, sometimes she asks what it is to write. It is important to realize, however, that in each of these various moves, Lê is boldly offering *Calomnies* as a test case. That is, she encourages us to think about everything *we* have read and the uses to which we have put it, inviting us to consider her own novel in that harsh light.

Until now, the uncle has used literature as a drug, as a kind of sedative: "Evenings, I go back to my room, I read while I eat, I read before I go to sleep. And to think they locked me up because my nerves were a little too highly strung. I didn't know that there was an excellent sedative: culture" (10, 2). Upon receiving the letter from his niece and learning that she is a writer, he imagines her activity at the other end of that pharmacological economy: "She's made herself a writer. A distiller of tranquilizers. A manufacturer of sedatives" (11, 3). He realizes that their respective roles in that economy, as reader and writer, are fundamentally different ones, despite certain similarities. Both are deeply committed to literature, and both regard literature as a drug; but where the uncle sees literature as a sedative, the niece on the contrary views it as a stimulant: "There's only one thing *she* and I have in common: books. That's what keeps her going, it's her business, her daily bread, her stimulant. For me, books are tranquilizers. Thanks to books, I play dead" (11, 2). It is in just that perspective that the effect of the niece's letter on her uncle becomes apparent. Causing him to turn away from reading and forcing him to become a writer, it deprives him of the balance he has so carefully constructed in his life, and it will lead him ever more deeply into despair.

Linda Lê examines the uses of literature in a variety of other ways, too, proceeding often by counterexample, in other words by evoking examples of the manners in which literature is *misused*. An extreme instance of that technique occurs in a passage where the uncle speculates about how the other members of the family (apart from himself and his niece, that is) think of literature. For the family, literature has no use whatever; still more alarmingly, they view it as a kind of dangerous contagion: "In this family, no one reads; reading causes headaches, reading is unhealthy: stay away from it" (78, 64). Like his niece, the uncle has served an apprenticeship to literature in order to construct a viable identity for himself apart from his family and in opposition thereto. That gesture, initially played out as revolt, soon assumes for both of them the status of vocation, and both will come to define themselves very largely through their literary activity, in the uncle's case as a reader, in the niece's as a writer.

Another example of the uses of literature is the niece's friend Ricin. He is an editor, and he owns a small publishing house. He is also a writer—but he is careful never to publish his writings, "for fear of prostituting his pain" (21, 12). Very early in her career, the niece had approached him, hoping that he would agree to publish one of her texts, and Ricin had refused, saying that she had not yet suffered enough. Since then, she and Ricin have remained in close touch as friends—though the niece sees their relationship as somewhat more hierarchical than that: "Ricin is my conscience, my lesson-giver, the unbearable brother who always has an insult ready" (21, 12). As she works her way through the difficult stages of her career, Ricin looks at her writings with a jaundiced eye. Nothing that she produces is good enough for him because his standards are far too lofty, too noble. Indeed they are clearly impossible standards, for, if one were to heed Ricin, no writer would ever allow anything whatever to be brought into print.

Ricin is particularly caustic in his evaluation of the other literary figures with whom the niece has been associated. Her former lovers, Bellemort and Weidman, were both writers, as I have mentioned, and Ricin dismisses them both out of hand. He criticizes Bellemort's books, saying that he lacks originality; and he argues that Bellemort had tried to appropriate the niece for his own uses, had tried to turn her into one of his characters. The question of appropriation is a burning one in *Calomnies,* because everywhere she turns it seems to the niece that someone is trying to take her over and turn her to uses for which she feels unsuited. Clearly, she sees the dynamic of her family life in this light, and likewise the entreaties of her "compatriot," the shoemaker. Yet it is appropriation through literature that she fears most keenly.

In that context, the "Counselor," her publisher, is the most egregious abuser. He seeks to mold the niece in the image that will best serve his own purposes, that is, as his protégée, and to commodify her and market her as a "Francophone" writer. He insists that she write a book about her father, and he is already thinking ahead to the film rights. He tells her also that the book must be a happy one, and that she must abandon the pathological tone of her current inquiries into her family history, for what she is engaged in is merely *calomnie,* slander: "Put your corpses away. Write some exercises in jubilation. Stop slandering yourself, slandering *us*" (31, 22). Here, Linda Lê wraps her meditation on the uses of literature in multiple layers of irony. The reader will appreciate that the notion of *calomnie* is centrally at issue in this novel, on a variety of levels.

One of the points Lê returns to frequently is that slander is very much in the eye of the beholder. That is, in this instance, the Counselor may be reacting to elements of the niece's writing that tend to put him (and others of his ilk) directly on trial—and for once his reading may be accurate. He proposes a handy solution to the niece. She will write a feuilleton romance, full of noble sentiment and complete with a lushly nostalgic evocation of colonial life. Should she feel unequal to such a task, that's not a problem:

The Counselor says, You will write an episode of *The Love of Their Life*. I will dictate it to you, if necessary. I will erase all those dark thoughts from your head, I will purify your brain. I will force-feed you with joy. I will teach you the mathematics of sentimentality, the hearts-and-flowers method. I will tear you away from from Ricin's influence. (134, 112)

Ricin, for his part, constantly warns the niece not to let herself be influenced by the Counselor, imploring her to sabotage the Counselor and the iniquitous ambitions he has for her. In those competing voices, both of which deplore the influence of the other, the niece realizes that the common thread is, precisely, influence itself—and more precisely still, literary influence. Ricin, Bellemort, Weidman, the Counselor: each of the literary men in her life has tried in some way to appropriate her. She also realizes that the question of influence is deeply bound up in literature. This is certainly true on a fairly obvious level, for every author writes on a horizon of literary influence, taking a variety of positions with regard to literary tradition. Yet it is also true on a more insidious level as well, since any aspiring author must come to terms with the literary marketplace and the networks of power and influence that, to a significant degree, govern it. That lesson is all the more bitter for the niece, being a woman and an immigrant, because all of her direct experience has taught her that the world of literature to which she aspires is ruled by French men.[12]

The webs of influence in which she is caught inspire feelings of shame in the niece. She feels that it is shameful to allow oneself to be manipulated by other, more powerful people; and despite all of her efforts to resist, she has let herself be manipulated by the literary men around her in a variety of situations and in different ways. She comes to doubt the legitimacy of her own writing, and most particularly the project she is currently working on, in which she is seeking to examine her relations with her father. When she gives a few pages of her work-in-progress to Ricin, he refuses to read them, and accuses her of cynically exploiting her father in order to further her own career (32, 23). From the context of that passage, and from everything else we know about Ricin, it is clear that his accusation is unjustified. Nonetheless, it is sufficient to instill a profound impression of guilt in the niece, an impression that will color her other reflections about her own work in significant ways.[13] Is she merely using her father as a pretext? Is she putting his sad figure on display simply in order to inspire spurious feelings of pity in her reader? Is she proposing the characters in her vexed family history in a sordid, sensationalist manner, like the freaks in a sideshow? Or is she simply following the example of her uncle, whose job while he was in the asylum was to wash the community's dirty laundry?

As she rehearses those questions, and others like them offering equally unattractive interpretations of her motivations, the niece comes to feel that the space available to her and her writing is becoming more and more constricted. On every side, she encounters criticism, objection, and outright slander. Those are abundantly provided, of course, by the influential men in her life; yet more perniciously still, the niece will adopt a severe—and nearly paralyzing—policy of self-criticism. It will leave her very little room for maneuver as she ponders the fundamental question that faces her here: what kind of a book *can* she write?

Her uncle, too, reflects on her motivations on many occasions, putting his niece on trial in his own mind. He wonders what prompts her to write, and, more specifically, what prompted her to write to *him:* "What has gotten into her? Is it because she loves taking risks? Is it her taste for novelistic situations?" (12, 3). Clearly, the notion of "risk" is an important one in this novel. The niece's approach to her uncle is a gamble, and its stakes are high. Likewise, her decision to write about her own family is one fraught with dangers of many kinds. It is also legitimate to assume that Linda Lê regards *Calomnies* as a risky undertaking because of the way it stages the dynamic of power and because of the questions *Calomnies* raises about the institution of literature and the tradition of the novel. Quite possibly too, she might worry that the reader's temptation to read an autobiographical discourse in this novel, relegating its other concerns to the background, will leave her too exposed personally on the one hand and, on the other, will reduce much of what she has tried to convey in *Calomnies* to a trivial status. What is a "novelistic situation," moreover, and how are we to construe it? To the uncle's way of thinking, it denotes a romanticized fascination with the extraordinary: "The danger that lies in wait for her is a lyrical intoxication, a sentimentality that will corrode her cynical faculties" (165, 138). It seems to me, however, that *Calomnies* reconfigures and rehabilitates that word, using it to denote those aspects of a novel that serve to interrogate the novel itself as a cultural practice. And in that sense at least, the uncle's suspicions concerning his niece's motives are accurate on both counts.

Other suspicions of his are perhaps less well founded: "She wants me to tell her stories, to irrigate her head with a new source of obsession, to substitute an illusion forged by my imagination for an illusion she created for herself and has carefully tended for years" (45, 35). He worries that his niece is merely seeking grist for her writerly mill, rather than the truth about her father, and that the story she is asking him to tell will be transformed under her hand into something that bears only a distant relation to the family experience they have both struggled to survive. The uncle sees the task the niece has set herself as a pair of alternatives, and he is afraid that she will not be courageous enough to choose the only one which he feels to be valid:

> She will have to choose between these two specimens of a father. Between a bestselling novelist's book, a book that puts on a showy display of erudition and seduction, a book written with facility, a book that enchants the reader, a book padded out with frivolous phrases and ending with a pirouette—she has to choose between that charming book and the other specimen, an austere book that encloses nothing but a little dried blood. (176, 146)

Though he feels obligated to respond to his niece's request in some manner, the uncle regards her literary project with deep mistrust; and he wonders if she is prepared to accept the full implications of the analogy she has suggested between his madness and her decision to become a writer: "*She* says she wants to dedicate herself to writing in the same way as I have dedicated myself to madness—this is an example of the kind of expression her letter is crammed with, it makes her sound like a renegade Carmelite nun. She says she wants to join the underground. Flee from life" (176, 146).

Initially at least, it is the uncle himself who will flee, retreating into the sanctuary of the public library, allowing himself to be locked in there at night unbeknownst to the other librarians, in order to write his "report." He will spend six nights there in all, writing without respite and sinking ever more deeply into hopelessness and desperation. He recognizes with chagrin that it was his niece's *writing* which brought him to this pass, compelling him to reconsider issues that he believed he had already come to terms with, once and for all: "It's that letter with the pretentious handwriting that put an end to my peace of mind. She sent me back to the family, to sickness. She forced me to look at myself in the mirror" (148, 123). And curiously, though reading has always until that point allowed the uncle to take a step back from his demons and relativize them, when he reads—and rereads—what his niece has written, the effect is precisely contrary. Moreover, that experience ruins all reading for the uncle, and he knows that from that point onward there will be no solace to be found in the books that surround him in the library: "In front of me are the long shelves full of books. I hear them whispering. Their murmuring doesn't reach me. They've abandoned me. They've dismissed me from their fraternal union. [...] Books can no longer do anything for me" (171, 142).

The uncle will faithfully hold up his end of this strange correspondence, despite his doubts about his niece's motivations and the tremendous pain that this confrontation with his own history will entail. "The report I'm going to send is unfinished," he muses (178, 148), for the uncle sees no possibility of closure in the story he is obliged to tell, no real end. It will be the end of *him,* however, because after he sends his report he will immolate himself in the library on a pile of books. It will be a small holocaust, compared to others that one might imagine, but nonetheless a noble one, since it participates in a venerable tradition of library fires in history and literature, from the Great Library at Alexandria to the final scenes of Elias Canetti's *Auto-da-Fé* and Umberto Eco's *The Name of the Rose*. It is only in the ashes of literature, the uncle suggests, that he will now be able to find peace: "No one will demand the truth from my charred remains. My body will be one with the books" (179, 149).

In the final scene of *Calomnies,* the niece receives the package containing her uncle's report. Like him, she has resolved to flee; but her flight will take a somewhat different shape than his—different, yet perhaps no less dramatic. Walking along with Ricin, her uncle's report under her arm, the niece has decided that flight is the only course of action left to her. She will leave her apartment, her neighborhood; she will leave Ricin; she will leave her uncle's report behind her, unopened and unread. Linda Lê stages that gesture of flight in the explicit of *Calomnies,* in a manner that is stark and uncompromising: "I hand Ricin the package I was clutching. *I'm leaving.* I turn back, I follow the dog's trail. He's moving fast along the tree-lined avenue. I quicken my step. I feel the rush of cold wind against my cheeks. *I'm leaving*" (181, 151).

Thus, the correspondence of the uncle and the niece will not be fully consummated. Or at least not within the narrower bounds of the fictional world in this novel. Clearly, however, the novel presents in some sense a locus of correspondence between these two voices and the questions that they articulate, even if that correspondence is characterized on both of its poles by hesitation, doubt, and uncertainty—and even if it is largely unresolved. No satisfactory point of closure can be found in the literal correspondence, and the same is true on the figurative level. It should be recognized, too, that the ending that Linda Lê has chosen for her novel contains a very similar lesson. Unlike other stories one might think of, there is no explosion of truth here. On the contrary, there is the suggestion that the concerns evoked in the novel are not susceptible to easy resolution, and must be examined, probed, and problematized still further.[14]

What does become apparent in *Calomnies* is how arduous the search for the truth can be, and we may interpret that as one of the parables of the novel that Linda Lê is telling here. Truth is often elusive, of course; it is often difficult to find—and unacceptable to us when we do find it. All the more so in the case of a slanderous truth, whether it be a question of the niece's true paternity or rather that of how a novel comes to be. In regard to the uses of literature, Lê seems to moot the question: literature ultimately failed the uncle in his efforts to come to terms with his existence; will it also fail the niece? Perhaps the principal concern of *Calomnies* lies elsewhere, in the representation of the search for slanderous truth, and in the insistent staging of that representation *as* representation. For one of the things that Lê is proposing here is a reflection upon the ways in which a novel may engage the world—the world of personal experience, the political and social world, the world of letters. That engagement must be mobile and contrapuntal, she argues; it must be austere and unflinching; it must be conscious of the motivations that subtend it, and it must put those motivations on display; it must be truthful—but it must not balk, either, at slander.

NOTES

[1] Jack Yeager provides an excellent overview of Lê's work in "Culture, Citizenship, Nation: The Narrative Texts of Linda Lê."

[2] See Yeager 259: "*Calomnies* appears to be Lê's most autobiographical novel to date, though indications are vague and imprecise; it is up to the reader to assemble the clues that seem to point to Lê herself. [. . .] Lê seems both to force and to prevent an autobiographical reading of her novel. This concurrent creation and destruction exemplifies the paradoxical position in which she finds herself: compelled to invent a new, composite identity, but with materials that bear the stigmata of the colonial past."

[3] Here and throughout, I have used Esther Allen's translation. The first page numbers refer to the original, the second to the translation.

[4] See Edward Said's reflection on the way marginality is conceived in contemporary American society: "Marginalization in American culture means a kind of unimportant provinciality. It means the inconsequence associated with what is not major, not central, not powerful—in short, it means association with what are considered euphemistically as 'alternative' modes, alternative states, peoples, cultures, alternative theaters, presses, newspapers, artists, scholars, and styles, which may later become central or at least fashionable. The new images of centrality—directly connected with what C. Wright Mills called the power elite—supplant the slower, reflective, the less immediate and rapid processes of print culture, with its encoding of the attendant and recalcitrant categories of historical class, inherited property, and traditional privilege. The executive presence is central in American culture today: the president, the television commentator, the corporate official, celebrity. Centrality is identity, what is powerful, important, and *ours*" (*Culture and Imperialism* 324).

[5] See Goffman xiii: "A total institution may be defined as a place of residence and work where a large number of like-situated individuals, cut off from the wider society for an appreciable period of time, together lead an enclosed, formally administered round of life. Prisons serve as a clear example, providing we appreciate that what is prison-like about prisons is found in institutions whose members have broken no laws." On the specific characteristics of total institutions, see 3-124.

[6] See Chambers, *Room for Maneuver* 1: "Oppositional behavior consists of individual or group survival tactics that do not challenge the power in place, but make use of circumstances set up by that power for purposes the power may ignore or deny."

[7] Here and elsewhere in the quoted material, the italics are in the original.

[8] See in this regard Gayatri Chakravorty Spivak 107: "The putative center welcomes selective inhabitants of the margin in order better to exclude the margin."

[9] See also *Representations of the Intellectual* 60: "A second advantage to what in effect is the exile standpoint for an intellectual is that you tend to see things not simply as they are, but as they have come to be that way."

[10] See *Calomnies* 10, 12, 33, 127.

[11] See *Slander* 2, 4, 23, 106.

[12] In this regard, see Trinh T. Minh-ha 8: "S/he who writes, writes. In uncertainty, in necessity. And does not ask whether s/he is given the permission to do so or not. Yet, in the context of today's market-dependent societies, 'to be a writer' can no longer mean purely to perform the act of writing. For a laywo/man to enter the priesthood—the sacred world of writers—s/he must fulfill a number of unwritten conditions. S/he must undergo a series of rituals, be baptized and ordained. S/he must *submit* her writings to the law laid down by the corporation of literary/literacy victims and be prepared to *accept* their verdict."

[13] See Trinh 7: "To point out that, in general, the situation of women does not favor literary productivity is to imply that it is almost impossible for them (and especially for those bound up with the Third World) to engage in writing as an occupation without letting themselves be consumed by a deep and pervasive sense of guilt."

[14] In such a perspective, see Spivak 77: "Whereas in other kinds of discourses there is a move toward the final truth of a situation, literature, even without this argument, displays that the truth of a human situation *is* the itinerary of not being able to find it. In the general discourse of the humanities, there is a sort of search for solutions, whereas in literary discourse there is a playing out of the problem as the solution, if you like."

IV

∽

ERIC LAURRENT'S
SCHLEMIEL

Everybody loves a schlemiel. Stumbling through our contemporary cultural landscape in a constitutionally benighted fashion, the schlemiel carnivalizes our struggles and our way of being in the world, holding a funhouse mirror up to us and daring us to recognize ourselves therein. He is certainly antiheroic, but to say that the schlemiel is simply an antihero is to trivialize the richness of his character. Ihab Hassan points out the vastness of the semantic field that the term "antihero" may embrace: "In fiction, the unnerving rubric 'anti-hero' refers to a ragged assembly of victims: the fool, the clown, the hipster, the criminal, the poor sod, the freak, the outsider, the scapegoat, the scrubby opportunist, the rebel without a cause, the 'hero' in the ashcan and the 'hero' on a leash" (Hassan 21). One recognizes aspects of the schlemiel in many of the figures Hassan cites; yet clearly the terms "antihero" and "schlemiel" are not synonymous. Camus's Meursault and Céline's Bardamu, for instance, are both antiheroes; yet neither is a schlemiel.

Sinking his thirsty roots deeply into the Ashkenazic tradition, the schlemiel is a special sort of antihero, and he performs a special kind of critique upon traditional European notions of heroism.[1] Unlike many antiheroes, his performance is fundamentally ludic in character. He dramatizes his ineptitude like a shadow-play, against the backdrop of the quotidian. He is constantly attentive to his own performance and alert to the fact that he is on stage. His play is articulative, moreover, in that he insistently solicits our participation therein, our reaction and our approbation. For each of the schlemiel's pratfalls, each imbecility, each bumbling, is intended to figure, in parodic and exaggerative fashion, the kinds of gestures we ourselves sketch out as we attempt to negotiate the labyrinth of the everyday. In a real sense, the schlemiel saves us from ourselves. And by virtue of that, he too is saved. He is a loser without a doubt; yet he is a beautiful loser, one who can turn the act of losing itself into a form of art.

In popular culture, the schlemiel has staked out a territory all his own through his various figurative expressions, from Charlie Chaplin to Jerry Lewis, Lenny Bruce, Charlie Brown, Woody Allen, and Forrest Gump. In literature, one thinks of Italo Svevo's Zeno, Henri Michaux's Plume, Jaroslav Hasek's Good Soldier Schweik, James Thurber's Walter Mitty, Isaac Bashevis Singer's Gimpel, Samuel Beckett's Watt, Saul Bellow's Herzog, Philip Roth's Portnoy, Heinrich Böll's Hans Schnier, and Bernard Malamud's Fidelman, to name just a few. The classic instance of the schlemiel is of course Adelbert von Chamisso's *Peter Schlemiel* (1814), the story of a man who sold his shadow to improve his social standing. When Chamisso's brother proposed a French translation of the German original, Chamisso wrote to him, insisting that the character's name should in no case be changed:

> Schlemihl, or rather Schlemiel, is a Hebrew name, and means Gottlieb, Theophil or Beloved of God. This, in the everyday parlance of the Jews, is their designation for clumsy or unlucky souls who succeed at nothing in this world. A Schlemiel breaks his finger in his vest pocket or falls on his back and breaks his nose. (Chamisso xiv)

While Chamisso's derivation of the word may not be exact,[2] the passage offers a good thumbnail sketch of the schlemiel, and of the particular kind of uncertain hero that Chamisso wished to construct.

In recent French literature, the schlemiel has returned in force, blundering through the novels of Jean-Philippe Toussaint, Christian Oster, Eric Chevillard, Olivier Targowla, and Eric Laurent. Among those writers, I believe that it is in Laurent's work that the schlemiel attains his purest and most felicitous expression. Laurent himself is a relatively young writer, born in 1966, and he has published six novels at the Editions de Minuit thus far: *Coup de foudre* (1995; Love at First Sight), *Les Atomiques* (1996; The Atomics), *Liquider* (1997; Liquidate), *Remue-ménage* (1999; Commotion), *Dehors* (2000; Outside), and *Ne pas toucher* (2002; Don't Touch). His books are impressive ones, both by virtue of their quality and their range. I shall deal here with *Coup de foudre,* an astonishing "first novel," and a richly intriguing piece of writing by any standard.

Coup de foudre is a comic novel, and more particularly a romantic comedy. There are moments of farce worthy of Feydeau and Courteline; and there are other comic moments sketched with a far more buoyant stroke, evincing that quality of "lightness" that Italo Calvino postulated as one of the cardinal virtues of good literature (3-29). Its hero—if hero he be—is named "Chester," and he shoulders the heavy mantle of his precursors in the schlemiel tradition with admirable brio. Through Chester and the innumerable vicissitudes with which he grapples, Laurrent offers a series of amusing meditations upon the status of the subject in postmodern society, and a more sober reflection on the possibilities of the novel as literary form in contemporary culture.

To all outward appearances, Chester appears to be reasonably well integrated in society as his story begins. Yet that integration proves quickly to be very precarious indeed, for in the space of a few pages, Chester is fired from his job; he is cuckolded and thrown out of his home; his mother dies; his car is towed away; and (the unkindest cut) his credit card is refused. He becomes, in short, an utterly marginal man.[3] It should be noted that these evils are visited upon Chester due to circumstances very largely beyond his control—but then what sort of meager control might he pretend to enjoy, schlemiel that he is? Chalk it up to kismet, rather, and a particularly cruel and absurd one at that. Chester embraces his bad luck like a vocation, and each paltry mischance that afflicts him, one after the other, confirms to him (and to us) that, if he is ill-equipped for success in this world, he is remarkably well-suited for a modest sort of martyrdom. The fundamental rule of thumb in his life is that if anything can go wrong in a given situation, it will go wrong. Witness just a few of the stations on Chester's via dolorosa: washing his hands in a sink, he breaks the spout and gets his finger caught in the water pipe; he falls down a stairway; he is almost murdered by a hired assassin; he tries—vainly, of course—to commit suicide in a trash compactor; he burns his crotch on a radiator; he almost drowns under an air mattress at the municipal swimming pool; he knocks himself unconscious; chasing a fly in his office, he falls and wakes up in the hospital; he falls into the Canal St. Martin; his seat at the Opéra breaks

under him; a jealous husband pursues him through the streets of Paris, shoot-
ing at him; he is run over by a taxi; his head falls into his computer screen.[4]

Briefly stated, Chester is a ridiculous man, a consideration that Eric
Laurrent stages in the very beginning of this text, with the epigraph he bor-
rows from Pascal's *Pensées,* "O most ridiculous hero!" Clearly, Laurrent's intention is to push that topos to its limit in *Coup de foudre,* and to test the narrative possibilities of the schlemiel, straining them to the breaking point. In that
sense, *Coup de foudre* is an excessive text, one that is based upon the principle
of vertiginous accumulation—even unto absurdity. That's one way to write a
work of literature, I suppose; and one can think of other experimental texts,
from Mallarmé's "Ses purs ongles" to Georges Perec's *La Disparition (A Void),*
where one essential conceit is pursued with similar dogged devotion.

Chester, too, is capable of great and single-minded devotion; yet his devotion takes a more carnal form than Laurrent's, for Chester is a lover of
women. Conventionally enough, Chester loves his wife; yet she is perfidious,
and loves another. Chester discovers that fact to his chagrin when he tumbles
head over heels down the staircase of his apartment building, bursting open
his neighbor's door, coming to rest at the feet of his wife and their neighbor
who are making love "more caninas" (20). To her credit, his wife asks Chester
to forgive her. But she quickly thinks the better of that, and throws him out of
his home and her life, hurling after him a heartless parting shot: "I forgot to
tell you your mother died this morning" (21). What more can a man endure?
Chester finds his moral nadir in the trash compactor, and it is at that moment
that he meets Luvainc Azerty, who takes him to task severely because his
suicide attempt has blocked traffic in the street, and thus caused Azerty considerable inconvenience. Upon hearing Chester's story, however, Azerty has a
dramatic change of heart: "Monsieur is a cuckold. Well shit, that changes everything" (31). For Azerty, too, has been a cuckold—by his first wife, if not yet
by his second—and he welcomes Chester into that compassionate fraternity
with open arms. His generosity knows no limits: being a highly placed and
powerful bureaucrat in some Ministry or other, he will introduce Chester to
his colleagues, give him a job (but no duties) in his office, and allow him to live
in one of the elevators in the Ministry, specifying only that Chester should
place an "out of order" sign on the elevator door for the sake of appearances.

He will also (and most importantly) introduce Chester to his second wife, the euphoniously named, impossibly pulchritudinous "Vénus." As the title of the novel might lead one to suspect, Chester falls in love with Vénus at first sight, and the rest of the novel will be devoted to the schlemiel courtship that he pays to her.

As a lover, Chester displays all the awkwardness that characterizes his behavior in other, more prosaic aspects of his life. In his first encounter with Vénus, he awakes from a dead faint to discover her graciously applying an icepack to his burned crotch (43)—not a particularly auspicious beginning for a romantic relationship, one would imagine. Given the opportunity to save Vénus from drowning, he is overcome by the beautiful vision of his inamorata emerging from the water, for all the world like Botticelli's *The Birth of Venus,* and he faints yet again, only to be saved by Vénus herself. "You almost drowned when you saved me," she remarks laconically, "I don't know what came over you but you fainted, clearly it's becoming a habit with you" (51). Finding (or pretending to find) Chester's importunities toward her difficult to bear, Vénus asks him to desist: "Chester, please, stop playing the besotted lover, it's a ridiculous game that you're beginning to take too seriously, you'll end up under my window playing the lute all night if it continues" (85). Chester takes that proscription as license—in any case, the prospect of being ridiculous has never deterred him before—and the following night takes up his post under Vénus's window, guitar in hand. Despite all odds, and his innumerable setbacks notwithstanding, Chester will remain steadfast in his love, and he will be rewarded. One of the last scenes in the novel sees him alone at last with Vénus in his pied-à-terre (that is, in the abandoned elevator in the Ministry building), his head firmly lodged between her legs, as Vénus urgently encourages him: "Chester devour me, I'm hungry for your hunger" (120). Not bad, for a schlemiel.

Characteristically, Chester triumphs through nullity. That is, it's his very nullity that separates him from the rest of humanity, and allows him to distinguish himself in Vénus's eyes and, importantly, in ours. Moreover, he is aware of his condition, and realizes that he is not quite like other people. Melvin Friedman has pointed out that this kind of self-knowledge is an essential trait of the schlemiel. Speaking about Norma Rosen's *Joy to Levine!,* he argues,

"Like all accomplished schlemiels, Levine has a sense of his own deficiencies and weaknesses" (147). Chester's nullity, and his own awareness thereof, is staged in the incipit of the novel, which finds him at work, seated in front of his computer, gazing otiosely into the screen:

> The computer screen was such a cerulean gray that it seemed to be a skylight looking onto the world outside. In fact, Chester began to see some clouds roaming about therein, whose shapes gradually became more precise: a hydrocephalic diplodocus, gently followed by a four-horned pachyderm, then by an incredibly hairy yak, wow! I'm really whacked [*naze*]. (9)

The word that he uses to describe his state, *naze,* is a colloquialism. It can mean "of poor quality," "spoiled," "tainted," "in bad shape," "out of service," or "drunk" (Cellard and Rey 558). Yet it can also mean "tired," "whacked," or simply "worthless." Here, Chester seems to use it to denote his fatigue: he is sleepy, and can barely keep his eyes open. Gradually, however, that word attains totemic status in the text, for Chester will use it to describe himself over and over again.[5] In other terms, the word *naze* comes to denote the general existential condition that afflicts Chester, his nullity, his schlemielhood.

The mirror scenes in the novel reflect Chester's growing recognition of that condition. Mirror scenes abound in literature from the myth of Narcissus onward, and most particularly in contemporary literature. They suggest a character's alienation from the world and, more alarmingly still, from himself or herself. Typically, the character fails to recognize the image reflected in the mirror, or his or her recognition is problematized in some fashion. It is legitimate to suggest that in *Coup de foudre* the first mirror scene occurs in the passage I just quoted, for a computer screen is a kind of mirror, at least figuratively speaking. Chester sees many things therein—a dinosaur, an elephant, a yak—but he does not see himself. More literal, and more troubling, is a scene where Chester is washing his hands in the bathroom of his workplace, in the company of a few colleagues: "He looked up: he was no longer in the mirror. The others didn't notice. He fainted" (16). Here, Chester's nullity stares him in the face because, like Peter Schlemiel himself, he is a man without a shadow. More encouraging is when Chester, having come to rest at the feet of his faithless wife and her lover, in a scene I alluded to earlier, stares at her shoe from close range: "He opened his eyes. A tiny dromedary's face was observing him, blinking. He recognized the anamorphosis of his own face, reflected in the shiny surface of a black evening shoe" (19). Just like his computer screen, his wife's shoe reflects in Chester's bewildered gaze the image of an exotic animal (in this case a dromedary); yet this time he succeeds in decoding that image. He recognizes himself—albeit in caricatural, impossibly carnivalized form— therein. The final mirror scene in the novel occurs during a cocktail party at the Azerty home, when Chester, inevitably enough, spills champagne on his trousers:

> He ran to the restroom, where he moistened the spot on his pants where he had spilled champagne. Then he took advantage of the mirror to pass some time. He stretched his epidermis under the neon light, his gaze following the path traced by his fingers, seeking a desquamation to peel off, maybe a seba-ceous eruption to provoke. His empty hand fell upon a rebel lock of hair, and put it back on the correct side of the part (40).

Not only does Chester recognize his image in the mirror, simply and unproblematically this time, he avails himself of the mirror in order to *compose* his face, orchestrating that part of himself that he presents most immediately to the world.

Clearly, these scenes are specular in the fullest sense of that term. Taken together, they describe the manner in which Chester's view of himself and his schlemiel condition evolve. His consciousness of self is difficult and halting in the early part of the novel, yet gradually and ineluctably he comes to know himself. The specular quality of these scenes is more pronounced still, however, for they recall—parodically but nonetheless precisely—yet another superbly marginal man, Albert Camus's Meursault. In *L'Etranger (The Stranger),* Meursault gazes into mirrors (or mirror-substitutes, like his tin bowl in prison) on three occasions. His evolution, just like Chester's, is tripartite; and its steps parallel Chester's own very closely indeed. First, he fails to see himself (though he sees other objects reflected in the mirror); then he recognizes his image, though problematically; finally, he recognizes himself clearly.[6]

Consciousness of self does not come easily for Chester. In part, this is because consciousness itself, literally construed, is so precarious for him. Chester is continually falling asleep: in his office (12), during a meeting at the Ministry (70), at the Opera (97); and never do we find him fully awake and engaged in his surroundings. By virtue of his somnolence, he rejoins yet another literary freemasonry (apart from those of the schlemiel and the cuckold, that is), that of the sleeping man. His precursors, heavy-lidded figures like Ivan Goncharov's Oblomov, Franz Kafka's K., Thomas Mann's Hans Castorp, the anonymous heroes of Bruno Schulz's *Sanatorium under the Sign of the Hourglass* and of Georges Perec's *Un Homme qui dort (A Man Asleep),* John Barth's Jacob Horner, and J. M. Coetzee's Michael K, are men who are very largely unequal, like Chester, to the demands that mere existence places upon them, and they seek their refuge in sleep. Or perhaps their true refuge is not in sleep but rather in dream, for dream offers those figures the vision of a world that is much more closely suited in every way to their particular needs. This is certainly true in Chester's case, as we shall see very shortly.

When the real world is too much with him and sleep fails (as it inevitably must sometimes, even for the drowsiest people), Chester will simply *lose* consciousness. As Vénus remarks with her habitual perspicacity, fainting is a habit with him. Mostly, it is in reaction to strong emotion that Chester goes belly up: when he fails to see himself in the mirror (16); when he burns his crotch (43); when he attempts to save Vénus from drowning (50); when he encounters her at the swimming pool (64); when he angrily pursues the fly in his office (77).

It is precisely during his moment of greatest emotion, with his head between Vénus's perfect legs, that Chester loses consciousness for the last time. Perfect moments can't last, after all, and this one is no exception to that rule. Overcome by sheer passion, one supposes, Vénus loses her grip on the table supporting her; she falls and fractures her head:

> Vénus Azerty slipped away from him. Falling over toward the side, she rolled into the folding chair, whose curule webbing, bending under the pressure, deflected her fall toward the fragile partition of the restroom, which broke, thus projecting the sink attached to it against the first panel of the shelves which, one ofter the other, came tumbling down, the first one sweeping away the second, and so forth, until the shock wave, after bouncing around the el-

evator, hit Chester who, dazed by the spectacle of Vénus Azerty's broken skull, failed to see the computer screen diving toward him, nor the cylindrical foam of the mattress breaking his fall. He saw no more than a night, sparkling with a thousand brilliant points, shining above the flames which the candelabra, on the third story, had lit in Vénus Azerty's hair. (121-22)

This penultimate scene in *Coup de foudre* returns us to the first scene, where Chester was dozing at his computer. Perchance to dream, indeed: shortly stated, every event in the story, each of Chester's egregious blunders, each of his triumphs large and small, takes place in the brief space of dream, between his yawn and the moment his head crashes into the computer screen. And the reader has just been made the victim of one of the hoariest tricks a novelist can play. In light of that very consideration, moreover, who is the true schlemiel here?

Well, *vida es sueño,* to coin a phrase; but also (and perhaps more importantly) *novela es sueño.* For if in *Coup de foudre* Eric Laurrent takes the sleepy novelistic commonplace of "it was only a dream" and brutally bludgeons us with it, it is the better to make us think—or *dream,* rather, in our turn—about his own novel and the tradition out of which it arises. It should be noted, too, that this is merely the final instance of a richly specular, metanovelistic discourse that echoes throughout the pages of *Coup de foudre.* Laurrent puts that discourse into play in the very first scene of his novel, where Chester's situation, as he stares into the screen of his computer, parodies that of the writer himself—especially, one would imagine, a writer faced with the daunting prospect of beginning a novel (and in Laurrent's case, his very first novel). Beginnings are never easy, after all, and the way Chester conjures *something* (a dinosaur, an elephant, a yak) out of *nothing* may be read as a ludic figuration of the novelist's particular alchemy.

Chester won't stop there, of course. He will shortly pull a variety of other rabbits out of the hat, or rather—like Laurrent himself—out of his computer:

An entire creation crossed the screen then, but a mad creation, a sort of rough sketch, and the few letters that Chester improvised on the keyboard, V, E, N, U, S, seemed like an effort to organize the world, a prime vocable seeking to

find a meaning in the original magma, a vast program whose perspective was
beginning to put him to sleep, really whacked. (9-10)

Laurrent's choice to introduce the idea of creation in the opening scene
of his novel is deliberate. Clearly, he intends for the reader to savor the ironic
tension prevailing between Chester's maunderings and his own writerly efforts. Whatever else one might say about him, Chester is clearly gifted with a
vivid, fertile imagination. He is a creator by vocation, even if that which he
creates may seem, to the profane eye, "mad." Perhaps a "mad creation" is just
what Laurrent is proposing here, too; upon reflection, that epithet suits *Coup
de foudre* rather nicely. The evocation of the "rough sketch" [*ébauche*] is a wry
touch, too, because it is a term that is often associated with the creative act of
writing. It serves to foreground the studiously provisional character of this
novel's beginnings, as if Laurrent wished to deflect the portentousness of first
things. Like Chester himself, Laurrent is "improvising" here—or so, at least,
he would have us believe.

It is important to recognize that the first gesture which Chester accom-
plishes in this story is an act of writing, as brief and improvisational as it may
be. Typing the name "Vénus" into his computer initiates everything that follows, calling his oneiric universe into being. She takes shape upon his screen
from the "original magma" as it were, like Botticelli's Venus arising from the
waves. And if the five letters composing her name may seem to him like "an
effort to organize the world," it is also legitimate to read them as the *literal*
foundation of this novel, the generative vocable out of which all the rest will
proceed. What does a novelist seek to do, if not to organize the world—or at
the very least *a* world, one that will fit between the pages of a book? It is no
coincidence, moreover, that as Chester looks out the window of his office while
seated at his computer, his haggard gaze encounters the Bibliothèque de France,
and thus, by metonymy, all of French literature. Once again, Laurrent invites
us to follow the ironic meanders of the comparison of Chester's situation and
his own with considerable glee—and perhaps some chagrin.

Toward the middle of the novel, Laurrent describes the office that
Luvainc Azerty, in his generosity, has provided for Chester in the Ministry. It
is an exiguous, ignoble, closetlike affair previously occupied by the cleaning
lady:

With the fingers of his fist, Chester appreciated the resonance of the desk. He opened the drawers. He also opened the doors of the closets. Everything was empty. No poster was tacked to the walls, either. It seemed that the room had been conceived only to furnish nothingness.

It was only when he closed the door again that Chester discovered the row of household utensils, a vacuum cleaner, some brooms, some brushes, some sponges, some rubber gloves, a blue housecoat, a whole range of cleaning products, some rags, a coffee-maker.

He tidied up. He made some coffee. Then he sat down at the desk, facing the window. The hall ran along in front of him. Then he no longer moved. (74-75)

Here, Chester's creative impulses are for the moment frustrated. And quite understandably so, for Azerty has carefully provided him with a non-space in which to perform his non-job. He tours his small world and, like Adam, takes its inventory; he performs the small gestures that such a world allows; he waits, and we wait with him. Clearly, not much happens in this scene, at least on the level of event. Yet here, too, it is legitimate to read a suggestion of analogy between Chester's situation and that of Laurent, because if one shifts one's perspective from the focus on the told to the focus on the telling, it becomes apparent that this room was indeed conceived "to furnish nothingness." On the one hand, the scene serves to underscore the emptiness of Chester's schlemiel existence. On the other hand, it serves to remind us that in any story there are necessarily moments that are emptier or more naked than others, moments that a storyteller must furnish or clothe nonetheless, as best he or she can. In other words, Laurent intends to draw our attention once again toward process issues, and to put his own process decisions upon display. In this case, those are simple ones, as if to suggest that in this moment of the text the author, like his character, has very little room for maneuver. A brief glance around the little room, a catalogue of its few contents, the evocation of a couple of trivial acts: this is narration by accretion, the most elementary kind of storytelling.

Chester's ennui is finally—and mercifully—relieved by (of all things) a housefly. As he stalks it heroically, with blood in his eyes, and to the catastrophic result that I mentioned earlier, something else about this story becomes clear. Chester has the talent to transform the most ordinary, anodyne situation into calamity. This is the alchemical gesture that Laurrent wagers on too, of course, right alongside his character, and examples of it abound in the novel. A good instance of this effect is when Chester, bored to tears in his hospital room after his unequal battle with the fly, decides that he wishes to read something. Something light, perhaps—Chester is not a great reader, one suspects, and indeed this is the only moment in the story where his desire to read is mentioned. Clothed only in his pajamas, he leaves the hospital intending to buy some periodicals at a newsdealer's shop. Once there, his gaze alights upon some pornographic magazines, that variety of periodical, precisely, which is most calculated to stimulate the sort of revery that Chester is prey to throughout *Coup de foudre*. It is a simple gesture that Chester wishes to accomplish, and a reasonably simple pleasure that he seeks to attain thereby. However, like most of his simple acts, its consequences will prove to be calamitous because, making his way back to the hospital and deeply engrossed in his "reading," Chester will succeed only in falling into the Canal St. Martin (79-82).

It's a question of fundamental imperative, I suppose: *schlemiel oblige*. It should be noted, though, that each of Chester's blunders has a spectacular quality to it. In other terms, if he undoubtedly has the gift of transforming banal, quotidian gestures into calamity, that calamity is consistently played out as spectacle. That is, despite his ineptitude—or rather through the very ostentation of its display—Chester is an artist. Laurrent exploits that topos lustily, embroidering the calamity scenes richly and presenting them to his reader quite patently as spectacle, as theater, and thus, in the fullest sense of the word, as *play*.[7] A good example of this is Chester's botched suicide attempt. When he comes upon the trash compactor truck in which he will try to end his sufferings, Laurrent describes the garbagemen and their actions, carefully staging the entire scene as theater:

> They looked like old-time actors, moving around the city in a sort of Taylorist parody, whose title, "Parisian Cleanliness," written in white letters on the side of the truck, and legible in spite of the putrid miasma covering them, fully expressed its comic intent, and to which, moreover, the whirling halo of the flashing lights on the garbage truck conferred a still more theatrical aspect,

even a carnivalesque one, considering the slow parade of cars which followed it, and whose progression it impeded. (29)

When Luvainc Azerty takes Chester severely to task for having caused, through his efforts at self-immolation, a "scene," his first words to him are particularly pungent ones: "isn't your farce almost over?" (31). It is a comic moment, of course, and one that takes its place felicitously in the broader economy of this comic novel. But it is also played out as comedy when, trying to accomplish the gravest act an individual can perform upon himself or herself, Chester on the contrary *creates* the comic.

As an artist, unwitting though he may be, Chester's noblest creation is undoubtedly Vénus. He calls her into being after all, and she is in a sense his character, his creation. In this perspective, it is no coincidence that, when Chester goes to the Opéra only to discover himself seated next to Vénus Azerty, the piece being performed that evening is Haydn's *The Creation*. And, clearly, Vénus is herself a work of art. Or rather a work of the arts, for if she is associated with the great classical traditions of music and painting through Haydn and Botticelli, she is also the very embodiment of a poem. Among all of her superb attributes, it is her hair that most enflames Chester's imagination. The word "hair" [*chevelure*] insistently recurs in the text; and it is a word whose strong Baudelairean connotations will not be lost on the reader. Despite the fact that Vénus's hair is described as "Venetian blonde" (35), whereas Baudelaire in "La Chevelure," it will be recalled, invokes an "ebony sea," the parallel is otherwise precise. Chester projects the same sort of desire upon Vénus's hair, as if it incarnated the entire, abundant sexuality of the woman whom it adorns. Like in Baudelaire's text, too, the hair stands in Chester's mind metonymically for that other "aromatic forest," the one veiling the pubis, the true (but bashfully unavowed) object of Chester's longing, and the home to which he will return—happy like Ulysses—at the end of the novel.

Until we learn, likewise at the end of the novel, that Vénus is a creature of Chester's imagination, she seems "real" enough to us. Yet interspersed among those of Chester's creative imaginings that we take provisionally for the real, there are moments that are obviously more phantasmic than others; and they tend to multiply as the novel progresses. Such a moment occurs when Chester takes the métro, with his head bandaged as a result of his misadventure in the swimming pool, finding himself in a subway car packed to the bursting:

> One could distinguish no more than a mass of beings, each one the siamese twin of the other, a mass so compact that it looked like a sea. Only the heads emerged, ruddy and apoplectic, one of them bandaged. Then the surface, at first flat, became agitated. A wave rose up in its center, and quickly evoked a giant breast; a nipple outlined itself on its apogee. It broke. A woman surged up, pushed out of the flood by the exasperated snorts of dozens of noses; and it was not until she was entirely above the crowd that Chester recognized Vénus Azerty. She was naked, the crush of the bodies having stripped her of her apparel, but the sinuosity of her long hair clothed her with a sort of chaste line. She was profiled against billboards advertising the price of scallops at the Printemps store, and the whiteness of her skin contrasted with the blackness of the manes of tousled hair lapping at her feet. Nobody said a word. Only a bandaged head, floating like a jellyfish in one end of the subway car, proclaimed "Vénus I love you." And then it disappeared, probably drowned. (65-66)

It is a vision of beauty, and once again, just as when Chester sees Vénus drowning, the vision owes much of its beauty to Botticelli. Vénus emerges from a "sea," a "wave," a "flood" here; and only her hair hides her nakedness. A vision of beauty is merely a vision nonetheless, and clearly in this case Chester is seeing things. Serious headwounds will do that to you, as will other kinds of trauma, the kinds that are all too legion in Chester's life. Later on in the hospital, recovering from the broken ankle he suffered while chasing the fly, Chester "sees" Vénus, in all her magnificence, in the otherwise unremarkable nurse who is coaxing him slowly back into consciousness (78).

That phantasmatic quality also colors Chester's final encounter with Vénus. The scene in his elevator at the Ministry is impossibly absurd in every respect: the setting; Vénus's impromptu arrival; her urgent desire for him; and most remarkably the notion that an inveterate schlemiel like Chester might finally win the lottery. We are quickly disabused of the latter notion, as Vénus falls and cracks her head open. And we are shortly stripped of our remaining illusions as well, when we discover that Chester dreamed his whole story. But, as Lewis Carroll so tantalizingly put it in the final chapter of *Through the Looking-Glass,* "Which Dreamed It?" The different levels of revery in Chester's story suggest that phantasm can be layered upon phantasm in a human imagination as strongly inclined toward the oneiric as Chester's own. Yet isn't the same also true of Eric Laurrent's imagination? After all, he is the one who imagines all these imaginings. And isn't it true of us as well, as this story is projected upon us? As in the imagination, so too in the novel, then: in the dynamic play of illusion and reality, it is sometimes rather difficult to know just where one stands.

That is certainly true of Chester, who often finds that things are very largely beyond his ken. Dispatched by Luvainc Azerty to Florence in order to find Vénus and drive her back to Paris, Chester looks for her in vain. Expanding his search into the countryside, he succeeds only in getting lost, a fact that he articulates with some bitterness: "Goddamn, I'm really lost" (47). He is indeed "lost" on every level: lost in a literal sense certainly, but also constitutionally lost and foundering in a web of circumstance that he cannot understand and over which he has very little control. Importantly, he is lost in his own story. He doesn't have a clue why Azerty sent him to find Vénus, nor why Vénus went to Florence. And nor do we, because Laurrent has not provided that information to us. In other terms, in this and the other moments in the novel when Chester bemoans his lostness, the reader may perhaps be forgiven if he or she keens that lamentation right along with him. For we too, like Chester, often become lost in the baroque, improbable twists of *Coup de foudre.* We are dallied with, misdirected, confounded, and tricked in the course of this novel, and it may dawn upon us, as I suggested previously, that Chester is not the only schlemiel here, for often we are made to feel just as inept as he.

No, Chester is not alone. We share his bewilderment, as Eric Laurrent projects schlemielhood squarely upon us. Yet turnabout is fair play, and through the multiple analogies of Chester's situation and his own, Laurrent builds up a vision of the writer as schlemiel, also. From time to time, his expression of those analogies goes so far as to suggest a conflation of character and storyteller. A good example of that is the scene early in the novel where Chester breaks the spout of the sink in his company's bathroom: "The water was spraying against the door now, that I can guarantee you, in a dull battering, though leavened by the pizzicato of its splashes, and get me out of here" (14). Who is speaking in the first person here? The "I" seems to be enunciated by the narrator, while the "me" appears to be Chester's speech; but nevertheless there is a curious doubling effect at work in this passage. It is legitimate to say, more generally, that the narrator's voice (which mediates that of the writer) and the character's compete throughout *Coup de foudre* because, while the novel is written in the third person, it uses free indirect discourse liberally. In this instance, however, Laurrent pushes that technique further, studiously vexing the narrator's voice against Chester's, daring the reader to disintricate the two, as if both character and narrator were caught up in the same impossible situation. Moreover, the reader is directly and explicitly implicated in that situation, too, through the mediation of the narratee, to whom the "you" is addressed. In short, Laurrent adumbrates the notion that writer, reader, and character are all schlemiels, each one a member in good standing of that abashed and benighted company.

But there may be yet a fourth term in Laurrent's schlemiel homologic. In the final moment of *Coup de foudre,* several firemen, having been called to the scene of the disaster, valiantly attempt to extricate Chester from the computer screen into which he has fallen:

> Easy does it, guys, pick him up gently there it's OK gently for God's sake bring that stretcher over what the hell are you doing? All right all right I'm coming. O.K. O.K. gently there. OK he's not too roasted after all seeing how it's burning in here. Yeah exactly we've got to get a move on. That doesn't mean that we can't do it gently. Hold on toss that computer over there. Listen I don't want to risk it he's half wedged inside it leave it we'll see about it later. Look, he's opening his eyes. How are you sir it's OK everything will be OK you're saved we're firemen. I think I left the tagliatelli on the burner. Huh? What? You understand what he said? No no. Me, I thought he was talking about tagliatelli. He must be delirious maybe it's more serious than we thought. It's probably shock. And Vénus? Huh? Who? Vénus the woman who was with me where is she? What woman sir nobody was with you you were alone. Goddamn he got a hell of a knock for sure. Hello traumatism! Total delirium. (122-23)

Like a writer who has been overtaken by his story or a reader engrossed in a book to the point of oblivion, Chester has fallen into his fabula, into a computer screen with the lone word "Vénus" inscribed upon it. His few utterances are interpreted by those around him as delirium. And on at least one of the levels of the articulation of illusion and reality in *Coup de foudre,* that diagnosis is quite exact, for he has merely imagined his adventure from beginning to end, while putting the world around him on hold. It should not surprise us. Chester is a schlemiel after all, and schlemiels of his ilk are known to jump the tracks every once in a while. If they crop up with troubling regularity in the contemporary novel, it is perhaps because, as Melvin Friedman has argued, they prosper "under circumstances which acknowledge anti-heroes and anti-novels and which give the spotlight to marginal men of every variety" (141).

Yet here, I think, is where Laurrent offers his final meditation on the figure of the schlemiel. For *Coup de foudre* could also be described as a "total delirium." It is, moreover, a carefully constructed, pleasantly demented example of that organized delirium which we call the novel. Once one of the dominant species in our aesthetic ecology, the novel now competes in an ever more unequal manner with other, newer, and perhaps more readily accessible cultural forms. For the last thirty years at least, a variety of gloomy mandarins have brayed their predictions of the novel's imminent demise. For my own part, I do not believe that the novel is dead; but its position in our culture is clearly more marginal than it used to be. That shifting process has been apparent even during the relatively few years in the novel's evolution where I have counted myself a dedicated reader of the genre. In the light of such considerations, I would like to suggest that, among his other concerns in *Coup de foudre,* Eric Laurrent is commenting upon the novel itself as form and upon its increasing marginality with regard to other forms, its eccentricity. His principal tactic is to stage that eccentricity in a highly exaggerative, parodic manner, and exploit it for ludic effect, carnivalizing the novel's efforts to regain the paradise it seems to have lost, in an attempt to turn the novel's very marginality into a real (if undoubtedly tenuous and provisional) strategic advantage. He will attempt to enlist us in that project, offering us the chance to play the dubious—yet somehow deeply satisfying—role of the beautiful loser. He swears to us also that we won't be alone: character as schlemiel; writer as schlemiel; reader as schlemiel; novel as schlemiel—hell, we're all schlemiels here. But happy schlemiels, Laurrent assures us, nonetheless; and therein lies the *novelty* of his pitch.

NOTES

[1] See Melvin Friedman: "He has always been an essential part of the Jew's exploded myth of heroism, a reminder of his fallibility and insecure position in the Diaspora" (141).

[2] Webster's, for example, suggests that the word comes into Yiddish from the Hebrew proper name *Shelumiel,* meaning "my peace is God." The name itself is a biblical one, occurring in Numbers 1.6.

[3] See Friedman: "The schlemiel remains a classic instance of the outsider or anti-hero who never ceases to lose his way—only partly to find it again" (153).

[4] See, respectively, 15, 17, 26, 29, 43, 62, 64, 77, 82, 98, 113, 115, 120.

[5] See 10, 11, 12, 47, 75, 83.

[6] See Camus 41, 125, 126.

[7] Walter Isle has argued that play must be ostentatious in some fashion, and inevitably contains "an aspect of self-pageantry" (Isle 69-70).

V

∾

JACQUES JOUET'S MAGIC MOUNTAIN

In somewhat less than twenty years, Jacques Jouet has produced one of the most remarkable bodies of work in French literature today. It is a corpus that numbers twenty-eight volumes to date, and which traverses the horizon of genre, including books of poetry such as *Le Chantier* (The Construction Site) and *107 Ames* (107 Souls), a collection of plays entitled *La Scène est sur la scène* (The Stage is on the Stage), a major critical essay on Raymond Queneau, meditations on language and its uses in both a lyrical vein (*Des ans et des ânes;* Years and Donkeys) and a lexicographical one (*Les Mots du corps;* Body Words), collections of short fiction like *Le Bestiaire inconstant* (The Fickle Bestiary), *Romillats* (Romillats), and *Actes de la machine ronde* (Acts of the Round Machine), and two novels, *Le Directeur du Musée des Cadeaux des Chefs d'Etat de l'Etranger* (The Director of the Museum of Gifts of Foreign Heads of State) and *La Montagne R (Mountain R),* both published in Le Seuil's prestigious "Fiction & Cie" series. Jouet is a literary experimentalist in the noblest sense of that term: each of his works seeks in some fashion to test the limits and possibilities of literature; each one comes to us anew as the product of an original reflection; and each book is animated by a keen, subtle literary intelligence.

Jouet's second novel, *La Montagne R* (1996), displays those virtues abundantly. In it can be found the whole range of concerns and techniques which together define Jouet's specificity as a writer, and I feel moreover that it is exemplary of certain broader trends in contemporary French fiction. The story it tells is simple enough in its conceit, and engagingly droll, too: the leaders of a fictional—yet transparently French—republic decide to build a 1500-meter mountain near the capital, both to provide jobs through a massive public works project and as a monument to national prestige. The project will go awry (as indeed it inevitably must), but not in the way we might expect. The novel is divided into three parts. The first is devoted to the speech of the President of the Republican Council, as he outlines that project to the legislature. It offers a canny parody of contemporary political discourse, particularly amusing for those readers who recognize that "politspeak" is a language which scoffs at national and cultural boundaries, and who are assailed by its egregious brayings on a daily basis. The second part takes place after the project has come to a halt. A young woman interviews her father, a minor contractor who had worked on the mountain for many years. She asks him about his daily life during those years, about the status of the workers on the mountain, particularly that of the many foreign workers, about the reasons for the accidents that happened on the site and which eventually brought work to a standstill. Here, Jouet deals with other political issues, such as race and class; yet he also sketches the very local and conflictive politics that may animate family relations. Finally, the people responsible for the mountain are put on trial, and the third part of the novel stages the testimony of a novelist who had been commissioned to write a fictional account of the project. He is a shadowy, elusive figure who realizes that certain affinities link the mountain and his own writerly task—and flaw them, too, in similar ways. National monuments, like novels, dig their foundations deep in the human imagination; yet in politics, as in literature, things are very rarely what we first imagine them to be.

Throughout *La Montagne R,* language is put on trial. Testing language in several different discursive contexts, in each of which language is strained to the breaking point, Jouet asks his reader to think about its limits as a heuristic tool and to question its potential as a vehicle of truth. He initiates this process on the first page of his novel, as the President begins his address to the Republican Council: "We must do something. We must. Something must be done, something must be accomplished. It must not be said that we have not done anything. We must do something more and better than anyone has ever done. And moreover, this famous something, we are going to do it" (9). Jouet's first target is thus an easy one, for it is a commonplace in France (and not only in France) that the language of the body politic is corrupt and largely empty—

so much so, in fact, that it has recently been gratified with its own generic term, *la langue de bois* [wooden language]. The President's utterance is a shining example of that sort of language: it is static, inanely iterative, and seems to serve a purpose that is, at best, merely phatic. The message it contains is a very simple one: "I am speaking"; its function is initiatory and it serves to set the tone for what will follow.

It is important to realize, however, that this passage constitutes the inaugural moment of Jouet's novel, too, and that ironic reciprocities prevail between the President's political speech and Jouet's literary discourse. That is, just as this passage is intended to give us a foretaste of the President's linguistic absurdities, so too it announces a more sober reflection upon the uses of language. Though the President's role is clearly that of a straw man in such a perspective, his attitude toward language is not as unrelievedly naive as one might suspect. For he is a critic of language, too. He castigates the language of his political rivals, deploring the "verbal words which our predecessors made habitual" (10). But of course his own "words" are merely "verbal" too, because the President is steeped in the linguistic conventions of his trade. He fancies himself a poet of sorts, and will not deny himself the pleasure of turning a metaphor or two. "The Republic is a becalmed galleon. It is up to us to make wind!" he perorates (11), nicely illustrating by his example the flatulent politspeak which is at issue in the first part of *La Montagne R.*

In the second part of his novel, Jouet turns his attention from the political domain to the personal. As young Mademoiselle Muratore questions her father about his role in the Montagne R project, Jouet invites us to question the kind of language that we use in quotidian, intimate settings. Telling her father that she has been commissioned by some vague "Americans" to do research on daily life in the Republic during the construction of the Montagne R, she asks him about those years. Her questions are banal to begin with, yet they elicit suspicious hesitations, resistances, and surjustifications from her father. As it becomes progressively clear that his role in the Montagne R was a depraved one from the outset, and that he was deeply intricated in the social and moral crimes which subtended the project, the language that the daughter and the father speak changes dramatically in tenor. The daughter's questions become more urgent, more accusatory, while her father answers ever more elliptical. Pushed to his limit, the father breaks off their conversation and tells her to leave, which she refuses to do, because she has not finished her interrogation: "Not until you've told me how you obtained it, that rotten contract for that rotten project of a rotten mountain that poisoned my childhood and the entire Republic!" (70). Like the first part of the novel, language here leads to catastrophe, but this time the catastrophe is of a personal nature. Pressed by his daughter's questions, the father confesses that he had committed an incestuous attack on her many years before, during the time of the Montagne R, and he suggests moreover that she was complaisant in that crime. If this is the truth, it is one which neither father nor daughter can bear to hear. That moment in the text stages yet another consideration about language: if language can suffice to describe certain crimes, whether civil or familial, it is also an agent of those crimes. And, far from palliating them after the fact, it serves to re-enact them.

The final part of the novel takes place ten years after the events of the first part, during a lengthy trial in which the President of the Republican Council and other figures involved in the Montagne R are brought to justice. More specifically, it is devoted to the testimony of a writer named "Stéphane" who had accepted a commission to write a novel about the project. Jacques Jouet's focus in this part is literary language and the ways it is perceived in the society that surrounds it. Since the setting of this portion of his novel is literally that of a legal proceeding, Jouet's technique of putting language on trial takes on additional pungency here. For a trial is above all a linguistic event in which different utterances are tested forensically in order to arrive at the truth. In the view of the court, however, Stéphane is the witness from hell: his answers to their questions are elusive, obscure, imprecise, conjectural, and deliberately misleading. The fundamental problem is that he doesn't speak the language of the court. Whether by choice or by necessity, he misconstrues their questions, responds figuratively when a literal answer is called for, uses humor to deflect the examination, and envelops his testimony in trope and rhetorical flourish. He insists to his advantage on the notion that literature is somehow apart from other sorts of language. The court itself subscribes very largely to that notion, for, unlike many other collaborators in the Montagne R, Stéphane is not among the accused. Indeed the presiding judge deplores that fact and suggests that if Stéphane had not been inculpated, "It was precisely because writers have always been the darlings of the Republic!" (93). In this final portion of *La Montagne R,* Jouet offers a rich pattern of suggestion centering upon the uses and abuses of literature, a range of considerations which I shall discuss in more detail later. For the moment, however, suffice it to say that his first intention in this part of his novel is to show how literary language is marginalized from the other kinds of language we speak, with more or less fluency, as we make our way through the world.

In considering Jouet's critique of language, it becomes apparent that one of the stances he takes is that of a literalist, for the language of his novel is solidly grounded in the *letter.* The precombinatory, alphabetical sign "R," suspended at the end of his title, piques the reader's curiosity. It is the founding integer of the hermeneutic code of the text, which Jouet develops and exploits to great effect throughout *La Montagne R.* Around it, Jouet weaves textures of association in which are imbricated all the major terms of his novel. Through that strategy, he invokes a theory of language which holds the letter to be the fundamental generator of meaning.[1] And he appeals implicitly to traditions both ancient and modern: literalist experiments like those of the Grands Rhétoriqueurs and the cabalist Abraham Abulafia, but also those of contemporary writers who, like him, have promoted the alphabetical letter as a richly suggestive signifier, figures such as Edmond Jabès, John Barth, Walter Abish, and Georges Perec.

Within the novel, it is the President of the Republican Council who launches the letter into the privileged position it will occupy. Arguing that "something" must be done for the Republic, he says, "Something, in point of fact, has a name, and this name is *the Mountain, the Republic Mountain,* it's *the Mountain R.* There's a name that breathes everything it knows. The mountain with a big R. Henceforth, we shall say *the Mountain R*" (9). Playing on both the graphic and the phonetic value of the letter R, which is pronounced in French just like the word *air*—"We shall build a mountain in the open air" (10)—the President unwittingly sketches out the set of ironic correspondences which doom the project in its very conception. For the Republic that this project is intended to glorify is nothing more than air; and neither air nor the Republic will support a mountain. Jouet carefully expands the semantic reach of the letter throughout the novel. In the second part, Mademoiselle Muratore compares the Montagne R project to the construction of the Palais de Versailles: "R like Royal, thus" (41). One of Stéphane's previous books is entitled *Révélations tardives sur ce qui se passa vraiment dans la carlingue* [Tardy Revelations on What Really Happened in the Cockpit] (95); and indeed the idea of "revelation" is a central one in *La Montagne R*. Near the end of the novel, the notion that the alphabetical sign marks the project fatally (which has been implicit up to that point) is formulated explicitly by one of the members of the court as he offers yet another interpretation of the letter R: "a Mountain R like rotten!" (96). Jouet casts the various significations of the letter R in a fashion that underscores their mutual complementarity, and he toils away productively in the semantic field which they define. Among them, however, there is one signification that is predominant by virtue of the fact that Jouet deploys it as the central metaphor of his novel: R as in *roman,* "novel." For this is, after all, a novel of a mountain. It is also a mountain of a novel—or rather a Montagne R of a novel, according to the remarkable literary contract that Jouet proposes to his reader.

That contract is a highly playful one, and its terms are ludic in character. Jacques Jouet casts *La Montagne R* as a collaborative game, one in which the writer's moves are intended to be reciprocated by those of the reader.[2] Jouet plays in a Nietzschean sense, that is, he adopts a playful attitude as a way of coming to terms with the job of writing a novel.[3] In a similar vein—and in the context of another mountainous novel—Thomas Mann borrowed Goethe's characterization of *Faust* as a "very serious jest" to describe his own intent in *The Magic Mountain,* suggesting furthermore that such a notion is broadly illustrative of the artistic impulse in general (Mann 721). My point here is that the sort of play Jouet engages in does not exclude seriousness of intent; quite to the contrary, it is play which facilitates seriousness. If my assertion seems paradoxical, it is only because we tend to think of play and seriousness as mutually exclusive categories. That view is a pernicious and reductive one, I think, insofar as it does violence both to play and to seriousness, marginalizing the former mode and trivializing the latter.

Closely examined, art gives the lie to the play-seriousness antinomy, and most particularly (since that is my focus here) literary art. On the one hand, as

Johan Huizinga argues in *Homo Ludens,* his seminal study of play as a cultural influence, "All poetry is born of play" (129). That is, literature arises in the play of language; it takes shape as a writer tests words against other words, configuring them in new ways, rejecting certain configurations and retaining others. On the other hand, play itself is a significant function, since it produces meaning. Despite its seeming gratuitousness, play is not "for nothing." Rather, it is a creative activity which we all engage in, to varying degree and at different moments, as we attempt to invest our experience in the world with structure; as Huizinga puts it, "All play means something" (1). Play is dynamic: the word itself connotes a motion and a latitude that serve to attenuate the constraints we encounter in our daily life. That is not to say that games are altogether free of constraints; but we accept those constraints freely when we play, whether it be a game of chess, or basketball, or charades. Or indeed when we read a novel. In other words, play affords us with a "useful freedom," to borrow Roger Caillois's term (12), a facility that we may turn to certain creative purposes. Finally, as Jacques Ehrmann argued so persuasively, play is communicational and articulative (56). It puts all of its constitutive elements—pawns and players alike—*in* play, and it constructs something significant out of that process.

The game that Jacques Jouet proposes in *La Montagne R* is just that sort of articulative system. This is perhaps most apparent in his insistence on the alphabetical letter, for the R of his title announces the play of the words beginning in R that I discussed earlier. Subtly and methodically, Jouet situates those words in a dynamic, articulative context wherein each successive word interrogates and nuances those that precede it and evokes new interpretive possibilities, each word a different move in a game of literary potentiality. In that sense, Jouet moves his characters around the board in a programmatic fashion, too. They offer different versions of the events that surrounded the Montagne R, accounts which conflict with each other on key points and put each other into question. There is no definitive, authoritative "story" here. The tales the characters tell compete for the reader's subscription on equal terms as Jouet plays on the hermeneutic code, dispensing narrative information and withholding it, but never guaranteeing it. In fact, the notion of the "story" makes sense in *La Montagne R* only if we accept Jouet's ludic contract.

For the very idea of the story has been displaced in this novel from the realm of the *narrated* into the realm of the *narrating:* more than anything else, *La Montagne R* tells the tale of the ways writers and readers engage each other in the play of literature.

Jouet's most powerful token in that game is Stéphane, and he plays Stéphane boldly in the novel, particularly in the third part. As the reader counters each successive move, he or she is called upon to think about certain fundamental considerations of literature, and most especially about the duplicity of fiction. For Stéphane is a supremely duplicitous figure. If the first part of his testimony at the Montagne R trial seems straightforward enough, the rest is lost in innuendo and deliberate obfuscation. Telling the court about his commission to write a novelistic account of the Montagne R, he projects himself disingenuously as a simple writer undertaking a simple task:

> At the time of the announcement, ten years ago, by the government of the Republic, of the great Mountain R project, I for my part confided, to the presidency of the Republican Council, and in writing, my intention to write a work of fiction which would take its material (all of its material, nothing but its material) from the conception and the realization of the project. This intention seemed to please the highest authorities. (89-90)

His record as a novelist is an enviable one, he mentions. Had he brought this project to fruition, it would have been his ninth novel. And for novelists especially, Stéphane suggests, nothing succeeds like success: "I had obtained this contract because my previous book had been particularly appreciated by some of my colleagues, and not by the least of them, who had made their appreciation known" (95).

Stéphane is not only a novelist, one learns. Like Jouet himself, he has worked in a variety of other literary genres. Biography interests him, for instance: he testifies that his current project is a life of Eugène de Mirecourt, "a very strange character, who hunted lice on Alexandre Dumas's head" (92). And history, too: Stéphane tells the court that he wished to write an account of Pierre Louis Moreau de Maupertuis's eighteenth-century expedition to Lapland (113). Yet certain lines in his writerly curriculum vitae occasion Stéphane far more unease, touching painfully as they do on the social and political realities that are at issue in the trial. The prosecuting attorney accuses him, for example, of having authored a mawkishly servile paean to the principal contracting corporation of the Montagne R, a text entitled "Ode à Bargéco," and he quotes a passage from that poem; its truly awful mock-heroic style provokes a moment of hilarity in court. Stéphane rises gamely to the defense of his verses, cannily locating that argument in a noble defense of poetry in general: "They were no worse than many others. Poetry is not something purer than anything else, nor less dirty" (100).

Stéphane's forays into other kinds of writing may have been still more nefarious, it is suggested. The prosecutor asks him if he had authored an anonymous journalistic exposé of the Montagne R project. He counters Stéphane's unconvincing demurral with evidence of stylistic analysis comparing the newspaper piece to Stéphane's other writings, a tactic which leaves Stéphane reeling: "The uses to which my prose were put hurt me more than anything. I wondered if, after that, I could still make my living as a writer" (122). Finally, the prosecutor charges Stéphane with having ghostwritten a speech about the Montagne R which the President of the Republican Council's delivered in camera, of playing Père Joseph to the President's Richelieu. Closely pressed, Stéphane is forced to admit that he had "participated" in the writing of that speech (122). And indeed, it becomes apparent that Stéphane was the *éminence grise* behind much of the political maneuvering involved in the project, scripting and precipitating events, rather than merely chronicling them.

Granted that consideration, the role Stéphane plays in *La Montagne R* is strictly figural of the one Jouet himself plays. And clearly, the game that Jouet proposes to the readers of his novel is one that hinges upon the notion of textual specularity.[4] At the simplest level, Stéphane's Montagne R novel is emblazoned within Jouet's own, each mirroring the other. When Stéphane describes the travails and writerly struggles he endures as he labors to write his virtual text, we readers are encouraged to reflect on the kind of work that resulted in the real text that we are holding before us. Yet the relations between these two texts are not perfectly reciprocal, and multiple ironies animate those relations, the most obvious among them being the fact that Stéphane, unlike Jouet, cannot finish his novel. In other words, the doubling effects that Jouet elaborates in *La Montagne R* are asymmetrical, carefully skewed to his own advantage.

And the way he exploits his character is double in the same fashion, for Stéphane serves as both example and counterexample. At certain moments, Stéphane's account of his project may be read as a faithful description of the kinds of concerns and issues that any successful novelist must face; at other times, his woeful maunderings are intended to suggest the worst nightmares of a failed novelist.

Early in his testimony, Stéphane tells the court in some detail about his ambition in undertaking the project:

> I didn't want to write a chronicle, but rather a novel. It would have been my ninth novel. I had no idea of the manner in which this novel would account for observed reality. What had fascinated me, in the annoncement of this un-bounded thing, the Mountain R, was precisely the similarity I saw in it with my experience as a writer. To write a novel is to be obliged to build a mountain, just like that, from scratch, on a lot next to your own property. You see it progress, every day, from your window, every day, even during vacations and holidays. A mountain next to one's life. One must count pages, estimate the number of words, make the chapters proportional. A certain fine accumulation ... in the lower levels the ungraded product, and the more one climbs to the surface, the more elaborate it is .... Each word must be as "written" as every other, each sentence carefully articulated with the whole. One knows that this will demand several months, sometimes several years, of loving effort.... If one dies in the middle of it, nobody will finish the project, unless one is lucky enough to be a worker like Balzac. (94)

The analogy that Stéphane proposes between the novel and the moun-tain is of course the same one which Jouet elaborates throughout *La Montagne R* as the principal metaphor of his text. The fact that Stéphane's vision and Jouet's coincide upon that central term suggests that we may take Stéphane at his word here. I would like to argue, moreover, that it is legitimate to read in this passage a theory of the novel which Jouet claims as his own. From a writer's perspective, a novel in progress looms up like the Montagne R does on the landscape of the République. It is artifice, but it imitates the real. Its dimen-sions are impossible ones, and its conception beggars its execution. The task of writing a novel is Sisyphean. What it chiefly demands is a labor of artisanry rather than art, work rather than inspiration. Most importantly, a novel is a *chantier,* a construction site. And Stéphane is not the only one to enunciate that notion in *La Montagne R.* Monsieur Muratore, the contractor, uses the word as he describes the kind of work he did on the mountain to his daughter:

> Yes, but, a construction site, you know, when you work on it, when it's done, it's not what the public sees. Otherwise, it would be too boring. No, the project when finished is an enormous quantity of little things, little tasks . . . certain of them take a week, others three days, others a morning, others a month and a half. . . . The only thing you know, let's admit it, is that you have worked on this project for several years of your life, and that during those years you have not done much else, it's true . . . nothing much other than finishing an infinity of little tasks. (40)

His discourse is closely similar to Stéphane's, and it likewise encodes— if more subtly—a theory of literary process as Jouet conceives the latter. It should be recalled, too, that one of Jacques Jouet's earlier books is entitled *Le Chantier,* and just like *La Montagne R,* it insists upon the idea of literature as *construction.*

Literature is constructivist in all of its phases, Jouet argues, in its production and its reception, in both writing and reading alike. If one accepts the hypothesis that the passages I have quoted are intended by Jouet to mirror the writing act, it is perhaps not stretching the point to suggest that he intends for us to see in them an image of the kinds of processes we undertake when we read a text, too. For if his novel offers a mirror to the writer, it also offers a mirror to the reader.[5] By using specular devices such as these, Jouet confronts us throughout *La Montagne R* with our own reading act, inviting us to reflect upon it, to watch ourselves as we test different interpretive strategies, attempting to build coherence and meaning. Once again, let me stress that Jouet's manner is playful, and that he encourages his readers to enter into a textual contract whose terms are ludic. He plays with the idea of the novel in *La Montagne R,* examining it from a variety of different angles and in a variety of different discursive modes, sometimes soberly and candidly, sometimes ironically or parodically.

One of Jouet's richest games involves the notion of *littérature engagée.*

The prosecutor attacks Stéphane ruthlessly on that issue, asking him whether he believes that novelists have political responsibilities in the world of ideas. No more than butchers do, Stéphane retorts, asserting categorically that "literature must never be used as testimony" (103). He launches into a rebuttal that vexes ideology against aesthetics, intending only that each should render the other still more murky to the eyes of the court: "When one speaks of a writer's 'political luck,' the politics one means is always the hardball kind! Me, I'm sorry, I'm interested in softball. I was willing to be responsible in the present moment, but I must also be responsible in History, in the history, especially, of my art, and those two responsibilities may sometimes conflict" (103). Stéphane's bad faith is in this instance so egregious, so craven, that it turns to comedy. For quite obviously, granted the dubious terms of his contract, his project was a political one from the outset. His novel was indeed intended to engage the social reality of the Montagne R directly, and to condition the public perception of that reality to the advantage of the authorities: his commission was principally that of a propagandist, rather than a novelist.

Once again, rich specular relations pertain between Stéphane's novel and Jouet's. But in this case the reflected image is that of a funhouse mirror, for Stéphane's novel presents a deformed, exaggerated, and essentially ludic image of Jouet's own. *La Montagne R* undoubtedly engages contemporary political concerns, interrogating the way the masters of the society of the spectacle stage their vision of the Republic for the plebeians. Yet it also disengages strategically: it would be a long stretch to call *La Montagne R* a "political novel," without nuancing that term far beyond its usual boundaries. The terms of Jouet's interrogation are, moreover, critical and oppositional from the start. The political dimension of *La Montagne R* clearly positions itself in the high satirical tradition of Swift and Voltaire. Whereas Stéphane deliberately sets out to speak the language of power on behalf of power, Jouet's intent is on the contrary subversive. The most fundamental difference between Stéphane's project and Jouet's is that the principal focus of Jouet's project is not politics, but rather literature itself and, in particular, the novel as literary form.

Here, too, Jouet offers Stéphane's work as both example and counterexample. Stéphane, like Jouet himself, is well aware that writing a novel is a risky business: "I wanted this novel to embrace a collective passion.

I knew I was taking a risk," he tells the court (96). Among the risks he faces as he undertakes his project, one is preponderant in Stéphane's mind: "Let's say that the only real risk was that the novel would never be finished. That's exactly what happened" (96). In that perspective, the many accusations with which the court taxes Stéphane—criminal conspiracy in the early stages of the Montagne R project, his subsequent role as accomplice to the President, his failure to denounce the local abuses he witnessed in the course of his work, and so forth—may be seen as pretextual. For Stéphane's real crime is textual in character: he failed to write his book. Most of his bluster in the courtroom is intended to deflect, elide, or relativize that vital fact. For each successful novel, he argues, five others are left unfinished. The problems a novelist must grapple with cannot be imagined by common mortals, and even the most accomplished writer may fail to foresee them: "To write is not to foresee. One must not confuse them," he whines (104). In the broader scheme of things it makes very little difference if he finished his novel or not, he suggests, because the fate of literature is necessarily uncertain: "A writer can work all his life without ever being appreciated" (97-98).

Despite all his efforts, however, the fact that Stéphane failed to complete his novel remains incontrovertible in the court's mind. Because nothing fails like failure, whether it be a question of a novel or a mountain. Had the President's Montagne R project succeeded, there would have been no need for a trial: he and his collaborators would have been lionized rather than vilified. But nobody likes a loser. For Stéphane himself it didn't have to be this way: even granted the fact that work on the Montagne R came to a halt in scandal and catastrophe, the option of acquitting himself more or less honorably of his task was nonetheless available to Stéphane. As a member of the court points out, he could have written an honest account of the failure of that project, "the successful novel of an aborted mountain" (96). Therein may be read the final move in the specular game that Jouet proposes to his readers, for of course Stéphane's failure is intended to stage *contrariwise* (as another genial literary gamesman, Lewis Carroll, would put it) Jouet's success. If Stéphane becomes in the end the unfortunate object of his society's scorn, it is principally because, unlike Jacques Jouet, he has failed to negotiate the Montagne R's terrain. That terrain features a steep upside, and its downside is a vertiginous, precipitous one. But that's the way it is with mountains—and with novels, too.

NOTES

[1] See for example Jacques Derrida's remarks about "the radical origin of meaning as letter" (*Ecriture* 99); Joseph Guglielmi, who speaks of "the promotion of the letter as motor of the production of meaning" (41); and Gabriel Bounoure: "These days, writing is all too frequently foully debased, but the letter (whose function is to destroy the effect of time) rediscovers, traced by the poet, its original character. Reinvested with their antique power, the symbols of the word and the graphic sign obey their metaphorical essence, that is, their transpositional vocation" (66).

[2] Michel Picard has elaborated a very useful model of reading as play, focusing on literature as a social game. See also Motte, *Playtexts,* especially 3-27.

[3] See Nietzsche 258: "I do not know of any other way of associating with great tasks than *play:* as a sign of greatness, this is an essential presupposition."

[4] I use that term in Lucien Dällenbach's sense. See *Le Récit spéculaire,* especially 37-38 and 51.

[5] I note in passing an exaggerated—if highly particular—example of that effect, one which stunned *this* reader. It is taken from Stéphane's testimony to the court: "Did I obtain the grant for which I had applied to the Warren Motte Foundation, for the trip and for writing this novel?" (114).

VI

∽

MARIE NDIAYE'S SORCERY

With ten books currently to her credit, Marie NDiaye has been hailed as a prodigy of French literature, for she published her first novel at the Editions de Minuit while still in her teens. Her writings have been received in the press with an impressive level of encomium, but they have not yet generated a great deal of interest among academic critics.[1] While NDiaye's novels display a variety of settings and techniques, a common concern animates all of them, insofar as each is focused in some manner upon the question of alienation and the problems experienced by an individual who finds herself or himself marginalized for reasons very largely beyond her or his understanding and control. Such is the case of *La Sorcière* (1996; The Witch), Marie NDiaye's sixth novel, which I regard as her most interesting, provocative book thus far.

La Sorcière is the story of Lucie, a middle-aged housewife. She lives in an unremarkable house in a drably homogeneous housing development in an ordinary, unnamed town in the provinces. Her husband, a superbly undistinguished man named Pierrot, makes a difficult living selling time-shares in vacation condominiums on commission. Their twin daughters, Maud and Lise, are on the cusp of adolescence, and they manifest toward their long-suffering parents the kind of behavior that is habitual with teenagers, from Combray to Colorado. In short, Lucie's story would be an utterly banal one—were it not for the fact that she is a witch.

That brief sketch of *La Sorcière's* setting may offer some idea of its originality, for one of the principal curiosities of this novel is the way it stages the fantastic against the backdrop of the quotidian, vexing one against the other in turn such that each interrogates the other, and ironically encouraging us to question the categories we use in order to come to terms with experience. That technique is used throughout the novel, and indeed NDiaye puts it into play in *La Sorcière's* very first words:

> When my daughters turned twelve, I initiated them into the mysterious powers. Not so much "mysterious" because they were unaware of their existence, or because I had hidden them from my daughters (with them, I never hid anything, since we were of the same gender), but rather because, having grown up in the vague and indifferent knowledge of this reality, they didn't feel that they needed to worry about it all of a sudden, nor to master it in any fashion, any more than they felt obliged to learn how to prepare the meals that I served them, and which belonged to a domain that was equally distant and uninteresting. (9)

The locution "mysterious powers" is a potent one with which to initiate a story, one that is guaranteed to jumpstart what Roland Barthes called the hermeneutic code of the novel, whetting the reader's curiosity and goading him or her to read onward in order to learn more. Yet as soon as NDiaye utters those words and evokes thereby the richly suggestive theme of the fantastic, she carefully subverts them. She projects the "mystery" into quite another perspective, that of adolescent indifference and ennui, wherein many of the things that adults find most extraordinary are systematically relativized and dismissed. The fact that Lucie's daughters feel (or pretend to feel) that her "powers" are as bland and fundamentally uninteresting as her cooking is symptomatic of the ways in which Lucie is misunderstood by those around her— and of the ways she misunderstands herself. It is also the first move in a game NDiaye will play in *La Sorcière,* pitting the fantastic against the mundane in a deliberately unbalanced struggle.

Lucie is a witch, then; but she is a most ordinary witch. She practices sorcery, but she feels that her gift is a very weak one compared to that of other sorceresses: "Truth be told, what I possessed was a ridiculous power, since it only allowed me to see insignificant things" (13). She can "see" things at a distance in the present: she "sees" her husband in his mother's house in Poitiers, for instance (58); and she "sees" him too in Bourges, after he has left her for another woman (140). Yet she cannot see into the future—or only very dimly and occasionally. Lucie's gift is one that is passed in unbroken tradition from mother to daughter; and, by an ironic twist that a geneticist might identify as alternation of generations, Lucie finds herself bracketed by highly talented witches, on the one hand her mother, on the other hand her daughters: "Maud and Lise had acquired in their turn the ability to see into the future and the past, the latest in a procession of female ancestors more or less talented, of whom the eldest and perhaps the most gifted of all was my own mother" (12). Lucie's mother is an exceptionally gifted witch, one who is capable of powerful acts of sorcery of various kinds. Yet she experiences her gift as a burden, finds it shameful and repugnant, and does everything she can to hide it. In that, she is mostly successful: "Nobody, moreover, could have looked less like a witch than my mother" (76). She did, nonetheless, initiate Lucie into the "mysterious powers" when she came of age, and she made Lucie promise that she would eventually do the same for her own daughters, in order that their sorceress dynasty be preserved.

Maud and Lise receive their benediction, however, with an offhandedness that bewilders Lucie: "—Come on, Mom, really, all this silliness . . . , said Maud, and that was their only way of marking their entrance into the immemorial parade of women with occult powers" (13). Nevertheless, despite their apparent indifference toward sorcery, Lucie recognizes quickly that her daughters are endowed with very exceptional powers indeed. Not only can they "see" in the past, present, and future, they can also fly, change shape, and even call down storms. They exercise those powers intuitively and effortlessly, laughing off Lucie's attempts to speak about the occult, dismissing her when she tries to tutor them. In short, the twins are infinitely more gifted than Lucie herself: "Seeing them, I finally understood what a real witch was like, and I began to fear and to envy Maud and Lise" (110-11).

Thus, Lucie finds herself doubly marginalized by her sorcery. First and most obviously, she is set apart from ordinary people by virtue of the fact that she is a witch, as impotent and pitiful as her gift may be. Second, Lucie is distinctly unequal to the great witches who precede and follow her, and she feels herself to be the object of her mother's and her daughters' tacit (and sometimes less tacit) scorn. Moreover, Lucie fears that her powers, such as they may be, are gradually eroding: "It seemed to me that each day my talent eroded a little bit more—and in view of that, I wondered if perhaps I wasn't cut out to be a real witch?" (139). A witch without much witchery: that's Lucie's situation in a nutshell. She tries her best to navigate between the everyday world and the occult, but she feels at home neither in one nor in the other. Mundane social interactions in her town leave her just as perplexed as do the most arcane rituals of sorcery. She is equally inept in cocktail party chat as in incantations. She cannot understand her daughters as suburban adolescents; nor can she understand them as witches. Toward the end of the novel though, and against appalling odds, Lucie will come to provisional terms with herself: "I'm *sort of* a witch, after all. On that at least, I haven't deceived anyone" (178).

If Lucie's powers are very modest ones, they will nonetheless mark her as someone very different from the people around her. She is feared and shunned by many of those people, most particularly men, beginning with her own husband, Pierrot. The reason for her marginalization is rarely rendered explicit by the individuals who shun her, and indeed Lucie experiences her sorcery as a sort of guilty secret. Unspoken alterity is the motor that drives many of Marie NDiaye's novels, a phenomenon that Lydie Moudileno has analyzed in her reading of the question of anathema in *En famille (Among Family)*, where a young woman named Fanny is excluded from her family because of some past sin that is never made explicit. The family dynamic turns constantly around that sin obliquely, without articulating it, and so does NDiaye's writing. K. Ambroise Teko-Agbo, noting that NDiaye herself is the daughter of a Senegalese father and a "French" (that is, Caucasian) mother, sees in Fanny "the black sheep that disrupts" (161), and argues that *En famille* offers a meditation on the problem of racial alterity and the difficult prospect of integration in the political culture of contemporary France. I feel that similar issues are at work in *La Sorcière*, but I believe that several other concerns are carefully interwoven among them.

One thing which appears to be certain is that the epithet "witch" is a catchall term that may conveniently cover a plethora of sins, as Jules Michelet pointed out long ago: "Note that in certain periods, by that lone word *Witch*, hate kills anyone it wants to. Women's jealousies, men's envies take up that handy weapon. A woman is rich? . . . *Witch*. A woman is beautiful? . . . *Witch*"

(24). By her own admission, Lucie is not a very accomplished person. She has little formal education and no profession, apart from that of wife, mother, housekeeper, and cook—and in each of those domains, she feels that she has failed. Her social life is very limited indeed: she has no friends except for a neighbor named Isabelle, and her husband is loathe to bring his business associates home for dinner because Lucie's qualities as a hostess are, in his eyes at least, sorely lacking.

Something about Lucie troubles other people and makes them wary of her. On the lone occasion in the novel when Lucie encounters a spontaneous gesture of solidarity from someone else, she is at a loss to explain it. Walking along in the main street of her town one day, Lucie encounters a stranger, described vaguely as an emigrant woman, who greets her in a manner that leaves Lucie both delighted and perplexed: "Hello, my sister" (62). Never having experienced a social situation like this one, Lucie responds to the woman's greeting using the very same words, and watches her as she disappears into a rundown apartment building: "I waited a moment in front of the doorway, shivering in my raincoat, vaguely hoping I did not know what—that the woman would appear again, that she would call to me once more in that nice manner, so sure of herself and unselfish? Could this stranger [*étrangère*] be my sister in one way or another, and how did she know it?" (63). What sort of commonality was the woman invoking? Was it merely a question of shared gender? Was she appealing to some shared ethnic or racial identity? Was it a question of one witch, in a vast sorority of witches, recognizing another? Or was it a case of a "stranger" or a "foreigner" (the word *étrangère* in the original leaves that distinction richly unresolved) appealing to another person who is likewise branded as being dramatically different from other people? Lucie is unable to resolve those questions, and NDiaye does nothing to help her reader resolve them, either. She prefers to suspend them, intending that the reader should examine them in the context of what follows in the novel. It should also be remarked that the passage itself is a very strange one in the broader narrative economy of *La Sorcière,* an anomalous moment that doesn't seem to fit in. By virtue of that, moreover, it is strongly performative in the dimension of the novel that is focused on the question of alterity.[2]

Lucie's other social encounters are far less gratifying than the one described above. An extreme example of those is offered in a passage near the end of the novel, where members of the town council, accompanied by two policemen—that is, designated representatives of the social order, in both its legislative and punitive incarnations—descend upon Lucie, accusing her of charlatanism and swindling. As they take her off to jail, Lucie is astonished to see how much they loathe her, and still more stupefied when she realizes that they fear her, too. She stands accused, ironically enough, of not being a real witch: "I have been accused of charlatanism! I have been accused, precisely, of not being a real witch, of passing myself off as something that I'm not" (181). In jail, one of the policeman vilifies her, yet he cannot bring himself to pronounce the word *sorcière:* "Everyone knows that . . . that women like you try to persuade people that they are not" (182). Availing himself of the time-honored method of dealing with witches, he sets fire to her mattress, and only then can he bring himself to enunciate the word, practically choking on it: "Cursed witch, he cried in a muffled voice. Cursed, cursed" (183).

The lesson is a harsh one, but it is limpid. Society has the final word on who is a witch and who is not. Lucie may worry about not being sorceress enough; she may view her powers as paltry at best; and she may fret that they are diminishing by the day: all of that is finally meaningless, for the issue does not lie with her. On the contrary, it is constituted authority and the power it wields—a power that mocks and dwarfs her own putative "powers"—that will adjudicate the question of whether or not she is a witch. In that perspective, the difference between being accused of sorcery and of pretending to be a witch is both trivial and otiose, because for society all that matters is the projection of the *word* itself onto the individual. Such an individual becomes the vessel of society's ill-repressed fears, and the vector of its violence. That is the phenomenon Michelet pointed to in his analysis of the origins of the witch, laying the blame squarely at the feet of one of the most powerful institutions of medieval European society:

> When did the Witch originate? I say without hesitation: "In the time of hopelessness."
> Of the profound hopelessness that the Church foisted upon the world. I say without hesitation: "The Witch is the Church's crime." (27)

The crime, then, is social in character, rather than individual; yet that is a distinction that provides little solace to the accused. As Lucie searches her conscience, trying to imagine what she might have done to make people hate her so, she finds nothing particularly egregious among all of her nebulous and generalized feelings of guilt. Yet it may become apparent to the reader that one of her crimes is the fact that she was born a woman. Sorcery is gender-coded in this novel, and NDiaye makes that clear in the text's incipit ("with them, I never hid anything, since we were of the same gender"). *La Sorcière* offers, among other things, a dispatch from the front in a grim gender war. Insofar as Lucie and her sorceress lineage are concerned, the fight is for basic survival, and it is for the most part clandestine and subterranean in character. Such is literally the case when Lucie begins to initiate her daughters into the sorceress tradition: "We went somewhere where we would be sheltered from their father's gaze, in the basement. In this big, low room, with its cinderblock walls, the pride of my husband by virtue of its very uselessness (old paint cans in a corner, that's all there was), I tried to convey to them the indispensable but imperfect power of my forebears" (10). Pierrot is aware of his wife's powers, but he feels only repugnance toward them. He doesn't speak about them (or only in moments of extreme anger, in order to revile Lucie), and he forbids Lucie to speak about them.

Clearly, one of the things that troubles Pierrot so deeply is that sorcery is closely associated with female sexuality. When Lucie "sees" people at a distance, tears of blood run from her eyes; and when her adolescent daughters begin to exercise their powers, they too begin to bleed.[3] The metaphorical evocation of menstruation is obvious here. Menstruation, like sorcery, is a subject powerfully hushed by taboo in a social discourse largely dominated by men, where it represents something that is misunderstood, demonized, and feared. The analogy of sorcery and female sexuality becomes more apparent still when Lucie remarks that she doesn't quite dare ask her daughters if they have used their new powers: "Modesty prevented me from questioning my daughters on that subject" (30). Read through that analogy, Lucie's behavior is understandable enough: like many parents, she hesitates to speak openly with her children on the subject of their nascent sexuality. Her compunction is not strictly identical to that of Pierrot, in that it is motivated principally by tact, rather than by dread; yet it is important to recognize that Lucie's stance is nonetheless conditioned in large measure by the phallocentric ideology of the society in which she lives. Women should be seductive, of course, according to such an ideology—but not *too* seductive. When women cross that boundary, what is normal and attractive becomes abnormal and repulsive. Deliberately focusing their all-too-abundant concupiscence upon men, they threaten the order of male power as a whole; they become, in short, witches. And one of the most nefarious consequences of such seductions is that men in authority might actually be tempted to forgive those women for being witches.[4]

Pierrot, for his part, girds himself manfully in order to resist such a temptation. He shares a house with Lucie—until he leaves her, that is—, but as far as the reader can tell, their relations in recent years have been coldly chaste ones. He feels a strong repellence toward her, for reasons that Lucie fails to comprehend, sensing only that the fault lies with her. Early on, she worries that Pierrot will come to feel the same kind of "irrepressible aversion" (16) toward his daughters as he does toward her. And indeed, that prospect is confirmed later in the story, ineluctably enough, after Pierrot has moved in with another woman, a blessedly bovine individual with whom he feels finally at peace. When Lucie goes to visit him in order to ask him what he intends to do about his daughters, he reacts with rage and ill-concealed terror:

> —So, your daughters? Maud and Lise?, I asked.
> But I regretted it as soon as I said it, and hunched back on my chair. Pierrot's pale and puffy face wrinkled in disgust. He was about to spit, then swallowed his saliva and wiped his mouth with the back of his hand.
> —Those dirty little witches!, he hissed, looking at me with hate in his eyes.
> He jumped up brutally and yelled, but without coming near me:
> —My life is here, leave me alone! Now, you get the hell out of here and use your damned diabolical powers to take care of everything else!
> —But they're only mediocre ones, I said, they're worthless, and you know it.
> He roared:
> —No, I don't know anything at all, and I don't want to know. Shut up, not another word about it, get the hell out! (149-50)

Certain other women campaign in the gender war far more aggressively than Lucie, and with more striking results. Her neighbor Isabelle, for instance, lives with her husband and son, but haughtily dismisses them both as idiots, even alluding to her son as "that little shit" (20) in her chats with Lucie. When eventually Isabelle finds the males in her family too burdensome to bear, she will leave them—not for another man, but rather to set off on a new life, unfettered and very much her own woman. On the lone occasion when Pierrot brings a business associate home for dinner, an unremarkable person named Matin, Lucie is at a loss to explain the attitude of almost slavish deference which Pierrot displays toward him. It turns out that just that very day Matin has taken the brave step that Pierrot has long dreamed of: he has left his wife. Yet when Lucie calls Matin's wife on the phone, she assures her that there is no cause for alarm, that her husband leaves home with predictable regularity, and that he always, alas, comes back.

The case of Lucie's own parents is an instructive one in this regard, too. They have been separated for five years, and both live in Paris. Lucie dreams of reuniting them, and will do everything she can imagine to bring about a reconciliation—to no avail, of course. Sorcery is what keeps them apart. Just like Pierrot, Lucie's father had for many years pretended to know nothing about his wife's considerable powers; and his wife, to her credit, tried always to exercise those powers with discretion. One day he had come home unannounced, however, and had glimpsed a serpent's tail that his wife had conjured. From that moment, understandably enough, things just weren't the same with them. Both Lucie's mother and father resist her efforts to bring them together again, and her mother in particular warns Lucie of the dire consequences that might ensue: "I won't be responsible for my actions if I see your father again" (130). She, like Pierrot and like Isabelle, has made a new life for herself, and she lives now with a man named Robert. Yet one wonders if sorcery won't eventually shatter that couple, too. During one of Lucie's visits, when the question of sorcery is raised, even though very obliquely, Robert is visibly shaken, and he takes pains to explain to Lucie, "You know, moreover, that I myself don't believe in . . ." (91). Her mother moves quickly to relieve the embarrassing situation: "We must not speak about certain things here." On another occasion, when the subject comes up again, Robert once more attempts to stifle it, and remarks in passing that his former wife had also been an adept of the occult: "How I loathe all that nonsense! My first wife, Josiane, used to consult a clairvoyant every month. I don't even look at my horoscope, I hate that foolishness. Josiane was very attached to it, however. And now your mother . . ." (174). One wonders if Robert, poor soul, doesn't feel that he has jumped from the frying pan into the fire. Like him, the rest of the men in the novel are condemned to grapple vainly with mysteries that are far beyond their understanding; and for the most part, those mysteries find their incarnation in women.

The women struggle, too, of course, and most particularly Lucie; yet the dilemmas they face are more diffuse, and perhaps more pernicious still, than those of the men. In rare instances, they triumph against the odds, at least provisionally. Such is the case of Isabelle, who offers the closest approximation of a liberated woman among all the women in *La Sorcière*. Nevertheless, the portrait of Isabelle that NDiaye paints is a cruel and somber one. Isabelle had been the first to build a house in Lucie's subdivision, and she reigns over her neighborhood imperiously, managing her neighbors' lives and coordinating the local gossip to devastating effect. As to the moral side of her character, she is described as a stupid, egotistical, and fundamentally unsympathetic person. Her physical appearance is scarcely more attractive: "Isabelle had a face that was red, impatient, pockmarked with old acne scars. She wore a gray sweater which outlined very exactly, almost scrupulously, the five rolls of fat that her stomach formed when she was seated. She was coquettish, but two of her premolars were missing" (20). Despite this, Lucie feels that Isabelle is her friend—perhaps her only friend. Indeed, when the stranger greets Lucie with a "Hello, my sister," Lucie reflects that it is Isabelle who is in fact her "true sister" (63), rather than anyone else.

Isabelle is the only person in Lucie's life to express any interest whatso-ever in her powers, and Lucie receives that interest like a rare gift. In order to ingratiate herself to Isabelle, Lucie proposes to teach her some elements of sorcery, "because nothing prevented me, after all, from passing on my gift to women other than my daughters" (18). Isabelle, however, is a distracted, un-receptive student. Moreover, she is interested in Lucie's powers only insofar as they might provide her with an immediate, personal advantage. The only exception to that rule is when she urges Lucie to gaze into the future in order to determine if her son, of whom she has not yet quite despaired, will one day attend the Ecole Polytechnique (the French equivalent of MIT or Cal Tech); and when Lucie fails to give her a satisfactory answer, Isabelle quickly loses whatever interest she may have had in sorcery.

A supremely self-confident person, Isabelle believes that she is destined for great things. She sees herself as a dynamic individual, one who is not afraid to seize opportunity by the forelock, one who is ready to *act* in the world. That kind of assurance leaves Lucie in awe, and serves to attach her still more closely to Isabelle. Even Maud and Lise, as blithely inattentive as they may be to all the other adults who people their world, are drawn to her, for Isabelle is a born leader. Having left her laughingstock of a husband, and having farmed out her dull-witted son in a Parisian boarding school, Isabelle deploys her leadership skills boldly, founding "ISABELLE O.'S FEMININE UNIVER-SITY OF SPIRITUAL HEALTH" in Châteauroux. That establishment is a kind of New Age ashram for women from eighteen to twenty-five years of age, conceived as a gynecocracy with Isabelle herself at the helm. She will offer Lucie a job there, proposing to pay her ten thousand francs a month, along with room and board, to teach a course entitled "Objective Knowledge of the Past and the Future for Oneself and for Others" (155); and Lucie will accept her offer.

Lucie's initial enthusiasm is only barely diluted when she meets her new colleagues, "poor kinds of women, thinly disguised as professors by the miracle of Isabelle's virtuosity" (160), young women in difficult circumstances whom Isabelle had recruited through the help wanted ads in the local newspaper. All things considered, Lucie is excited by the prospect of her new job, and she wonders if she hasn't finally found her place in life: "in a curious startling of pleasure and hope, I reflected that I might just find a kind of happiness at the Feminine University" (163). Of course, such a positive finality is not to be. The separatist utopia is fraught with a variety of problems, both incidental and structural, and Lucie's own role therein will end abruptly when male author-ity, in the guise of the town council and the police, come to arrest her. Isabelle adds her voice to the lusty chorus of accusation and calumny—predictably enough, once one recognizes the fact that Isabelle's most salient character trait is a talent for survival. So much for collegiality, friendship, and female solidarity.

All of these vicissitudes are played out in *La Sorcière* against the backdrop of the most unrelieved banality imaginable. Apart from the fact that she is a witch, the daughter of a witch, and the mother of twin witches, Lucie's existence is ruled by the mind-numbing rituals of the suburban quotidian. Throughout the novel, NDiaye carefully elaborates a vision of everyday, middle-class life quite deliberately constructed out of commonplace and cliché, in a bleak panorama of the utterly ordinary. Such a setting is calculated to heighten the effect of the fantastic, of course, when that element appears; but another interesting consideration in *La Sorcière* is the way the fantastic puts the banal on trial, interrupting it, destabilizing it, and contaminating it in such a manner that readers of the novel may be prompted to rethink the distinction we habitually draw between the ordinary and the extraordinary. Thus, NDiaye stages an ironical agonistic of those two categories. On the face of it, Lucie is a very ordinary housewife, grappling with very ordinary problems. But of course she's a witch. Compared to other witches, however, and notably those in her own family, Lucie is very ordinary indeed; and the meager sorcery she is capable of proves of no use whatever as she struggles to come to terms with the vexations of her everyday life.

The description of that life which NDiaye offers is flattened, stultifying, and all too familiar. Lucie's horizon of possibility is limited in a progressively constricting geography defined by her town, her neighborhood, her house, her kitchen. Materially speaking, she doesn't seem to lack much, yet she believes nevertheless that her life is impoverished. In that, she takes her cue both from her husband and her daughters. Pierrot commutes daily to the "Garden-Club," where he is a salesman. He makes his money on commissions, but he is a poor salesman and he feels that he doesn't earn enough. He is a Willy Loman for the 1990s, that is, a figure denuded of whatever small savor he might once have possessed—processed, precooked, and ready for unappetizing and strictly utilitarian consumption, like a microwave dinner. Pierrot's daughters are snobs, directing their snobbery in its first and most torrid blast against their parents; yet Pierrot is proud of their taste for the good things in life, and does everything he can to provide his daughters with them. He is ashamed of the place he occupies in the social order. He is ashamed of his house, finding it drab and common. Most profoundly, though, he is ashamed of his wife. All of that leaves Lucie with very little room for maneuver:

> What could I do? I kept house, having been unable to find a job in our little town since we had arrived, two years ago; with perplexity, I watched Maud and Lise grow up; and I tested my poor powers, those of a failed witch, catching here and there glimpses of the future, which only worried me, rather than teaching me anything useful. (38)

Clearly, there are many areas in which Lucie has failed to come up to the standards that her husband expects of her. Chief among those areas—and perhaps because it's a question of relatively simple activity that she should long ago have mastered—Lucie feels that she has failed Pierrot as a cook. As Isabelle lingers on in Lucie's kitchen one day through the cocktail hour, braying her inanities in an unrelenting litany of narcissism, Lucie reflects that once again she will be obliged to prepare Pierrot's evening meal hastily, and she thinks ruefully of "all those good dinners which he had rightfully expected and which I had not been capable of cooking for him soon enough" (20-21). When Pierrot brings Matin home to dinner unannounced, Lucie quickly sends her daughters to Isabelle's house with a fifty-franc note, to get three pizzas from the cornucopia of fast food in Isabelle's freezer (40). Her gesture in this case is precisely characteristic of her more general dilemma: here is a sorceress capable only of the most ordinary kind of legerdemain, the kind that mocks both the normal and the paranormal in its absurd futility.

In order to persuade us that Lucie's world is the one that we, too, know (or think we know), NDiaye furnishes it here and there with easily recognized tokens of the real. The simplest instance of that technique is the occasional use of brand names—Renault, Citroën, Coca-Cola—borrowed from the elementary lexicon of the consumer society. A more intriguing example is offered by a passage in which Lucie, along with her mother, Robert, and Pierrot's mother, listen to the radio and hear the news that Yitzhak Rabin has just been assassinated. That reference to the real tantalizes the reader, and guarantees in a sense the referentiality of Lucie's world. We can even locate that moment with some precision on November 4, 1995, and imagine the rest of the temporality of *La Sorcière* as pivoting upon it. However, NDiaye is clearly playing here upon our semiotic needs, for she quickly problematizes that moment of her text and layers it in irony. Pierrot's mother misunderstands the news report, thinking that the man who has been assassinated is a man from Poitiers, Monsieur Rabine from the Rue Vaillant-Couturier; and consequently when Robert remarks with astonishment that Rabin's assassin was apparently not an Arab, she finds that less than surprising:

> —The world's going crazy, it seems that it wasn't an Arab who killed Rabin, I just don't understand anything anymore.
> —There aren't many Arabs in Poitiers, said the mother. (132)

Well, no, of course there aren't many Arabs in Poitiers—and most particularly not since Charles Martel defeated the Saracens there in 732. The mother's misunderstanding is innocent enough, and indeed it is comic, but it also suggests a dizzying and far more troubling confusion of the temporal and spatial orders we normally rely on to situate events and thereby position ourselves in the world. If reality itself can be so easily misconstrued, what are the consequences for the representation of reality put on display in *La Sorcière?* NDiaye exploits that question exhaustively in her novel, presenting a fiction which swears it is real, a story peppered nevertheless with elements that are patently and obviously calculated to remind us of its fictional character, cloaking those elements however in the guise of the most trivially believable banality, yet insisting that we examine the dubious underpinning of that banality, and so forth, in a vertiginous and studiously constructed dynamic of contradiction. Call it poetic license, if you will, and kindly regard it as the kind of playful, aphoristic questioning of human experience and its interpretations that is the bread and butter of many contemporary novelists.

Lucie's daughters negotiate the labyrinth of the real far more intrepidly and efficiently than their mother. Indeed, they seem to find very little challenge in the world around them and, like many adolescents, they find the representation of the real that television offers far more attractive than the world itself. They watch television ravenously, even bulimically[5]; but they are astute enough to see through the curious mediation of the world that it presents. In short, the twins are savvy readers of the real and its various representations. They are also, of course, great sorceresses already; and they don't hesitate to project their powers even on television itself, that household appliance which conflates most felicitously the ordinary and the magical. No remote control for these young witches, or rather not one of conventional kind: in yet another example of the way the fantastic interrogates the banal in this novel, they prefer to turn the TV off by telekinesis (136).

Lucie herself is awestruck by the dimensions of her daughters' powers, and it is through them, too, that NDiaye chooses to introduce some of the more startling of the fantastic effects in her story. Maud and Lise seem to be capable of effortless motion in space, for instance. During a visit to Lucie's father, Lucie looks out the window and sees her girls in the street, wondering how they had left the apartment so quickly; in the blink of an eye, they are back in the next room (101). They are moreover practiced shape-changers, it would seem. Having fallen asleep in the train, Lucie awakes to find her daughters gone, and looks out the window to find two crows flying alongside, recognizing her daughters in plumed disguise (111); and later, walking along in the street with them, when Lucie goes to take their hands, she encounters feathered wings instead of flesh (136).

Marie NDiaye encourages us to read such events simultaneously on the literal and the metaphorical level, savoring as we do so the contrast of the fantastic and the ordinary, and attempting also a mutual conciliation of those two regimes. On the one hand, the twins do perform things that are leagues beyond the capabilities of normal folk, things that cannot be explained in any rational manner. On the other hand, as adolescents, they frequently escape from the gaze of those adults who are responsible for keeping them in sight; and their moods are terrifyingly mobile—so much so that they may seem constantly to mutate into other kinds of beings entirely, and back again, without warning. By the same token, the most devastating act of sorcery that Lucie's mother commits can be interpreted in two ways. Having been forced by Lucie to meet her ex-husband in a hotel by the seaside, she responds by transforming him into a snail, sending him back to his daughter in a small cardboard box. Read literally, that event is irretrievably strange and uncanny; read metaphorically, it is closely figural of the kind of violence that divorced parents inflict upon each other, especially when seen through the eyes of their bewildered children.

Lucie is bewildered by many things in her life, of course, but perhaps most of all by the fact that nobody—neither her parents, nor her husband, nor her children, nor her friend Isabelle—seems to *need* her. Things have fallen apart for her, she feels, things are not the way they ought to be. By all rights, she ought to be loved in return by the people to whom she has devoted so much affection; and in a better world, she would be loved like that. Like many of us, she glimpses a world of that sort in her dreams, particularly one night when she dreams of her mother:

> That night, lying in my husband's little bedroom, I dreamed that my mother came and kissed me on the side of my lips, then I woke up with a painful feeling of disappointment, realizing that I was alone.
>
> How happy I would be if my mother came into the bedroom, I told myself fervently, and sat on my bed for a few moments!
>
> I found it difficult to believe, awaking from the clear, sweet visions of my dream, that reality wasn't like that. (125-26)

The cruel disparity between Lucie's dream and the reality of her life comes home to her in an especially poignant manner here. The idea that her mother might display affection toward her seems to Lucie quite simply impossible when she awakes; and sorceress though Lucie may be, she cannot inhabit her dream for very long, nor still less turn it into reality. At the risk of belaboring the obvious, though, I would like to point out that dreams, among many other things, are places where the utterly fantastic and the most convincingly real can coexist peacefully, and can even harmonize felicitously.

So, too, of course, are novels. That striking concoction of the fantastic and the real is perhaps the principal potion that NDiaye brews in *La Sorcière*. It is a very heady one, and the fact that NDiaye offers it to us with such ostentation leads me to suspect that she is thereby gesturing toward the particular literary alchemy of this novel. That is, the contrast between the natural and the supernatural is arresting to such a degree that we are obliged, throughout *La Sorcière,* to reflect upon it; and more precisely still, we are encouraged to consider the specific terms of the narrative contract that enables it. Like Lydie Moudileno, I see a strong pattern of metaliterary discourse in Marie NDiaye's writing.[6] In *La Sorcière,* however, that discourse is more occulted than in many of NDiaye's other books, and she will subtly suggest to us on several occasions in the novel that we must exercise a modest level of sorcery in order to render it manifest. Such an occasion occurs in the first pages of *La Sorcière,* where Lucie is initiating her daughters into the "mysterious powers," still sanguine as to their interest in her teaching, and indeed in her. Lucie believes that she detects in the twins "a touching desire to solve the puzzle" (10); and she feels that her role in this pedagogical process is to *speak,* with rigorous economy, and hope that her speech will stimulate her children's inherited, but still latent, talent for augury: "I had only a few words to speak. They had to observe me and—with their entire person, with every bit of their little being issued from my own—try to assimilate the painful process of divination" (12). In short, she is calling upon her daughters to become hermeneutes; and through that same voice, NDiaye is calling upon her reader in a similar fashion, asking her or him to consider the enigmatic quality of this novel.

In a passage toward the end of *La Sorcière,* that sort of solicitation becomes clearer still. Once again, Lucie is cast in a role that is pedagogical in character. Teaching her course in Isabelle's "Feminine University," Lucie feels dismally ill-equipped:

> After several days, I realized that if I wished to make a place for myself in the Feminine University, I had to find a kind of painless technique, which would satisfy my students without draining me of my own forces. It was then that I began to make up that which I presented to those naive young women as the true elements of their past or future lives. And their faith in the seriousness of Isabelle's establishment was so great that they never contradicted me, even though they were often surprised that they failed to remember certain childhood scenes. I invented these scenes with conviction, artfully illuminating my gaze with glimmers of magic and forcing myself to act in a bizarre manner.
>
> —Thus, I said to myself, it's easier for me to be a professional scoundrel of a witch than a real one. (168)

Lucie's description of her pedagogical methodology may bring a rictus of abashed recognition to those of her readers who earn their living in the academy. What intrigues me still more, however, is the fact that Lucie's technique is precisely descriptive of the one that NDiaye deploys in her novel. Like Lucie, NDiaye relies on her imagination in order to capture her audience's attention, conjuring up a world through sheer invention; she constructs that world with a great deal of conviction and artifice; the representation of everyday life therein would be a thoroughly convincing one, too, were it not for the bizarre effects that interrupt it and call it richly into question.

One may be tempted to concur with Lucie: perhaps it *is* easier to be a professional and villainous witch than a real one. Yet it is just possible that such a distinction may prove finally to be a trivial one, both for Lucie and for NDiaye. Insofar as Lucie is concerned at least, toward the end of her struggles she comes to regard "real" sorcery with skepticism: "I came to doubt that I had ever possessed a gift other than that of fabulization, and that the sort of powers that the women of my maternal family thought they wielded even existed" (169). Clearly, though, that gift of fabulization is a singularly puissant one—and it is moreover just the gift which NDiaye puts on stage in *La Sorcière*. There are many kinds of fables in this novel: fables of the individual, fables of family, fables of society and its discontents; fables of gender and sexuality, fables of alterity and alienation; fables of the natural and fables of the supernatural; fables of the writer and fables of the reader. Interweaving those fables and coaxing them into a dynamic of reciprocal complementarity, Marie NDiaye gradually conjures up an apparition of the novel itself as sorcery; and I imagine that I am not alone among its readers to have fallen blissfully under its spell.

NOTES

[1] I have been able to locate only two extended discussions of NDiaye's work, both devoted to her fourth novel, *En famille* (1990). In "*En famille* or the Problem of Alterity," K. Ambroise Teko-Agbo alludes to the favorable reviews which greeted that book: "The unanimous, enthusiastic welcome accorded the work by French literary critics—a rare feat—was all that was required to establish the reputation of the young NDiaye as an exceptional writer"; and he adds his own voice to that

chorus of praise, suggesting that NDiaye "displays a particular care in the craft of writing and an incontestable mastery of the art" (158). Lydie Moudileno, in "Délits, détours et affabulation: L'écriture de l'anathème dans *En famille* de Marie Ndiaye," speaks of the sophistication of NDiaye's language and the richness of her novelistic imagination, comparing her to Proust and Kafka (442).

[2] See Teko-Agbo 163: "Here is where Marie NDiaye's fiction stands out. She valorizes by revealing the problem of the strange and invites us to reflect on the place of the strange and the stranger in our societies. With what eyes do we look upon the stranger?"

[3] See for instance 10-11, 12, 25-26, 50, 57.

[4] See Josane Charpentier's account of witch trials in the southwest of France: "An important precaution was to avoid at all costs being touched by the witch. Even the sound of her voice could be maleficent. There was also a strange power in her eyes, and sometimes the judges at whom she gazed lost every sense of indignation and, moved by pity, let her go free; this was inconceivable for any judge worthy of that name and that high responsibility" (24).

[5] See for instance 31, 60, 135.

[6] In her reading of *En famille,* Moudileno argues that Fanny's sense of exclusion from her family may be figural of NDiaye's own feeling of marginality with regard to the literary institution and its attendants, and even with respect to her own publishing house, the Editions de Minuit. See Moudileno 450-52.

VII

⁀

JEAN ECHENOZ'S YEARBOOK

Since the publication of *Le Méridien de Greenwich* (The Greenwich Meridian) in 1979, Jean Echenoz has constructed a body of work that includes nine novels to date, and which should already be recognized as one of the most arresting and intriguing oeuvres in contemporary French literature. His books have received considerable attention and accolade in critical circles[1] (including a Prix Médicis for *Cherokee* in 1983), and they have been warmly received by general readers as well. Each of Echenoz's novels puts on display his remarkable gifts as a storyteller, as Echenoz experiments with a variety of narrative traditions and genres, interrogating them, reconfiguring them, and turning them to his own purposes. In *Le Méridien de Greenwich* and *Cherokee,* Echenoz invokes the conventions of the detective novel, peopling his texts with con artists, gunsels, tough-but-kindhearted molls, and other stock characters of the genre. He exploits that genre's narrative power in a canny manner, perversely and ironically, playing on the reader's expectations and desires. No explosion of truth awaits us at the end of these novels, but rather the realization that the real import of the stories we've just been told engages broad issues of literature and its uses. *L'Equipée malaise* (1986; *Double Jeopardy*) performs an analogous operation on the genre of the action novel, as a pair of ludicrously benighted adventurers attempt to foment revolution in Malaysia. *L'Occupation des sols* (1988; *Plan of Occupancy*), a very short book, offers a novel stripped to its bones. In a stark, dramatically minimalist style, Echenoz tells the story of a man who is trying to come to terms with his wife's death. In *Lac* (1989; Lake), Echenoz focuses his writerly lens on the espionage novel, as Franck Chopin, entomologist and part-time spy, stumbles through the secret world. A space shuttle mission is at the center of *Nous trois* (1992; We Three), until that story is displaced, like other "conventional" fictions in Echenoz's writing, by more pressing concerns. The pretext of *Les Grandes Blondes* (1995; *Big Blondes*) is a talent search for tall, blonde women. Here too, however, the real object of the exercise is elsewhere: to locate one tall, blonde woman in particular who has gone underground without a trace. *Je m'en vais* (1999; *I'm Gone*), Echenoz's most recent novel, is the story of a middle-aged art dealer who abruptly decides to leave his wife. His subsequent peregrinations are futile, circular, and comic; they include an expedition toward a North Pole as cold and arid as his own emotional life.

Among all of Echenoz's stories, however, the one that I find most compelling is a story that each of his novels tells, if in very different ways: the tale of the novel as literary form and of how that form labors to express itself on the stage of our vexed, anxious, and thoroughly postmodern culture. In *Un An* (1997; A Year), that story assumes a rather curious shape. The heroine of *Un An* is Victoire, a young woman who, fearing that she may be accused of the murder of her lover, flees Paris for the southwest of France. She'll spend a year there, wandering from place to place, and her material circumstances will gradually and ineluctably worsen, until she is reduced to living on the brutal edge of French society as a homeless person. When finally she returns to Paris, she'll discover that things were not quite what they seemed when she left.

Echenoz tells this story with the laconism, the dry wit, and the pungent precision that have come to be the hallmarks of his style. All of his novels are characterized by a strong hermeneutic code, and *Un An* is no exception. Like any detective, Victoire must decipher the confusing intricacies of her situation in order to arrive at the truth—or at least some pale semblance thereof. *Un An* also engages contemporary social reality in France more powerfully than Echenoz's previous novels. As Victoire stumbles progressively downward in the social hierarchy, Echenoz reflects upon the problems of the homeless, whom the French designate by the loathsome, recently-coined acronym "SDF" (*sans domicile fixe,* or "without fixed abode"). *Un An* indicts the society that allows its members to become so utterly disenfranchised; and if a crime is at the focal point of this novel, it is clearly a political and social one.

Un An is very broadly governed by the principle of incertitude, both on the level of the told and on the level of the telling. Victoire's efforts to learn the material facts of her situation mediate and echo ironically the reader's efforts to find narrative truth—and the struggle of the one mocks and relativizes the struggle of the other. In that perspective, Victoire's wanderings in the provinces may be read as a wry commentary upon the many kinds of interpretive contingencies, dubious hypotheses, and uncertain inferences that the reader of *Un An* necessarily entertains as the novel develops. In other words, the reader's itinerary in *Un An* is similar to that of Victoire, because the reader, too, follows difficult, forking narrative paths. There is nonetheless a carefully considered logic here. For, beyond the tale of Victoire's vicissitudes, *Un An* also tells those of writing itself, enabling Echenoz to speculate closely upon the fate of the novel as literary genre, and upon its horizon of possibility on a cultural stage which is becoming, in his view, ever more impoverished by the day.

The title of Echenoz's novel adumbrates a variety of considerations, which the text itself will confirm. First of all, the extreme laconism of the utterance *un an* ["a year," or "one year"] announces a text that will be characterized by economy of expression, a minimalist style in which traditional narrative flourish and embellishment are eschewed in favor of what Echenoz feels to be a more essentialist approach. The ethos of reduction subtending that style will find its echo in the thematics of the novel, as Victoire's material situation becomes progressively more reduced. The apparent simplicity of the title points in similar fashion to analogous effects of style and theme: Echenoz tells this story in a straightforward, largely declarative prose; and on the face of it, Victoire herself is a simple person, caught in a dilemma that is very largely beyond her ken. The formal symmetry of the title is striking, both on the graphic level and on the phonetic level. In both contexts the resemblance of the words *un* and *an* suggests a text that will be colored by other, broader kinds of symmetries. The evocation of time in the title will be amply confirmed in the novel as well: the narrative organization of *Un An* is strictly chronological, renouncing analepse and prolepse, invoking instead a rigorously unforgiving linear time. The indeterminate article and the lack of further modification of the noun in the title prepares the reader for a text marked by narrative diffidence, indeterminacy, and, in certain key moments, a refusal to elaborate.

Echenoz puts those principals into play in the very first lines of his novel as the incipit of *Un An* opens onto a world where character, reader, and perhaps writer, too, will be called upon to grapple with doubt and uncertainty: "Victoire, awaking on a February morning remembering nothing of the previous night, then finding Félix dead right beside her in their bed, packed her suitcase before going to the bank and taking a taxi to the Montparnasse train station" (7). The precipative narrative instance, the event that kicks the story into gear, is a familiar one; and the question posed—whodunit?—is likewise classic. Yet the laconism with which Echenoz inaugurates the hermeneutic code of *Un An* serves more than anything else to put that literary commonplace on display, naked, denuded of its conventional trappings, in order to call it into question. The small world sketched out in this first sentence is clearly already one in which irony will rule, for these characters—one quick, one dead—are designated by names that seem dramatically inappropriate, granted their circumstances. Evocation of time and space is approximative here, and the question of causality is, for the moment at least, suspended in the domain of the unnarrated.

Like so many protagonists of fiction before her, Victoire will set off on a journey. Yet that familiar narrative topos is itself fraught with irony, for what she intends as a flight *away* from a dreadful truth will in point of fact lead directly back to it—or rather to a version of it that she cannot possibly imagine. Neither Victoire nor Echenoz himself can escape from narrative teleology, though between the first pages and the last of this novel, Echenoz does his level best to disguise that teleology, constructing a wandering, apparently random itinerary for Victoire on a landscape that she chooses precisely because she knows nothing about it:

> When this story begins, Victoire doesn't know Bordeaux at all, nor, more generally, the southwest region of France, but she knows February all too well, because, like March, it is one of the worst months in Paris. It wasn't a bad idea to leave Paris during these months, but she would have preferred to do it in different circumstances. However, having absolutely no recall of the hours preceding Félix's death, she worried that she would be suspected of provoking

it. Most of all, she didn't want to have to explain herself, because of course she would have been incapable of doing so, not even being sure in her own mind whether she was entirely innocent. (8)

In other words, Victoire's ignorance about where she's going recapitulates her lack of knowledge about the circumstances of Félix's death. She flees from one situation to the other, blindly.

She will penetrate ever further into the heart of darkness that the Aquitaine represents for her, and for many Parisians. Gradually, it becomes clear that if Victoire's intention is to lose herself in the geography of southwestern France, it is nonetheless Echenoz's intention to make his reader feel lost, too. For he assumes his reader to be as unconversant with that geography as is Victoire, and he consequently provides the kind of information that, while it seems helpful, serves in fact to emphasize the unfamiliarity of the narrative landscape. "Without wishing to offend anyone," Echenoz opines, "Mimizan-Plage is rather less attractive than Saint-Jean-de-Luz" (49). Shortly thereafter, as Victoire sets off on a bicycle into the vast *terra incognita* of the Landes, Echenoz remarks: "The countryside of the Landes is so flat that one immediately thinks of bicycles" (50). He will embroider that *verfremdungseffekt* more elaborately as Victoire loses herself still further, enunciating toponyms that he hopes will mean little or nothing to his reader beyond their strangeness, Gascon place-names like "Nérac," "Onesse-et-Laharie," and "Trensacq" (56-60) which, while they may correspond to real places, do not figure on the map of France that most of his readers can draw from their experience.

Victoire achieves her desire to escape into an unfamiliar world, if at considerable material and moral expense: "In the days that followed, her everyday life took on a character that she had never known" (55). Not only does she have to navigate through a landscape that is unfamiliar to her, but she has to deal with a variety of unfamiliar problems contingent upon her ever-worsening financial circumstances. As Victoire becomes more and more impoverished, so too does her story, which Echenoz progressively strips of description, interpretation, and commentary in order to focus ever more closely on bare event. In time, it becomes clear that Victoire's "story" is that of aimless wandering, to all appearances one that is devoid of logic: "Her itinerary would thus have very little coherence, but rather seemed like the fitful flitting of a fly trapped in a bedroom" (63). The indeterminacy of Victoire's peregrinations stands in a symmetrical relation to the narrative indeterminacy of *Un An;* simply put, the reader finds it difficult to find direction in this story, or any sense of where ultimately it will lead. Just as the places Echenoz evokes are very largely unmapped in the reader's imagination, so too does Victoire grope through an indeterminate space that bears no recognizable relation to the topographies of her previous experience: "In the days afterward, lacking a map, she oriented herself however she could, following road signs and with no precise goal" (96).

In like manner, Echenoz asks his reader to negotiate a narrative path where conventional points of reference are very largely lacking, following a diegetical trajectory that seems to be aleatory and directionless.[2] Moreover, the various sorts of incertitude that surround the issue of spatial reference in *Un An* are intended by Echenoz to set in motion broader effects of narrative indeterminacy. The most obvious and immediate diegetical principle of this novel is that of intrigue, yet Echenoz formulates that principle in a deliberately reductive way, beginning with the refusal to *tell* the circumstances of Félix's death. The confusion that the reader may experience when faced with the insufficiency of plot-related information finds its textual analogue in Victoire's own failure to understand how Félix died:

> Facing forward, next to the window in a smoking compartment, Victoire tried to arrange and classify her memories of the night before, but was unable to reconstruct the chronology of the evening. She knew she had spent the morning alone after Félix had left for the studio, then she had lunched with Louise before running into Louis-Philippe at the Central, toward late afternoon. It was always by chance at the Central, and frequently in the late afternoon, that Victoire encountered Louis-Philippe, whereas he, wherever she might be and at whatever time of day, always knew where to find her, whenever he wished. She remembered having had a few drinks with him, then returning home, perhaps a little bit later than usual—after that, alas, nothing at all. Anyone else in Victoire's shoes would have gone to family for advice in such a situation, but not Victoire, who was without a family and had burned all her bridges. (9-10)

Throughout the novel, Echenoz plays lustily on his reader's desire to *know*—and in this, at least, his narrative strategy is a familiar one. The amplitude of his game, however, is far vaster in *Un An* than in a traditional mystery novel; and the way that Echenoz encourages, directs, and finally subverts the reader's efforts at narrative inferencing is far more brutal.[3] Our natural tendency is to draw conclusions from the information a story provides us. Traditional novels of intrigue provide information little by little, in strictly calculated doses, and reward our hermeneutic efforts by confirming our inferences along the way. Echenoz turns that convention on its head in *Un An,* postulating contingencies of plot only to demonstrate in the next breath that they are impossible. Moreover, he studiously emblazons that very process of narrative inferencing in the text, and exploits it for ironic effect, for instance when Victoire wonders if Gérard, a young man she has met in Saint-Jean-de-Luz, has stolen some money she had hidden in her room: "First, this is how things stand: nothing proved beyond a doubt that Gérard was responsible for the money's disappearance [*disparition*], any more than Victoire herself was responsible for Félix's death, but in neither case could one clear away the aura of suspicion or neglect certain serious presumptions" (44). For Victoire, the theft necessarily evokes "suspicion" and "presumptions"; and the same is true of the reader, granted the fact that Victoire herself mediates the reader's hermeneutic role here and elsewhere in the novel. The analogy of the two crimes, theft and murder, is clear too, as is the ironizing effect of that analogy, which hinges paronomastically on the word *disparition,* which can mean either "disappearance" or "death" in French. Try as she might, however, Victoire will not succeed in untangling the problem, and all of her interpretive efforts will be in vain. So too the reader's efforts will founder because Echenoz refuses to divulge who stole the money, or indeed who killed Félix.[4]

That principle of fundamental narrative incertitude shapes *Un An* throughout the text. It is incarnated in the novel by a shadowy figure named Louis-Philippe, an acquaintance of Victoire who comes to her unexpected and unsolicited on several occasions in the story, and who seems to hold the key to the problems that beset her. Victoire is utterly in the dark concerning the circumstances of Félix's death, her own involvement in it, and the efforts of the authorities to track her down. Her stock of knowledge, like that of the reader, is impoverished, and it corresponds to the progressive impoverishment of her material situation. She looks to Louis-Philippe to provide information that will allow her to act productively; yet the only information Louis-Philippe provides when he visits her is negative. He comes to her in Saint-Jean-de-Luz, turning up out of nowhere with no explanation as to how he found her there: "Essentially, he told her, according to the information he had been able to obtain, Victoire was not really a suspect in Félix's death, but since some doubt remained, it was better that she remain in hiding. Stay away, stay unseen as much as possible. Her responsibility in the matter would undoubtedly not be dismissed. Louis-Philippe would keep her informed of the way events developed." (36). Maddeningly enough, though, he seems to know a great deal more than what he tells her.

In that sense, the dynamic that prevails between Victoire and Louis-Philippe is analogous to that of the reader and the writer in *Un An,* pitting as it does someone who wants to know, who vitally *needs* to know, against someone who knows, but is not telling. The capricious character of Louis-Philippe's interventions in Victoire's life emblematizes the kind of narrative capriciousness that seems to animate the novel. Echenoz highlights that function, too, taking care to underline the gratuitous, apparently unmotivated, and thus troubling aspect of Louis-Philippe's appearances: "Louis-Philippe's presence at the Albizzia was inexplicable, and it worried Victoire" (47). On one occasion, when Victoire is tired, hungry, and very nearly at the end of her tether as she hitchhikes to Toulouse, an unidentified man gives her a ride. Only after she alights does she wonder if it wasn't Louis-Philippe himself: "However, she was certain that she had recognized Louis-Philippe's voice, behind the wheel of his Fiat" (71). It is only in his final appearance that Louis-Philippe offers anything of substance to Victoire; and even then that substance is lamentably thin in fact and detail: "Félix's case was closed, he told her, it's no use thinking about it anymore. They had finally closed the case, dismissing any responsibility on Victoire's part" (104).

When Victoire, believing herself to be exculpated of Félix's murder, finally makes her way back to Paris, she discovers a perverse, hopelessly contradictory version of the "truth" that she—and the reader of *Un An* along with her—had labored so vainly to find. In the final scene of the novel, she visits a café that she used to frequent with her friends, encountering there none other than Félix himself, with another woman on his arm:

> Félix, who looked the picture of health, didn't seem to manifest any emotion at all when he saw Victoire approaching. So, he merely exclaimed, where were you? I've looked for you everywhere, let me introduce Hélène. Victoire, smiling toward Hélène, refrained from asking Félix why he wasn't dead, which might have altered the polite mood of the encounter, and instead ordered some dry white wine. And Louis-Philippe, she said, have you seen him around recently? Ah, said Félix, you didn't know. I'm sorry. I'll leave you alone a moment, said Hélène. I'm sorry, Félix repeated quietly as Hélène withdrew, I thought you knew. We never really understood what happened to Louis-Philippe, we never really learned, I think somebody found him two or three days afterward in the bathroom. That's the problem when you live alone. It happened just after you left, just about, what is it now, a year ago, a little less than a year. I even thought for a while that that was why you left. But no, said Victoire, of course not. (110-11)

The novel ends there, not in an explosion of truth but rather in a negation of the possibility of truth.[5] Victoire has been deceived or deluded; she has either been tricked and manipulated, victimized by a cruel conspiracy, or she has taken leave of her senses during a year's time. Within the diegetical economy of *Un An,* moreover, those issues are undecidable. It is important to realize that the reader of the novel has been had, too, for what has been until that point postulated as narrative truth—Félix's death, Louis-Philippe's existence—proves here false; and our *deception* when faced with that is largely similar to Victoire's own.[6]

One of the most obvious effects of that final gesture is to call those same categories, narrative truth and falsehood, deeply into question. The iteration of the principle of incertitude—"you didn't know"; "I thought you knew"; "We never really understood"; "we never really learned"; "I even thought"—finds its only resolution in Victoire's laconic "no." That word resounds with a double finality here, slamming the door on other, more conventional narrative possibilities that Echenoz holds out, tantalizingly, until the last moment. He suggests thereby that we must look elsewhere for this novel's point. If

Félix's death was a fiction and all of Victoire's struggles during her year of wandering have been premised on a fiction, it follows that the reader of *Un An* has been the victim of a fiction, also. On a first level, we should not be astonished by such a consideration. Novels are meant to deceive, after all; and most of the time we readers are willing collaborators in our own deception. Yet we feel, perhaps, that the kind of deception that writers of fiction practice must adhere to certain basic rules of fair play; and we may feel too that Echenoz has not followed those rules here. For my part, I believe that he deliberately steps outside the common boundaries of novelistic convention in order better to suggest what ground the novel as literary form may claim in our culture. Dramatically disabling the commonplace of "fictional truth" as he does at the end of *Un An,* he forces his reader to reflect upon the basic contradiction that subtends that notion, and upon the kinds of demands we place upon novels as we apprehend them. In other words, the eccentric conclusion of *Un An* may lead us to reconsider a cultural practice that, in Echenoz's view at least, is itself eccentric and ever more marginal by the day.

It is in such a perspective that the story of Victoire's wanderings takes on its full pungency. Echenoz constructs that story with close attention to detail, playing simultaneously on two discursive fronts. On the one hand, he postulates Victoire's struggles as an emblem of a generalized social disease, suggesting how fragile the stability of any given individual is in late capitalist society. On the other hand, as Bruno Blanckeman has argued, Echenoz suggests that Victoire's wanderings are figural of the way the novel as literary form wanders on our cultural topography, seeking a cultural insertion that is no longer taken for granted.[7]

Like many protagonists in contemporary French fiction (one thinks of characters in the novels of Jean-Philippe Toussaint, Marie Redonnet, Christian Oster, Olivier Targowla, and Eric Laurrent, for instance), Victoire is a marginal, radically alienated figure. Unlike those others, however, her alienation is not a result of individual proclivity, choice, or constitution; rather, it devolves upon the harsh contingencies of material circumstance. In the early pages of the novel, as Victoire heads south on the train, she looks out at the landscape: "There, through the bay windows, alone with her bottle of mineral water, she observed that homeless landscape which proclaimed merely its own identity, no more a countryside than a passport is somebody, no distinguishing marks" (12). Echenoz uses that passage to prefigure the dilemma that Victoire will encounter as she plunges precipitously through the social hierarchy of contemporary France. The characterization of the landscape as "homeless" clearly foreshadows the homeless condition that Victoire will fall into; and the dehumanizing effect of such a condition is suggested by the analogy of landscape and individual, both stripped of identifying signs.

As long as Victoire's money holds out, she can preserve some semblance of independence and autonomy, living in a rented house in Saint-Jean-de-Luz and in a variety of small hotels and pensions elsewhere in the southwest of France. She keeps herself apart from other social groups during this period. But later, lacking money or any means to obtain it, she is constrained to seek others out. In Toulouse she encounters a group of homeless people; yet even there Victoire finds social integration to be problematic, at best. For even if she herself is homeless, her physical appearance at that point of her wanderings is not yet that of a wholly destitute person: "Though she was living on the streets like them, though she was miserable, nevertheless in certain details she undoubtedly did not correspond to the usual profile of vagabonds" (73-74). Moreover, her inclination to avoid contact with others as she hides from authority works against her in this case, and she finds herself marginalized even *within* the small group of social pariahs that she frequents in Toulouse: "As long as she remained on the margins of that group, some of them would look upon Victoire with mistrust, suspecting her of whatever they might" (73). The irony of her situation is clear: shunned and excluded by mainstream society because of her otherness, she is also shunned by the smaller social unit that the homeless people constitute—and for the very same specious reasons.

In two cases, Victoire will find some kind of social integration, if merely temporary and highly conditional. For reasons of security she decides to forge an alliance with two homeless people in Toulouse, a couple who go by the names of Gore-Tex (so named after his only treasure, a parka lined with that material) and Lampoule. Gore-Tex has a dog, by whom he affects to be called "Papa." Together with Victoire, then, they seem to form a nuclear family. But as Echenoz describes their interactions, it is clear that he is offering their unit as a cruel parody of the traditional family, one that is ludicrously dysfunctional and inadequate to the needs of its members. It becomes apparent, too, that the official powers cannot tolerate the threat that such people represent, and Victoire and her friends will be run out of Toulouse. At that moment in the text, Echenoz takes the opportunity to formulate a broad and explicit indictment of the way society reacts to the problem of homelessness, casting his remarks in a hieratic language that parodies the egregious rhetoric of the administrative class:

> Then it came to pass in a number of municipalities that elected officials, more than the citizens, became weary of seeing vagabonds, often accompanied by their pet animals, invading their well-kept cities, strolling in their parks and their marketplaces, in their pedestrian malls, selling their miserable magazines on the terrace of their beautiful cafés. Thus a goodly number of mayors conceived ingenious laws prohibiting mendicity, laying about in public places, the assemblement of unmuzzled dogs, and the hawking of newspapers, under the threat of a fine and incarceration, along with incarceration fees. In short they undertook to incite the beggars to jump off a cliff, preferably someone else's cliff. (76)

After wandering about the countryside in ever more straightened circumstances, Victoire encounters and joins forces with a pair of men named Castel and Poussin who have been homeless for three years, since they were both laid off from their jobs in the electronics industry. Here again, the social organization of this newly forged group ironically questions that of the family as it is conventionally conceived. Castel and Poussin adopt Victoire, as it were, and exercise a parental benevolence toward her. The men are homosexual, which is a lucky thing for Victoire herself, as Poussin points out to her one day: "Because otherwise we would probably have raped you, and then what in the world could we have done with you?" (88). They live relatively happily—and indeed, compared to other moments in Victoire's story, idyllically—in the countryside, fishing, hunting, and committing small larcenies to provide for themselves. Yet here, too, just like in Toulouse, official authority will intervene to crush their social unit. The police, alerted to the existence of these homeless people by a civic-minded hunter, appear at their hut at dawn one morning. Castel and Poussin are arrested, but Victoire escapes in extremis,

149   JEAN ECHENOZ'S YEARBOOK

and takes once again to the road.

From that point, her fortunes wane still further, as Victoire is precipitated into utter indigency and destitution. Her hygiene and physical appearance suffer to such a degree that she can no longer get around by hitchhiking: "Victoire became dirty and soon bedraggled, more and more people seemed to have less and less inclination to pick her up hitchhiking, all the more so since she seemed no longer really able, when they did pick her up, to say where she was going" (96-97). Realizing that the socially integrated people whom she encounters assume that her physical appearance corresponds directly to a mental impoverishment, Victoire chooses deliberately to act out the role that society has scripted for people of her ilk: "In order to give good measure and so that people would leave her alone, Victoire began to behave like a retarded person, like she imagined a retarded person to behave, and in fact people often took her for one" (97). In order to survive, that is, Victoire takes pains to confirm the prejudicial stereotype of homeless people that mainstream society has constructed in order to obviate its responsibility toward them.

Echenoz's final indictment of the way the homeless are treated is staged on the individual level rather than on the collective one. When Victoire returns to Paris, she goes to see her friend Louise, in order to ask her if she can put her up for a few days while she gets her life back together. Louise works at the ticket counter in a railway station, and she transmits her refusal of Victoire's simple request through the small "hygienaphone" in the glass ticket window, administratively and with all the human kindness that is normally delivered through such a medium. "It is surprising," comments Echenoz, "that this circular hole in the glass, conceived to communicate messages exclusively about trains [. . .] can convey such points of view without the whole system exploding" (108-09). His remark is a laconic one, yet it is nonetheless scathing in its condemnation of a world where personal solidarity is just as illusory as is the collective solidarity purportedly guaranteed by the much-hallowed but essentially bankrupt social contract.

Victoire's social alienation is thus for all intents and purposes absolute. It is important to realize, however, that that phenomenon is accompanied and intensified by a gradual, ineluctable, and still more troubling process of alienation that takes place on the level of the self. Victoire is a lucid person, and like most lucid people she frequently thinks about herself and her situation. In the course of the novel, though, her thoughts become increasingly vexed by an apparent failure of correspondence between her own vision of herself and the reflection of herself projected by an indifferent society. Moreover, on those occasions when she is confronted by a literal image of herself, she finds it more and more difficult to recognize what she sees. Three mirror scenes in the novel testify to Victoire's psychological evolution. First, gazing into a mirror in the train to Bordeaux, Victoire sees a face that corresponds to her own and that obeys the commands she gives to it: "Then she examined herself in the mirror: a young, slim, nervous woman of twenty-six, looking determined, a green, inoffensive, wary gaze, dark hair arranged in fluid curls. She easily erased all trace of emotion from her face and made all its sentiment vanish, nonetheless she felt very worried, and she went back to her seat" (9). Later, in her apartment in Saint-Jean-de-Luz, just after she discovers that the money she had hidden in a drawer has been stolen, she suddenly catches a glimpse of her new, haggard self that dismays and frightens her: "Passing in front of the mirror, she stopped, and then, startling at the reflection of her face, she dropped the drawer at her feet" (42-43). Finally, during the time when she bicycles aimlessly through the Landes, Victoire comes face to face with an image of herself that she cannot make to cohere, a stranger's face that has very little relation to the person she always believed herself to be:

> Then something happened which she never imagined: in a drugstore mirror, since she barely had a change of clothing, nor makeup, nor anything to wash herself, nor any money to buy those things, she realized that her appearance had begun to decline. She approached the mirror: even though she had never tried it, always deferred that idea, it was obvious that with her current appearance it was too late to look for a job or something, and the day after that someone quite naturally stole her bicycle. (59-60)

Taken together, these three scenes recapitulate the kinds of psychological changes that Victoire experiences as a result of her circumstances. Little by little, she becomes persuaded that she has become another person, one quite different from the one she thought she knew. That new person is governed by different constraints, moreover, and none of the old rules apply. The new face she sees in the mirror is not the face she saw in the train; it is not the face of someone who is determined to act in order to save herself, if only through flight. On the contrary, it is the face of somebody who suffers and submits, somebody who regards the theft of her most precious possession as a "natural" occurrence, an event that is right and proper in the order of the world. It is in such a manner, Echenoz argues, that society convinces the homeless that they are responsible for—and indeed richly deserve—their own destitution.

As Victoire wanders in limbo, so too does this novel seem to wander.[8] Peripatetic and seemingly unmotivated, the narration gives an impression of strangeness. Constructed as it is on the principle of narrative incertitude, *Un An* strongly resists the kinds of conventional interpretive strategies that readers may bring to it; refusing common effects of plot development and diegetical causality, the novel proclaims its own alterity with regard to literary tradition. In short, Echenoz carefully constructs his novel as a marginal artifact, and through that marginality elaborates a discourse whose purpose is to put the mainstream novel on trial. The central argument in his brief is the question of narrative economy, an issue that Echenoz formulates metaphorically and ironically in a vaster, far more literal reflection on economy that resounds throughout his novel. Félix's "death" is the event that precipitates this story, but it is not in itself sufficient to make Victoire, a person who after all does not lack intelligence and resourcefulness, a social pariah. Rather, her gradual fall into homelessness hinges exclusively on economic considerations: simply and most obviously, she becomes poorer and poorer. Echenoz chronicles that fall with exquisite attention to detail, annotating each step in the process with remarks about Victoire's finances, like the entries in a bank statement, commenting ironically upon the intrications of money and social status.

When Victoire flees Paris, she takes with her 45,000 francs, hoping that that sum will allow her to live reasonably well in clandestine manner until the circumstances of Félix's death are clarified and she is exonerated of responsibility. After the theft in Saint-Jean-de-Luz, she is left with 10,000 francs, and she is forced to give up the small house she had rented there. Not yet willing to take draconian measures to conserve her finances, she takes a room in a hotel, telling herself that she would find other means of obtaining money: "At the worst she could always get a job as a salesgirl or cashier, find a lover less indelicate than Gérard, even as a last resort become a part-time prostitute, we'd see" (46). Yet she does not takes those steps, and later, in Mimizan-Plage, she finds that only 3,014 francs remain to her:

> As long as her three thousand francs allowed her to meet her needs, Victoire stayed away from big cities. The nights were becoming milder, and she got used to sleeping outdoors more quickly than she would have imagined, and to finding quiet spots. To nourish herself, she went to cheap restaurants early on, but she quickly stopped doing that, less because of money than because of space: one leaves a restaurant only to go home, to leave in order to go nowhere means feeling doubly outside. Thus she began to eat entirely alone, turning her back to the world. (58-59)

As her resources erode still further, Victoire is finally constrained to abandon the countryside and go to cities to find other homeless people who might teach her some basic protocols of survival. Eventually and inevitably, her money runs out entirely: "She possessed merely a pair of sneakers, a pair of jeans, and layered sweaters under a quilted coat, but she had very little spare underwear, which she washed whenever it was possible to do so, but quiet places to wash were few and far between" (61). By this time, her economic options are very few indeed. She obtains some money by begging, but when she finally considers the prospect of prostitution in a serious manner, she realizes that it is too late for that, because her physical appearance is now far too degraded, and she is no longer a marketable commodity.

One of the most interesting effects in *Un An* is that, just as Victoire's finances become more and more impoverished, so too does the narrative economy of the novel, as if the two phenomena were mutually contingent. One way of accounting for this is through the progressive impoverishment of Victoire's imagination. That is, as Victoire becomes more and more concerned with the bare exigencies of survival, she is less and less apt to reflect upon less pressing concerns, and Echenoz's chronicle of her struggles reflects that evolution. I feel, however, that the gradual thinning of narrative detail and commentary signifies on another level as well. To the degree that Echenoz strips his story of conventional kinds of novelistic description, flourish, and commentary, he forces his reader to come to terms with the novel as bare literary form, in a form, precisely, that is barely sufficient. His narration becomes starkly declarative, his language becomes more concrete and less figural, the horizon of his story becomes more and more reduced, leaving his reader with very little room for maneuver. The close analogies that prevail between Victoire's destitution and that of *Un An* allow Echenoz to adumbrate a parable of the novel, one that allegorizes the novel's increasingly marginal position in contemporary culture.

I believe that such a reading of *Un An* is legitimate, despite the fact that metaliterary discourse is not explicit in the text, at least in the places we commonly look for it. There is no intertextual allusion in *Un An,* for instance. Nor is there any representation of the activity of writing, something that in itself marks *Un An* as being qualitatively different from most of the novels of the avant-garde in the last forty years or so. There are very few effects of literary recursiveness in the text. Books are mentioned on rare occasions: among the personal effects that Victoire takes with her from Paris are "two books, a Walkman, a little tin elephant" (22); and on one occasion, we are told that she takes a book to bed with her, but Echenoz refuses to elaborate further than that (39). Explicit evocations of the act of narration are few and far between. One exception to that rule is the fiction that Victoire embroiders in order to explain her situation to Castel and Poussin, after having listened to *their* stories: "Their story inspired Victoire to imagine one that might explain her own situation. Divorce, fired from her job, eviction, minor offenses, homelessness, trouble with the courts, and directionless wandering. Yeah, she concluded, I think I've gotten lost" (89). Clearly, Victoire has realized that fiction has its uses, when one is otherwise bankrupt. And Poussin's reaction to her story seems to confirm the idea that fiction's best chance of survival, now, is to wager on its own alterity: "That's not so bad, said Poussin. If we didn't get lost, we'd be lost" (89-90).

That kind of narrative gesture, however, is a highly anomalous one in the economy of *Un An*. The typical trappings of metaliterary discourse are very largely lacking here—and suspiciously so, granted Echenoz's previous writings and the concerns expressed therein. A variety of critics have commented upon the way Echenoz renovates novelistic form in his earlier work, taking familiar forms and turning them against themselves.[9] In Bruno

Blanckeman's view, that technique manifests itself in *Un An* in a somewhat different way: "In *Un An,* more still than in his other novels, he distances himself from the other categories of implicit references: detective story, hardboiled novel, spy story. The tightened brevity of the text imposes this loss of models, though it leaves their traces visible" (910). I concur with that assessment, and I also feel that *Un An* is the most dramatic interrogation of novelistic possibilities and limits that Echenoz has formulated thus far. We readers are called upon to apprehend that interrogation, however, in ways that seem counterintuitive and tortured, following an itinerary that is as labyrinthine as Victoire's own. Provisionally at least, we must read that discourse in the negative mode, through a story that contradicts its own premises, sabotages the idea of narrative truth, and seems to mock the familiar heuristics that we deploy in our efforts to make sense of it. If one accepts the idea that the story of Victoire's homeless wanderings mediates a reflection upon literature itself, though, *Un An* quickly opens onto richer interpretive fields wherein Echenoz's most compelling argument may become apparent. Just as constructive individual identity is very much at the mercy of capricious social forces, so too is that social construct which we call the novel—and the fate of both, in the current order of things, is extraordinarily precarious.

NOTES

[1] See for instance Pierre Lepape's comments in the pages of *Le Monde* in 1990. He calls Echenoz "the most remarkable novelist of the 1980s," suggesting further that "if one had to tell the story of this period, one would do it with Echenoz's books."

[2] See Bruno Blanckeman's remarks about Victoire's wanderings: "The itinerary thus narrated refers in fact to a programmatic wandering, a cyclothymic fate for a time of crisis" (905).

[3] On the notions of play and game in Echenoz's work, see Cloonan 213, Houppermans 85, and Leclerc 64.

[4] See Dominique Jullien's remarks about Echenoz's early novels: "The principle of the novels is that everything happens but nothing goes on. While in the detective story every detail eventually finds its place in the solution, here on the

contrary we are given too many pieces of the puzzle, so that we feel the uneasiness (a pun obviously encouraged by the French title, *L'Equipée malaise*) of a story both overcrowded and vacuous. [. . .] Loose ends become the very principle of the narration" (339). See also Blanckeman's observations about narrative logic in *Un An:* "Echenoz erases in effect any principle of causality: events and behaviors occur one after the other without reason, by summons as it were, rather than by necessity. The beginning and the end of the novel sketch thus a common immotivation" (909).

⁵ Pierre Lepape situates effects like this at the center of Echenoz's literary strategy: "Echenoz affirms nothing; he doesn't even affirm that he affirms nothing: he is the novelist of the suspension of meaning, of the smiling demolition of dogmas, of unstructured space and floating time" (34).

⁶ See also Houppermans 90-91: "It is moreover on the level of narrative instances that the reader's unease threatens also to manifest itself, beyond, as it were, the pernicious events, and their parade of foreshadowings, and beyond the usual decay of the modern world according to Echenoz."

⁷ See Blanckeman 904: "Between novelistic conformity and novelistic experimentalism, the tale husbands its wanderings, like its main character. A young woman leaves her city, flees her life, becomes idle, becomes marginal. If it establishes an itinerary thus, the novel also proposes an aesthetic hypothesis: the homeless person as metaphor of the story."

⁸ See Blanckeman 911: "Like the fiction that carries her along, Victoire circulates in an indeterminate social space, where the pressure of the usual rules still makes itself felt, but inefficiently."

⁹ William Cloonan, Dominque Jullien, and Martine Reid have all addressed the issue of generic parody in Echenoz's novels (203-05, 337, and 988, respectively).

VIII

❧

CHRISTIAN OSTER'S
PICNIC

With nine novels published at the Editions de Minuit since 1989, Christian Oster has established himself as one of the most interesting figures in a cohort of new French writers who are gradually redefining the novel as literary form. Many of these writers are Oster's stablemates in the Minuit stud, while others are affiliated with publishing houses such as Gallimard, Le Seuil, and POL.[1] Their experiments involve a profound questioning of conventional narrative protocols, a dramatic recasting of the reciprocal articulation of writers and readers, and a sustained meditation upon the uses of fiction. All of Christian Oster's novels are interesting texts in such a perspective, but I shall focus here on *Le Pique-nique* (1997; The Picnic), his fifth novel, for I find that it exemplifies most broadly the various themes, techniques, and writerly idiosyncrasies that characterize his work as a whole.

Le Pique-nique is the story of a man and his child who set off on a picnic in the Sénart Forest, near Paris. The incipit of the text stages a curious effect of narrative uncertainty:

> The man to whom I would like to give some importance here, I shall call him simply Louis. Or Charles. Or Julien. Around noon on a Saturday, then, Louis, I think that this time he'll be Louis, I prefer Louis, was walking at a necessarily slow pace beside Pauline, his daughter, five years old, in a forest near Paris, in a season which one will choose to be still mild, the end of summer for instance, or the very beginning of autumn, so that in the trees the shape of the leaves, and not the nuances of their colors, should assume a characteristic turn. (9)

Describing the landscape, the narrator warns us not to look for detail: "Such a sketch, however, will remain mostly vague" (9). That's a point well taken, for what is true of the landscape is also true of this novel, whose narrative contract is dominated by indeterminacy, where logic and causality are blurred, and wherein the reader—like the protagonists—may well become lost.

We know very little about Louis. He is about forty years old and lives with his five-year-old daughter, Pauline, in Paris. His wife is alluded to, briefly, on a couple of occasions when Louis nostalgically evokes her memory. Clearly, she no longer figures in Louis's life, but we are never told what became of her. That refusal to tell is merely one integer in a literary algorithm that wagers heavily on irresolution and doubt, paving an indistinct narrative highway littered with lacunae and very largely denuded of traditional signposts. Louis himself is sad, passive, and utterly bemused by life; he is moreover a *singular* man, "not quite like other people, and who in an already long life has nevertheless succeeded in not doing very much" (185). Louis has no friends, except for three army buddies whom he has not seen for twenty years, and whom he is supposed to meet in the forest for a picnic. He doesn't like men very much, we learn. All things considered, he prefers women—but, by his own admission, he doesn't know many women. That he and Pauline should become lost in the forest is inevitable, for Louis is constitutionally lost in the labyrinthine meanders of his life: "At that moment, once again, he didn't know what to do in this forest, where henceforward nothing recalled communion, solidarity, the particular species that humans represent" (48).

Louis cannot find his own way out of the forest, but, felicitously enough, others find *him*. First, a young woman forest ranger, euphoniously named Blanche Hazanavicius, whose beauty seduces Louis as much as her competence. Then Dujardin, one of his army buddies, a man as alienated and friendless as Louis himself. Once outside the forest, however, it becomes clear that Louis is still just as lost as he was before, and that his literal situation in the forest was merely a simulacrum of a far more distressing existential condition. He is bewildered by the conventions of society, and unable to decipher its arcane codes. He finds that he has nothing to say to Dujardin after twenty years, and when he tries to understand Dujardin's social gestures, he loses himself in his interpretive efforts, each more convoluted than the one preceding it. He realizes that Dujardin needs his friendship, but all Louis can think about is Blanche, who may or may not be thinking about him.

In short, Louis is a wanderer—but not by choice, it is important to note. On the contrary, he is constantly looking for the way out of his aimless state. Indeed, it's that very possibility of egress that he sees in his reunion with his former friends: "Louis imagined precisely the meeting with Christian, Philippe, and Dujardin, now, as a break in the indifferent order of things, a fractal event which might coax him out of himself and his solitude" (33). The problem is that the landscape confronting him is one that is undifferentiated; it presents very few asperities, and those, upon close inspection, prove to be for the most part illusory. The narrator's description of the forest, for example, suggests just the sort of smooth, flat surface that Louis encounters wherever he turns: "in forests, each leafy formation, seen from a distance, presents merely a silhouette which is blurred by its intrication with others, offering to the stroller, should he or she stop to gaze at the branches, merely an approximative profile" (9-10). That passage, along with others like it in *Le Pique-nique,* should properly be read on another level as well, that of metaliterary discourse. For it may also be seen to encode a set of ironic reading instructions that Christian Oster proposes to his reader in order to help him or her find a path through a novel which, on the face of it, presents a panorama of bleak indirection. In other words, Louis is not the only wanderer in this story, by a long shot. Like him, the narrator seems to wander in the telling of the tale, adrift in narrative possibility and a generalized irresolution of voice. The reader looks in vain for traditional diegetic cues that might adumbrate an identifiable narrative itinerary; in this book about being lost, the reader may have the impression, in the early going especially, of being at a loss.

I believe that such is precisely the impression that Oster seeks to project upon his reader. It is useful, moreover, to examine the notion of what it is to be "lost" that serves as the motor of this novel, both in the dynamic of production and that of reception. For Oster uses that notion in several different ways, turning it this way and that, exploiting its various possibilities, vexing literal meaning against figural, and ultimately revealing his novel as a playful agonistic of writing and reading. First and most obviously, Oster deploys that idea in a literal register. He points out that being lost is a contingent notion, for it is only when Louis *recognizes* that he has lost his way that he truly becomes "lost": "If he felt himself to be lost, it was quite simply because he *was* lost" (36). Approaching that same idea from another angle, Oster asks us to consider what it means to "lose" someone in a literal sense. When Louis awakes from a short nap in the forest, he finds that Pauline has wandered off, and all of his efforts to find her prove fruitless. It is here that Oster engages the second level of his meditation, a figural one where the notion of being lost is cast as an existential condition. He suggests that Louis's solitary, alienated state is long-standing and indeed constitutional. The fact that Louis has "lost" his wife—though we don't know how, nor in what sense of the word—weighs heavily upon him, and seems to inflect upon his every gesture; he blunders through his life just as he blunders through the forest. When Pauline disappears, the idea of his own "lostness" comes home to Louis in resounding terms, both literally and figuratively, for he recognizes that he has become "a man who, since the disappearance of his daughter, knows that he is utterly lost, and in whom the apprehension of space, as if by itself, has become a dead function" (63). The anguish that this recognition inspires in Louis is massive, and he understands that it is in fact merely the crystallization of a sentiment that has haunted him for many years: "A sadness possessed him, which he quickly recognized. He knows this sadness, he has already experienced it. It is his. It has accompanied him for a long time, discreetly, but under reproof it sharpens. And, in the pressure of fear, it changes skin" (69). The crisis of this novel comes at the very moment when Louis is forced to confront the central fact of his existence, that he is utterly and radically estranged from the world in which he lives.[2] Finally, Oster interrogates the idea of being lost on the metaliterary level, asking his reader to reflect on the reading of *Le Pique-nique* as a model of certain very basic literary functions. Upon first consideration, the reader is faced with an apparently indeterminate narrative, one whose twists may seem largely aleatory and unmotivated. One can lose one's direction in the intrigue of this novel; just as certainly, one can become lost in individual sentences, whose syntax is often a wandering, tortured sort. I feel, however, that Oster is asking his reader to consider whether such a process, closely inspected, might not explain some kinds of pleasure that we take in some kinds of texts, and that perhaps our pleasure is in losing ourselves in order eventually to find ourselves again, within the safely defined limits of fiction.

For if in the first instance Louis stands in for the reader, mediating his or her experience of this novel, so too, later, does Blanche Hazanavicius, the forest ranger. In contrast to Louis, Blanche knows the forest: "She was attached, moreover, to this forest. Her duties linked her to its trees, quartered her on its paths. This forest was her station" (106). She makes her way through the forest superbly, on horseback, God-like. That which seems labyrinthine and hopelessly intricated to Louis is clear to Blanche, for she is completely at home in the forest. Louis's panic contrasts with Blanche's cool serenity; his befuddlement is opposed to her lucidity; he is inert and paralyzed by events, whereas she is a person of action. Most importantly, Blanche knows how to *read* the forest. She is not duped by its apparent meanders, nor is she intimidated by its vastness. The paths that lead through it are for Blanche as clearly traced as the Autoroute du Sud. She is able, in short, to interpret the forest's signs—while Louis himself is incapable of even recognizing those signs as such. She will lead Louis out of the Sénart Forest; and she may eventually offer Louis a way out of his solitude, as well. In analogous manner, if the reader is willing to follow Blanche's example, he or she may be able to find a way out of this novel.

Blanche intervenes in the story when everything seems lost, just at the moment when Louis has despaired of finding Pauline. That sense of lostness pervades the thematics of the novel, as I have suggested, and it is also inscribed in the novel's structure. The chapters in *Le Pique-nique* are numbered from one to thirty-four, but there is no thirteenth chapter; that is, chapter twelve is followed by chapter fourteen. That particular lacuna (among the many lacunae one notes in this text) is invested with a great deal of meaning, "negative" meaning as it were, and I should like to examine it here in some detail. Chapter twelve ends with Blanche setting out to find Pauline; in chapter fourteen Blanche brings Pauline back to Louis. What would seem to be a key event in the narrative, the moment when Blanche finds Pauline, has been elided here, and Oster seems to suggest that the chapter in which it is recounted has itself been lost. It is an example of what Gerald Prince has called the "unnarrated" or "nonnarrated."[3] Analogous examples of this phenomenon may come to mind: the "caves" scene in E. M. Forster's *A Passage to India;* the blank page in Sterne's *Tristram Shandy;* the map of the ocean in Carroll's *The Hunting of the Snark;* the empty book Voltaire evokes at the end of "Micromégas"; and, perhaps most directly, the elision of the fifth chapter and the fifth part of Georges Perec's *La Disparition (A Void)*.

If the absence of a sign is always the sign of an absence, it is important to read this lacunary moment as a privileged signifier in the economy of the novel as a whole. In an early essay on Edmond Jabès, Jacques Derrida argued that the figure of ellipsis should be understood as pointing toward the book itself as a construct or an idea.[4] That seems to me to be perfectly characteristic of the "lost" chapter of *Le Pique-nique.* In this book about losing and becoming lost, many things go missing, and this elided chapter encapsulates that topos efficiently, marked as it is by the sinister number thirteen. The lacuna interrupts the narrative in a radical, inevitable manner; yet that very process of interruption may upon reflection allow us to understand this text more fully.[5] Louis has tried and failed to find his daughter. Blanche succeeds where Louis fails, but Louis has no earthly clue how she achieves that. And neither, crucially enough, does the reader of *Le Pique-nique.* Just as nobody knows precisely what M. Grandet does when he repairs to his counting-house (even the narrator of *Eugénie Grandet,* otherwise omniscient, declares himself ignorant on that issue), so it is impossible to know how and in what circumstances Blanche finds Pauline: some things, clearly, are beyond the ken of common mortals. Yet it is also human to wonder about things we are not told, and Christian Oster plays savantly upon our readerly curiosity in this moment of his text. He encourages us to speculate on various narrative possibilities, to draw inferences from the narrative logic surrounding this missing chapter. Briefly stated, he is proposing this moment of his novel as a highly exaggerated instance of the sort of interrogative process that any reading entails.

Readers are curious people, and one of the reasons we read is to satisfy our curiosity. Texts prompt us to ask questions, and we are deeply pleased when those questions are answered. Yet no text answers every question we might put to it. In certain cases, the questions themselves are illegitimate ones, since they fall outside of the limits the text establishes for itself; one cannot ask, according to the classic example, what name Achilles used when he hid among the women. In other cases, however, our legitimate questions are met by a text's refusal to tell. That is the phenomenon which Oster puts on display so ostentatiously in *Le Pique-nique*. It should be recognized that he does this not merely anecdotally, but rather as part of a generalized pattern of narrative taciturnity, one which is deeply embedded in his authorial strategy. When Louis thinks about his wife, for instance, Oster is quick to suggest that he will not provide any additional information about her, however eager the reader may be to hear it: "Of course Pauline wasn't born with that sense of the comic, just like that, in spite of the fact that her mother was also a humorous person, and moreover, but that's another story, Louis reflects now" (97-98). We may wonder whether she died, whether she left Louis for another man, whether she joined the Foreign Legion—but we will wonder in vain, because Oster very deliberately stages that problem as belonging to the domain of the unknowable.

In a real sense, then, *Le Pique-nique* is dominated by a carefully elaborated uncertainty principle that Oster exploits for aesthetic effect. In the way it functions, the "missing" chapter of the novel can be usefully compared to the Lucretian *clinamen,* since like the clinamen it interrupts the scheme of things surrounding it, and by very virtue of that interruption declares its own significance. In *De rerum natura,* Lucretius postulates the clinamen as a locus of free will and uses it to refute the deterministic atomic theory of Democritus, arguing that a swerve away from linearity may call a whole chain of causality into question. In similar fashion, Oster suggests in his novel that unanswered questions provide the reader with room for maneuver and a kind of creative freedom that may allow him or her to negotiate the labyrinth of this text with some degree of success. Once again, the key figure here is Blanche. She intervenes in Louis's story just as the clinamen intervenes in the fall of the atoms, in an aleatory manner, unexpectedly, and without explanation. Louis himself cannot account for her, and his friend Dujardin, who happens by just as Blanche is about to leave, doesn't appear to notice her. Yet Blanche's agency in this novel is a capital one, through the role she plays in the drama of lost-and-found. Having found Louis, having found Pauline, Blanche writes the number of her cellular telephone on a piece of paper and gives it to Louis before riding off, to be used "If you should ever get lost again" (80), a kind of ultra-modern Ariadne's thread.

When Dujardin finds Louis, he leads Louis and Pauline out of the forest and takes them to his own house in a Parisian suburb. Oster describes the surroundings as utterly familiar ones, yet Louis experiences those surroundings as strange and incomprehensible, both inside and out. A superhighway howls its "superhighway horror" (147) next to Dujardin's yard; the kitschy furnishings of Dujardin's home appall Louis; paralyzed by timidity, Dujardin has nothing to say to Louis, and Louis finds nothing to say to him. When Louis puts in a telephone call to Blanche, he tells her that he is not lost this time, though all of his rhetoric proclaims the contrary; and Blanche, with her characteristic astuteness, is quick to recognize that:

> You're not bothering me, she says however. So, you've got yourself lost?
> Louis answered no, then he said something. It was a question of finding one's bearings [*se retrouver*], of finding oneself [*se retrouver soi*], he began awkwardly, he became confused, he decided to speak about his car, that was more reasonable. (174)

Fumbling his words, Louis cannot articulate his wishes. But Blanche reads him correctly and, granted the thematics of lost-and-found that Oster has elaborated, piece by piece, in his novel, so do we. Through Louis's maladroitness, Oster plays on the verb *se retrouver,* which can mean "to meet" when the context is plural, but which literally means "to find oneself again." As Louis stumbles over his syntax, the possibility that first suggested itself to him in the forest, dimly, becomes finally clear: to find Blanche once again, in order eventually to find himself.

That passage is emblematic of a broader ludic strategy which colors *Le Pique-nique* from beginning to end, furnishing this otherwise dark tale with welcome highlights. In the forest, Louis is caught up in a ludic dynamic that he cannot fathom, like a rat in a maze. Wherever he turns, Louis encounters the same sort of dilemma: constrained by circumstances that are beyond his understanding, he is called upon to play a game whose rules are arbitrary and obscure. Faced with such a situation, Louis nonetheless recognizes that one of the uses of play is to enable one to pass the time, when all else fails: "One must wait. One must play. One must occupy oneself" (175). He is moreover a man who knows how to play certain other kinds of games, and most especially (despite his awkwardness on the telephone) language games. He plays a kind of riddle game with Pauline for instance, something the French call a *charade à tiroirs:*

> Not daring to begin a game with Pauline that would be so engrossing that he would be unable to break it off in order to answer the telephone, Louis stayed near the phone, suggesting to his daughter that they play riddles together, an exercise that this child, already attentive to the fascinations and surprises of language, had recently mastered. My first one, began Louis, is red and white, with a little green tail, and is sometimes eaten at dinner as an appetizer. My second one is the opposite of slowness. My third one is something that can be read, when somebody is a little bit older than you, on the faces of watches. My entirety allows one to be warm in wintertime, at home. (169-70)

It is important to note that there are two levels of play going on here simultaneously. Just as Louis proposes this game to Pauline, so too does Oster propose it to his reader, furnishing the answer to the first question, *radis* [radish], but letting the reader guess *hâte* [haste], *heure* [time], and the solution to the riddle, *radiateur* [radiator]. In addition, Louis's sense that Pauline is already intrigued by language is clearly reciprocated in Oster's hope that his reader will share Pauline's delight in the "fascinations" and "surprises" that language provides.

That passage, and others like it in the novel, may be seen to emblazon a function that is broadly distributed throughout the text, and it may be read as a parable of the novel as a whole. Appearances notwithstanding, *Le Pique-nique* is a comedy wherein various levels of play are continually vexed one against the other, sometimes in a straightforward manner, at other times ironically—but always in mutual articulation. In many ways, *Le Pique-nique* is a centrifugal text, as Louis's constant wandering and the "missing" chapter thirteen suggest. Yet Louis's aspirations, however he frames them (to find Pauline, to reconnect with his friends from the army, to get out of the forest, to find some kind of emotional solace with Blanche) clearly constitute a quest toward the center of things, and that quest is essentially ludic in character.[6] The same is true of Oster's own quest, for he seeks to establish a ludic contract with his reader, a contract whose terms are mediated and exemplified by the actions of the characters in the novel. That is, Oster is inviting us to engage in a game that is based on literature and its conditions of possibility, a game that he proposes as pleasurable and amusing, but which does not lack seriousness of purpose and import. Through the story of Louis and his trials, Oster is asking us to think about how stories come to *be*.

In the late 1930s, Johan Huizinga, the distinguished medievalist, postulated a bold theory of aesthetics in which he argued that all culture arises in play. I shall not test that vast and seductive thesis here, but the fundamental claim he stakes for literary culture, that *poiesis* is a play-function (Huizinga 119), seems particularly apposite in the case of *Le Pique-nique.* Closely examined, Oster's novel may be seen as a set of carefully imbricated games played out on various thematic, syntactic, and metaliterary stages. Oster encourages us to play, for instance, with the distinction we habitually draw between fiction and reality. On a first level, the forest serves as a metaphor of fiction, and, more precisely, *this* fiction, where Louis's disorientation recapitulates our own. Even within the forest, however, certain events seem to Louis more unreal than others. His initial encounter with Blanche is a good example of that. She appears out of nowhere, and inscribes herself on Louis's horizon of consciousness like a vision. Oster abstracts that event from its context and deliberately frames it in a manner that is different from everything that precedes, suggesting that the scene might constitute "a vignette, an old engraving entitled *The Meeting in the Forest,* whose publisher might have wished to modernize its aspect and flesh out its meaning by adorning it with a bit of dialogue intended to seduce the potential buyer and satisfy his or her curiosity" (58). His tactic is a canny, subtle one. In one apparently simple gesture, he designates that encounter as a fiction embedded in a fictional register that suddenly seems somewhat more "real" by force of contrast; he puts on display the process of embellishment that fiction relies upon; he alludes to the profound hermeneutic impulse that motivates readers; and he reminds us that fiction is a commodity circulating in an economy and directed toward potential consumers—in point of fact toward us. In other words, Oster is playfully directing our attention to the dynamic of textual production that is occurring before our eyes, and that readers, lost in fictions, tend quite naturally to forget.

Once out of the forest and dubiously ensconced in Dujardin's house, Louis wonders why Dujardin didn't seem to notice Blanche in the forest, though she was right before her eyes—or was she? In retrospect, Louis is forced to admit that his perceptions in the forest may have deceived him at times: "Though he himself, Louis, during his wanderings in the forest, had felt several times that he was seeing or believing things that were not there" (142). Elsewhere in the text, too, Louis meditates on the problematic distinction of the real and the unreal, casting those categories explicitly in literary terms:

> In fact Louis knows exactly what he intends to do, or what he would like to do, now that he has found his daughter, or rather now that the loss of his daughter has been revealed as pure fiction, at the most his daughter inexplicably wandered off for a few long moments, but surely wasn't lost, what Louis wants to do now is to be alone with his daughter and with this piece of paper that is not a fiction, no, and which, in the bottom of his pocket, constitutes the sole trace of this woman rider's brief appearance in his life. (96-97)

If the experience of having lost Pauline, viewed after the fact, seems like a "pure fiction" to Louis, he nevertheless regards the piece of paper with Blanche's telephone number on it as the material guarantor of an encounter that he might otherwise be compelled to interpret as fictional. That is an issue that can only be adjudicated empirically, of course; and Louis's hesitation in placing a call to Blanche is founded in his dread of discovering that he imagined the entire encounter. That hesitation furnishes yet another locus of play for Oster and his reader, for if we disentangle ourselves from the multiple layers of fancy that he interweaves here, we realize that in fact the encounter *is* a fictional one, imagined by someone in the broader imaginary landscape of a novel. Moreover, fiction "works" in just that way, by imaginings through imaginings.

The little piece of paper with Blanche's phone number may be taken as an objective correlative for the novelistic intrigue itself—here both romantic and *romanesque*. Oster focuses our attention on it closely, because, more than anything else, it is the thing that links Louis's imagination, Oster's, and our own. Louis's narrative imagination is relatively naive, but the pleasure he takes in stories of his own making is abundant. Alone with his daughter at Dujardin's house, he tells Pauline a story: "he introduced a happy ending to which, as a grand finale, he added a party with all her little friends, represented at a moment's notice by some forks and spoons that Louis found in the kitchen" (163-64). Left to his own devices, that is, he will end his tales happily; and clearly he hopes that the story of Louis and Blanche will end as felicitously as the story he shares with Pauline. The narrative imagination that Christian Oster deploys, however, is somewhat more sophisticated. He plays ironically on Louis's storytelling; and he plays tensively on the reader's sense that something must happen in *Le Pique-nique,* one way or the other. There is a battle of narrative wills at work in this text, an agonistic that is ludic in nature, and one which is largely unresolved. The promise that the little piece of paper represents will find its confirmation (Blanche *will* answer Louis's call, she *will* come to his rescue once again, at Dujardin's house, just as she did in the forest); but the question of whether this novel ends "happily" or not will be left nonetheless very much open.

Another site of ludic exchange in *Le Pique-nique* involves syntax. Oster proposes a meditation on two levels, local and global, involving on the one hand the syntax of the individual sentence and on the other hand that of the novel. His intent is to make us realize the reciprocal affinities that play between those levels, and that may account for what we know as "style." Often, especially when recording Louis's thoughts or speech acts, Oster constructs his sentences according to a principle of aggregation, with little or no coordination, piling clause upon clause until the whole edifice threatens to collapse, as in this passage where Dujardin calls a friend on the phone, using its automatic dialing function:

> Dujardin was perhaps not so solitary after all, mused Louis, and maybe he was acquainted with more people than he was willing to admit, who knows, unless on the contrary, knowing only a very few people, he wished piously to remember them in that ebonite hollow, close to his hand or to his bosom, where, in order to embrace them symbolically, he might think that an index finger would suffice, his own, with a fingernail at its end, rather than the telephone

index that one usually leaves next to the phone, an index rendered obsolete by
that absolutely modern device. (130)

There are several moves in the game here. Most obviously, Oster wishes
to persuade us that Louis's "lostness" is more than anything else a state of
mind; Louis's thoughts wander, just as he himself wanders in the forest, without any apparent direction or clear goal. The syntax of the sentence is tortured, just as Louis himself is tortured by his solitude and his sense of being
apart from the world in which he lives. The syntactic indecision one notes
here, the recursive gestures, and the evocation of multiple interpretive possibilities are all closely reflective, in microcosmic form, of *Le Pique-nique*'s structure. That is, this passage, like the one describing the riddle game, may be
viewed as a *mise-en-abyme* of the novel as a whole. Finally, the passage effectively projects Louis's own wandering upon the reader, for we become lost in
the errant syntax of this sentence, looking ahead for some way out, looking
back to see where we went astray.

That last phenomenon is particularly evident when Louis tries to un-
burden himself to Dujardin. Whereas Blanche is a gifted interpreter who
knows how to decipher Louis's conversational maunderings and identify what
the poor man is *trying* to say, Dujardin on the contrary is utterly baffled by
Louis's language, which leaves him virtually speechless:

> Me, Louis suddenly said, I don't have many friends.
> Ah, said Dujardin.
> No, said Louis, surprised at himself, but who said nonetheless, thus, I
> have a few friends, of course, but not very many, but it's difficult, he admitted
> to his own astonishment, I like women too much, even though I don't know
> many women. Above all, I don't like men very much, he added, properly stu-
> pefied, or rather I didn't use to like them, I'm only beginning to appreciate
> them as time goes by, but at present I lack them, I lack men, men friends. And
> moreover, he forced himself to conclude, decidedly astonished that he could
> confess such things to Dujardin, then accepting, after all, that he could open
> himself a little bit to this sort of friend, feeling that, even if he couldn't hope
> that Dujardin would receive his confession in a positive manner, he was sure
> that he wouldn't hold it against him, moreover, I'm thirsty.

There, that's a thought, said Dujardin, suddenly almost mirthful, I'll get us something to drink. (121-22)

Both Blanche and Dujardin can be seen as mediative figures of the reader in *Le Pique-nique.* But Blanche is the reader at his or her best and most resourceful, while Dujardin serves to mediate those moments in the text when the reader, like Louis himself, becomes miserably benighted. Moments of tortured syntax recur insistently in *Le Pique-nique,* and indeed the syntax of the novel as a whole is closely analogous to that of the passages I have quoted. For *Le Pique-nique,* too, meanders maddeningly, unstably, indecisively, and its direction is obscure. It is difficult to assign pertinence to narrative event here; narrative prominencing seems to have been flattened. The few, sketchy adumbrations of teleology function parodically rather than frankly, pointing toward narrative possibilities that either result in dead ends or lead us back to where we began. The errant itinerary we follow in this novel obliges us necessarily to reflect upon Oster's narrative technique; and we may come to realize that what is going on in *Le Pique-nique* is the elaboration of a model, exaggerated for parodic and ludic effect, of certain very essential narrative conventions. In that regard, the image of the forest assumes capital importance. Like Borges's labyrinth, like John Barth's funhouse, like Georges Perec's jigsaw puzzle, Oster offers the forest to us both as an image of his own text and as a master image of the broad literary tradition out of which *Le Pique-nique* arises.

Such considerations dawn progressively upon the reader, as it slowly becomes clear that Christian Oster is proposing the story of Louis and his problems as a parable of yet another story, whose protagonist is the reader; and therein lies the final move in Oster's ludic strategy. As I have suggested, our reading experience is very largely mediated through the characters in this novel. From time to time, Oster provides us with reading instructions, wryly encoded in his description of the characters' situation, for instance when Louis is searching for his friends, early on in the novel: "Louis felt that, along with Pauline, he must explore the forest with more rigor from now on, in order to find them" (27). The "rigor" that Louis has to apply if he is to be successful is the same sort of quality that we must bring to our reading, according to Oster. More generally speaking, the actions of the characters in *Le Pique-nique* reflect the kinds of reading protocols we test one after the other—with varying degrees of success—as we make our way through the novel. Sometimes those reflections are flattering to us, sometimes they are distinctly unflattering. At certain moments, the reader is bound to feel as lost as Louis, or as nonplused as Dujardin; at other moments, he or she may feel as incisive as Blanche. One thing is certain, however: our reading of *Le Pique-nique* is constructed through those "others" in a playful dynamic of reciprocity. We see ourselves through those others, we look at ourselves looking at them; and, through that process, we may recognize a projection of ourselves, that figure who may very well be, as Sander Gilman has suggested, the real "other" whom we seek as we read.[7]

It is in just that perspective that one may interpret *Le Pique-nique* as an irredentist fable. But it is one with a distinct twist. Oster tantalizes the reader with the expectation that Louis will "find himself" at the end of this story. As Louis drives off with Blanche, however, that issue remains undecided: "Then Blanche turned toward Louis and asked him if, now, they could leave. And then Louis looked her in the eyes. And then it was like always, he didn't see anything, he didn't learn anything at all, but he said Yes" (189). On the one hand, the lack of resolution is right and proper, granted the general economy of *Le Pique-nique;* like all of Christian Oster's other novels, and like much of contemporary literature as well, this is a text which argues that questions are infinitely more intriguing than answers.[8] On the other hand, Oster wishes to persuade us, I think, that the import of *Le Pique-nique* is elsewhere, residing closely in our own experience. That may explain why Oster places so many obstacles in our way, frustrating our attempts to deploy familiar reading strategies in order to come to terms with the novel. Encountering those obstacles, we are continually confronted with our efforts to surmount them. In other words, as we read *Le Pique-nique,* Oster incessantly leads us, sometimes gently, sometimes brutally, back to our own reading. That reflexive gesture, of course, is precisely the kind of move that Oster himself makes, over and over again, in the telling of this tale. Moreover, it announces the principal claims that Oster intends to stake here concerning writing and reading. If one accepts the hypothesis that *Le Pique-nique* is a story about the fundamentally recurvate shape of literature, certain other considerations become clear. Readers do get lost in novels, Oster suggests, whether that novel be Balzac's *Eugénie*

Grandet or Robbe-Grillet's *Dans le labyrinthe (In the Labyrinth)*. So do writers, for that matter, who are faced with a bewildering array of narrative possibilities, a garden of forking paths that lead not outward, but rather *inward*. And indeed, in Christian Oster's opinion, it is just that itinerary of inward, reflective wandering which accounts for the pleasure of the text, both for the writer and for the reader.

NOTES

¹ The Minuit writers I'm thinking of are François Bon, Eric Chevillard, Patrick Deville, Jean Echenoz, Christian Gailly, Eric Laurrent, Marie NDiaye, Yves Ravey, Marie Redonnet, Eugène Savitzkaya, Jean-Philippe Toussaint, and Antoine Volodine. Among other writers one might mention are Emmanuèle Bernheim, Emmanuel Carrère, Marcel Cohen, Annie Ernaux, Jacques Jouet, Leslie Kaplan, Isabelle Lévesque, Danielle Mémoire, Pierre Michon, Alina Reyes, Patrick Roegiers, and Olivier Targowla.

² See Jacques Roubaud's eloquent formulation of that feeling of radical alienation, in another meditation upon loss, *La Pluralité des mondes de Lewis (The Plurality of Worlds of Lewis):* "For no world, in fact, is ours, that's what the constant functioning of our mind, against every inclination toward hope, tells us" (105).

³ See *Narrative as Theme* 30: "We are also familiar with another, closely related category that may be called the unnarrated, or nonnarrated. I am not thinking of what is left unsaid by a narrative because of ignorance, stupidity, repression, or choice. Rather, I am thinking of all the frontal and lateral ellipses explicitly underlined by the narrator ('I will not recount what happened during that fateful week') or inferrable from a significant lacuna in the chronology or through a retrospective filling-in: given a series of events e1, e2, e3 . . . en occurring at time t or at times t1, t2, t3 . . . tn respectively, one of the events goes unmentioned."

⁴ See *Writing and Difference* 296: "Thus understood, the return to the book is of an *elliptical* essence. Something invisible is missing in the grammar of this repetition. As this lack is invisible and undeterminable, as it completely redoubles and consecrates the book, once more passing each point along its circuit, nothing has budged. And yet all meaning is altered by this lack. Repeated, the same line is no longer exactly the same, the ring no longer has the same center, *the origin has played*. Something is missing that would make the circle perfect. But within the

ellipsis, by means of simple redoubling of the route, the solicitation of closure, and the jointing of the line, the book has let itself be thought as such."

[5] See Maurice Blanchot's "L'Interruption," where he argues that "Interruption is necessary in every sequence of words; intermittance enables the becoming; discontinuity guarantees the continuity of understanding" (870).

[6] See Derrida, *Writing and Difference* 297: "But is not the desire for a center, as a function of play itself, the indestructible itself? And in the repetition or return of play, how could the phantom of the center not call to us? It is here that the hesitation between writing as decentering and writing as an affirmation of play is infinite."

[7] See *Inscribing the Other* 14: "The fictive personalities we are constantly generating are rooted in the internalized dichotomy upon which we construct our world. Thus there is always an Other for us, no matter how we define ourselves. The ultimate Other is the doppelgänger, the Other which is our self, but a self projected into the world."

[8] See Gayatri Spivak's remarks about postmodern literary discourse: "Whereas in other kinds of discourses there is a move toward the final truth of a situation, literature, even without this argument, displays that the truth of a human situation *is* the itinerary of not being able to find it. In the general discourse of the humanities, there is a sort of search for solutions, whereas in literary discourse there is a playing out of the problem as the solution, if you like" (*In Other Worlds* 77).

IX

∾

JEAN-PHILIPPE TOUSSAINT'S TV GUIDE

Droll and sharply focused on the little vexations of everyday life, *La Télévision* (1997), Jean-Philippe Toussaint's fifth novel, takes its place in a body of work that is beginning to look like an epic of the trivial. Its narrator is a most reluctant hero, engaged in a comically unequal struggle with his own constitutional penchant for passiveness, diffidence, and immobility.[1] Like Toussaint's other protagonists, the narrator of *La Télévision* is anonymous; apart from his name, though, information about him is supplied in abundance. Some of that information is largely administrative in character. He is a fortyish university professor from Paris, spending a sabbatical year in Berlin in order to write a book on Titian, and particularly the painter's relations with the emperor Charles V, "a vast essay on the relations between the arts and political power" (15). He is married, with a young son, and his wife is expecting another child. Other data are more intimate. He mentions that he used to place sex above swimming in his pantheon of favorite activities (but below "thinking," of course, like any good academic); yet now he wonders if he doesn't prefer swimming to sex (12). The narrator stayed behind in Berlin when his family went on vacation to Italy, promising himself that he would put that time to good use. Having completed his research, he was ready to begin writing his book. Instead of that, however, he began to watch television; and he watched it constantly, indiscriminately, and bulimically.

La Télévision begins with one of the most radical gestures of renunciation one can make in our culture: "I stopped watching television" (7). The narrator's decision is grounded in a variety of closely reasoned considerations, both practical and philosophical. Though it will shortly become clear that decisiveness is not one of his principal virtues, as his resolution erodes ineluctably into velleity, it is nonetheless interesting to examine his reflections, for it is through them that Toussaint stages the crucial problematics of his novel. Taking stock of his life, the narrator realizes that he had been watching TV too much and that he didn't have time for anything other than TV:

> For hours every evening I remained immobile in front of the screen, my eyes fixed on the discontinuous glimmering of the changing scenes, invaded little by little by the flux of images that lit up my face, all of these images blindly directed toward everyone at the same time and addressed to nobody in particular, each network, in its narrow channel, being only one of the links in a gigantic pattern of waves which broke daily upon the world. (21-22)

It is the *image* that obsesses the narrator, and more particularly the raw, uncontextualized image that television projects.[2] As an art historian, the narrator is professionally attentive to images and how they signify. Yet despite his sophistication he cannot construct meaning from the images he sees on television: they are too indiscriminate, floating signifiers in a broader discourse that fails to cohere according to any of the codes—aesthetic, historical, social— that he is used to.

He senses that, while television pretends to give us the real, the images it bombards us with are empty ones from which the real has been very largely evacuated: "Television does not offer the spectacle of reality, though it has every appearance thereof [. . .], but rather of its representation" (13). Clearly, the narrator has read his Guy Debord.[3] And like Debord, he realizes that the permanent spectacle which television constructs is one that inverts the conventional relations of truth and falsehood: "I reflected that it was nevertheless thus that television presented the world to us every day: falsely" (205). Therefore, on TV, the real becomes the false, the false the real; and the spectator is left to negotiate a semiotic landscape that bears, at best, only a parodic relation to the world outside.[4]

Moreover, television banalizes human experience, the narrator feels. It takes event and abstracts it from history, strips it of meaning and deploys it as an undifferentiated integer in an infinitely self-perpetuating combinatoric of the senseless. It is important to note that the narrator does not take issue with banality itself. Quite to the contrary, he is a man who is intrigued—and utterly bemused—by the small things in life. He finds meaning in the little social rituals and trivial occurrences that most of us neglect by virtue of their very obviousness. Like his narrator, Toussaint himself is deeply interested in the banal, and in *La Télévision,* as in the novels that precede it, he focuses his gaze squarely upon it, in an attempt to invest the quotidian with significance.[5] The spectacle enacts a process that is precisely opposite in the narrator's view, taking the particularity of event and the heterogeneity of meaning and reducing them to pap in a cultural Cuisinart, through what Debord refers to as the spectacle's "movement of *banalization*" (43).

The narrator levels several other charges against television. It fosters alienation; it makes people passive; it doesn't leave time for thought; it causes people to be indifferent and keeps them in a state of artificial awareness (25-26). Most insidiously, he believes, it encourages people to spend more time commenting upon their actions than in performing those actions. He speculates upon television's nefarious effect on artistic creation, and on the way it invites artists to speak about works they *might* create, rather than comment on works they *have* created (54). The narrator feels that paralyzing effect intimately, because of course he has not written one word of his book on Titian.

The struggle between television and the written word is the problem upon which *La Télévision* hinges. In the narrator's view—and in Toussaint's, too—it is a vital problem, one that engages not only the local manifestations of culture, but also cultural survival. Television competes directly with literature in the cultural marketplace, Toussaint argues, and the result of that competition will determine the way we conceive our world. Staging that competition at the center of his novel and staking the fate of that novel boldly upon his polemical wager, he intends to tip the odds in favor of the written word, through the use of satire, irony, and humor—precisely the kind of subversive verbal strategies that television, in his opinion, eschews. In the course of the novel, it gradually becomes apparent that *La Télévision* is not "about" television, nor is it about one man's grapplings with television; rather, it is about literature and its uses, and more specifically about the uses that remain to literature in its current embattled state.

Toussaint will attempt to enlist the reader in this debate through the way he describes his narrator's dilemma, making it clear that it is a question not only of writing, but also of reading. For if the narrator is a writer (or rather he *would* be, if only he could write), he is also a reader, one who is deeply committed to literature in all its forms. When he compares literature to television, he concludes that the former offers people a far vaster field of possibility than the latter, leaving ample room for thought, inference, and interpretation, in short, for all the maneuvers in which an intellectual takes pride: "Whereas books, for instance, always offer a thousand times more than what they are, television offers exactly what it is, its essential immediacy, its ongoing superficiality" (159). The choice is clear for him, then. Yet the day after swearing off television cold turkey, he feels "a lack" (112). He does have time to read once again, but to his chagrin he finds himself reading the television listings in the newspaper. And television continues to vex his life in ways that are stranger still: in a moment of stunned recognition, the narrator reflects upon the ominous purport of the initial letters of Titian's given name, "Tiziano Vecellio" (248).

He sees TV wherever he turns, poor soul. Gazing out into the Berlin night from his apartment window, he realizes to his astonishment that all of his neighbors are watching television:

> I watched all of these luminous screens change together before me, or at least in great successive, synchronous waves that undoubtedly corresponded to the different programs that people were watching in the different apartments of the neighborhood, and, seeing this, I experienced the same painful impression of multitude and uniformity that the spectacle of thousands of camera flash bulbs going off at the same time in a stadium during a great sporting event gives me. (44-45)

Later, when he goes to visit a friend, he watches an episode of *Baywatch* adapted for German television. Looking out the window, he notes that the people in the apartment across the street are watching the same program (201-04). For the narrator, this is a chilling, uncanny moment: is he watching *Baywatch,* or is *Baywatch* watching him? It brings, too, a sobering recognition of television's cultural force, because despite the fact that *Baywatch* is commonly regarded as the most cretinous, most utterly vacuous program on TV, everyone seems to watch it.[6] Yes, everyone watches TV—but very few people are prepared to acknowledge that dirty little secret. To the contrary, within the narrator's circle of friends, everyone claims not to watch TV, or to have sworn off it, or to watch it very, very rarely: "Nobody watched television, in the final analysis (except me, of course)" (141).

Television stalks the narrator even when he's working (or trying to work). Visiting a museum, he looks at the video screens on the security guard's desk and sees on one of them an image of one of the paintings that initially prompted him to write a book on Titian (236). The burning issue here is that of *mediation*. The narrator's situation as he gazes into the video screen is emblematic of his broader dilemma as an intellectual and a critic of culture: TV gets there before he does, more quickly, more immediately. It expropriates the cultural artifact and leaves nothing—or very little—behind. The critic finds himself distanced from his object of study, seeing it only in heavily mediated form, through a glass, darkly.[7] That same situation haunts the narrator in other circumstances as well. Reading microfilm in a library or doing a bibliographic computer search on "Musset" at Beaubourg (78-84), he stares into a screen, a handy simulacrum of TV. He sees words there, certainly, words that might facilitate the other words that he wishes eventually to write; but these words are televised, and the narrator finds it difficult to come to terms with them. At home, laboring to write the first sentence of his book, he looks into the emptiness of his computer screen—a postmodern correlative of Mallarmé's "empty paper which whiteness forbids"—but no inspiration comes, and all he sees there is his own failure to create (48).

Even his own extinguished television set belabors the narrator. Poking around his apartment one evening, he catches himself staring into its darkened screen; what he sees there is himself, "in the center of the screen" (122), the butt of a hopelessly intricated joke. Contemplating the portrait of Charles V on the security guard's video screen, he finds the emperor "unrecognizable," and closes his eyes momentarily: "I opened my eyes again and, when I glanced once again at the video screen, it was my own face that I saw appear in the reflection on the screen, my own face which began to surge slowly out of the electronic limbo of the monitor's depths" (237-38). These moments contain, I think, a hard lesson. One can turn TV off, but it might just as well be on, for in either case television ceaselessly projects the riddle of the sphinx upon us, reflecting back to us our own banalized image.[8] And indeed that is the sense of every image of television in this novel, whether it be staged explicitly as a mirror scene or not. As the narrator strains to read the image that television projects, to penetrate beneath the flatness of its surface, he is continually confronted with the parodic representation of his own otiosity. What he really sees in that image on the screen, then, is a commentary on writing and its difficulties, writ large. That same image is emblazoned in specular fashion throughout *La Télévision*—and the narrator is not the only benighted academic who will recognize himself in it.

For a text that deals principally with the fate of literature, there is very little intertextual allusion in this novel. The narrator evokes Musset, as I mentioned, on several occasions; he refers in passing to Roger Martin du Gard's *Les Thibault (The Thibaults)* and to a new German translation of Proust. The Dutch novelist Cees Nooteboom makes a brief cameo appearance, too, when the narrator runs into him in a city park. But, at least in terms of explicit references to other writers, that's about all. Toussaint's four previous novels, like *La Télévision*, all invest heavily in metaliterary reflection; yet there, too, one notes a paucity of overt intertextual allusion. Questioned about the relative lack of cultural reference in his work by an interviewer, Toussaint offered a curious response: "No, in spite of the temptations, I shy away from that, I refuse that game in order to find my own path, where culture is almost inimical" (Ammouche-Kremers 33). In *La Télévision,* it is obvious from the first pages onward that Toussaint takes an adversarial stance toward the kind of culture that TV constructs. With regard to literary culture, however, his position is rather different. Clearly, he is attempting in his novel to argue a brief for literature's viability as a cultural medium; yet he wishes to elaborate that argument on his own terms, following an independent and very idiosyncratic "path." Rather than adducing other writers' work in an effort to convince his reader of literature's undiminished cultural strength, he intends that his own novel should *perform* that lesson through the force of example. His wager is not lacking in audacity. And many of Toussaint's readers may not be persuaded by it. Nonetheless, it seems to me that such is his strategy here, for better or for worse.

Symptomatically enough, while there is very little reference to other bodies of writing in *La Télévision,* there is an insistent pattern of allusion to

Toussaint's own works. Some of those allusions are fairly oblique, but many are more explicit. In this novel, for example, the narrator calls his wife simply "Delon." Seemingly a last name rather than a first name, and of undifferentiated gender, it recalls Toussaint's first novel, where the narrator's companion is a woman named Edmondsson. More obvious still is the passage in the early pages of *La Télévision* where the narrator remarks, "I place baths very high, actually, on the scale of pleasures that life offers us" (12). Near the end of the text, the narrator relaxes luxuriously in his bathtub, listening to the *lento* of Beethoven's last string quartet (256). Together, those two moments frame the autoallusive weft of *La Télévision* and remind the reader that Jean-Philippe Toussaint made his mark on the literary horizon in France with a novel called *La Salle de bain (The Bathroom)*. The title of Toussaint's third novel is inscribed in the narrator's evocation of "thousands of camera flash bulbs" (44-45). The novel that precedes *La Télévision, La Réticence* (Reticence), is alluded to on several occasions, first slyly, then more directly. The narrator mentions that he is constitutionally reserved (28), and reserve is the most salient trait of the narrator of *La Réticence*—as well as that text's most characteristic discursive strategy. Later, when the narrator informs his wife by telephone that he has stopped watching TV, she asks him for his reasons, but he declines to elaborate further, explaining in an aside to the reader that those were reasons "that I would have been very reluctant [*réticent*] to give her" (112). He notes too that, while people will lend their books, records, videocassettes, and even their clothes to other people reasonably freely, "people were very reluctant [*réticents*] to loan their television" (141). And when the director of the foundation sponsoring his sabbatical year asks him how his work is going, he answers his question "with reticence," remarking moreover that "I have always been somewhat reticent when asked to speak about my work" (71).

That passage performs an interesting critique on Toussaint's novels in general, and on *La Télévision* in particular. On the one hand, Toussaint's oeuvre as a whole is a singularly reticent one. His narrators are diffident in the extreme: they tell their stories despite themselves, as it were, and only at the expense of an effort that is almost beyond their powers. On the other hand, the "work" that the narrator of *La Télévision* envisions—for the moment at least—is writing, and much of the metaliterary dimension of this novel is bound up in a sustained meditation on writing *as work*. Vivid ironies color that meditation at every point. For, clearly enough, Toussaint's "work" is also writing, and in one sense the task the narrator has set himself is an analog of Toussaint's own. In that perspective, Toussaint deploys his narrator as a stalking-horse, using that man's struggles in order to suggest his own conception of writing and its vicissitudes. Yet, unlike Toussaint, the narrator's writerly efforts do not bear fruit—and one understands readily enough why he is "reticent" corncerning his work. One of the functions of autoallusion in *La Télévision* is to remind the reader that two very different kinds of writer are at issue here: if the narrator cannot write his book, that same charge cannot be laid at Jean-Philippe Toussaint's doorstep. At certain moments in the novel, then, Toussaint casts his narrator as exemplary: the problems he faces as he tries to write his book on Titian are real ones, problems that any writer must confront. At other times, the narrator's gropings, maunderings, and surjustifications are intended by Toussaint as counterexample, a ludicrously exaggerated depiction of a failed writer's martyrdom.

In both cases however, whether Toussaint is offering his narrator to us frankly or parodically, the central question is that of the *work* which writing demands. The narrator is an academic, after all. Any academic knows that work is tough (especially, perhaps, if like the narrator, one works very little). There are no easy solutions available, either: the only way to get one's work done is, well, to *work*. The dilemma is tautological; still more egregiously, it's unfair. The narrator of *La Télévision* senses that unfairness with every nerve in his body, for his essential vocation is to do nothing. By his own account, that nothing is a something which demands considerable mastery:

> I did nothing at all, moreover. By "nothing," I mean only doing the essential, thinking, reading, listening to music, making love, strolling, going to the swimming pool, picking mushrooms. To do nothing, contrary to what one might at first imagine, demands method and discipline, openness of mind and concentration. (11)

In point of fact the narrator will do almost anything in order to avoid work. After putting his family on the plane for Italy, he returns to his apartment, vowing to begin writing his book the next morning, bright and early. In order to prepare himself for that momentous step, he engages in a frenzy of activity, cleaning up the accumulation of papers on his desk, classifying his voluminous and hopelessly unmanageable notes, sweeping his office floor, taking the rug out onto the balcony to give it a sound beating (18-21). Toussaint describes those rituals of preliminary procrastination with some hilarity; yet one senses that, for anyone who has ever practiced them, they are more than a little harrowing, too.

Come the morning, the narrator will not work, of course. Instead, he will devote the days ahead to behaviors that he can substitute for work, wrestling with his conscience in an effort to convince himself that he is using his time productively. Spending an afternoon in a city park, he indulges agreeably in two of his favorite pastimes, thinking and swimming:

> I was stretched out on my back in the water, reflecting on my study, my two hands limp and relaxed floating next to me, and I watched them with a benevolent curiosity, my wrists slackened, each finger, each joint eased in the marvelous liquid element in which I bathed, my legs extended and my body suspended, my package lightly emerging from the water, like a very simply arranged still life, two prunes and a banana, which a very mild wave sometimes partially covered. In short, work. (74)

Yet that industrious contemplation of his own genitalia, however inspirational they might seem, brings little real solace to the narrator. For the only way he can get his mind to focus on the problem of work is to construe it as an eternally deferred abstraction: "I continued to think of my work in that manner, as a delicious and distant eventuality, a little bit vague and abstract, reassuring, which only circumstances, alas, momentarily prevented me from finishing" (193).

Clearly, if the narrator wishes to justify his own sloth, he must work harder at it. With all the intellectual resource he can muster, he constructs elaborate, intricate arguments to explain his failure to work, gradually building up an imposing edifice of self-deception and bad faith. Assuming once again the only position for which he is truly suited, supine, he basks in the sun, meditating on the mutual affinities of work and reverie, luxuriating in an orgy of sophistry: "However, wasn't working precisely this, I told myself, this slow and progressive opening of the spirit and this total availability of the senses that came over me little by little?" (89). Isn't the act of thinking about work, in other words, work enough? A corollary to that thesis occurs to him in a flash of insight, one which appears to blunt the horns of his dilemma: "not writing is at least as important as writing" (90).

Would it were so. If one could just hold onto that shining proposition firmly, one might believe in it deeply enough to make it *work*. But there's the rub, after all: work itself. In his moments of weakness—and they are, alas, legion—the narrator suspects dimly that merely thinking about work will not get his book on Titian written. Moreover, more chillingly still, he wonders on occasion if that very process of reflection is not in fact counterproductive to the task at hand:

> The rule, once again, seemed to confirm itself. I had not yet formulated it clearly to myself, but its pertinence had already appeared to me in a shadowy manner on many occasions. One's chances of successfully finishing a project are inversely proportional to the time one devotes to talking about it beforehand. For the simple reason, it seemed me, that, if one has already luxuriated in the potential joys of a project during the stages preceding its realization, there remains, at the moment when one has to begin it, merely the pain inherent in the process of creation, of burden, of labor. (53-54)

How else to account for the fact that when he finally sits down to write, despite his exhaustive preparation, he finds himself with nothing to say? That moment, long anticipated and lovingly imagined over many arduous months, is the narrator's dark night of the soul. "Seated in my study," he says, "I looked at my computer glowing before me, and I reflected that my desire to finish this essay had quite simply passed" (52).

In short, he's blocked. He realizes that fact, moreover, which only accentuates the tragic character of his situation. One imagines that this is not the first time in his career that the narrator has wrestled with the writer's worst bogeyman. He's not the first writer to do so—nor, one can predict with confidence, the last. Moreover, the narrator of *La Télévision* is the most recent avatar of a venerable literary type. In the contemporary French tradition, for example, one can point to Roquentin in Sartre's *La Nausée (Nausea)*, a historian, also, who loses his enthusiasm for his writing project; or to Joseph Grand in Camus's *La Peste (The Plague)*, who for years on end writes and rewrites the first sentence of his novel because nothing less than perfection will serve to enable the rest. Like Grand, the narrator of Toussaint's novel will struggle manfully against his condition, engaging in a Sisyphean labor that is as noble as it is absurd. By dint of an almost superhuman effort, he succeeds in writing the first two words of his book: "When Musset." Yet when his wife calls him on the telephone and asks him how it's going, he tells her he has written half a page (107). In a charitable perspective, one might suggest that he is motivated in this instance by modesty, rather than by duplicity, because, in his current state, those two words represent volumes.

Squarely facing his block, the narrator tries a variety of ways to negotiate it, each resulting in defeat: "In the days that followed, I no longer tried to work quite as systematically on my essay. I chose instead an angle of attack that was less voluntary, more diffused, more subterranean" (164). But that subterranean strategy will not avail, either—and we recognize in any case that the literature of our time is littered with the bodies of underground men. Upon her return from Italy, Delon comments upon her husband's work, with the awesome trenchancy that spouses of academics habitually display. Speaking of their young son, she remarks, "At the rate you're writing, he'll be an adult by the time it's published" (254). The reader of *La Télévision* is perhaps less sanguine still than Delon, for the final pages of the novel portray the narrator trying to write in his study with not one, but two TVs braying in the background.

Jean-Philippe Toussaint, for his part, demonstrates quite a bit of sympathy toward his character, even at those moments when the narrator is the vector of the author's sharpest ironies. That sympathy hinges on the task they share, writing, and specifically upon the issue of writing as work. In an interview that appeared in 1994, Toussaint responded to a question about the way he writes with the following comments:

> I write in a more or less definitive way, and I take an awfully long time over the beginning; It's always the most elaborate, most reread, most revised part. I remember that for *L'Appareil-photo (The Camera)* I spent more than a month on the first paragraph. In spite of the fact that I already had my inaugural idea: to juxtapose two independent and rather uninteresting events. After four months, I had just about written the first part. Thereafter, and each time it's practically the same, everything came together until the rapid acceleration of the end. Then I write much faster. But since I always need to feel like it's a question of a quest [*une recherche*], when things begin to come too easily, I call a halt to the book. (Ammouche-Kremers 28-29)

Several things are worthy of note here. Toussaint's avowal of the difficulties he experiences in the liminal phase of his novels is particularly pungent when one reads it in juxtaposition with *La Télévision:* one might suggest that the narrator's struggles in that novel are a kind of *demonstratio ad
absurdam* of the process that Toussaint describes here. His remarks about the
rhythm of his writing are interesting, also. To the degree that that rhythm
accelerates, Toussaint becomes suspicious of his writing. Writing must not
come easily, he argues, invoking implicitly the aesthetic principle of *difficulté
vaincue;* it is only through a laborious negotiation with difficulty that good
writing can come about. Toussaint believes firmly that writing must be a
recherche. Surely the Proustian overtones of that word are not lost on him,
and I think it is legitimate to assume that he intends it to designate a dynamic of rigorous inquiry and innovation, a very deliberate, painstaking itinerary of literary experimentation that cannot concede anything at all to the
facile. Briefly stated, Toussaint conceives writing in a resolutely materialist
perspective: not as vocation, nor as a matter of inspiration, but rather as hard
work.

He insists more directly upon that notion at other points in the interview. "Until now," he says for instance, "everything has always come to me
through work. Thus, I would decide to begin writing; I would get ready,
would get up early, would sit down at my desk and force myself to remain
there" (Ammouche-Kremers 29). Toussaint's vision of writing here recalls
Stendhal's celebrated prescription, "Twenty lines a day, genius or not."[9] For
Toussaint, it is essential that the process of writerly work be inscribed in the
text itself, at every level. Each of his novels, from *La Salle de bain* onward,
deals with that issue, if in somewhat different manners; and some, like *La
Télévision,* offer a figured chronicle of writing as work. Speaking of *La
Réticence,* for example, Toussaint remarks: "I see that book as a metaphor of
creation; as a metaphor of the writer's work, of his imagination" (Ammouche-
Kremers 31). As Toussaint plots it out carefully on the local maps of his texts,
such a strategy goes beyond the more familiar devices of metaliterary discourse, I believe, insofar as it focuses closely upon the literal, material—and
apparently trivial—gestures of writing. For the crucial question in Toussaint's
novels is how one coaxes words to roost upon a page.

Or, in the case of the narrator of *La Télévision,* how one fails to accomplish that. To all appearances, Toussaint relies on the rhetorical force of counterexample in this novel, ironically comparing his experience of writing with that of his narrator. Yet by his own account, Toussaint is no stranger to writer's block. When asked about his current projects, a couple of years after the publication of *La Réticence,* Toussaint had this to say:

> After *La Réticence,* I no longer had the desire to write, I even experienced a kind of disgust sometimes. [. . .] For the last year and a half, not only have I written nothing, but I find writing, even writing a letter, extremely painful. If once I entertained the idea of a certain perfection in writing, today I'm seeking a kind of nonacademic awkwardness which, paradoxically, seems to be even more difficult to attain. (Ammouche-Kremers 35)

In light of that confession, would it be stretching the point to suggest that, in addition to the considerations I have outlined thus far, *La Télévision* is also a story about Toussaint's own struggle with writer's block? If one accepts that hypothesis, it becomes clear that Toussaint describes his narrator's dilemma from a special vantage point, one in which proximity and distance alternate in canny ways. On the one hand, Toussaint invites us to feel the anguish that a writer experiences when the words won't come, dwelling minutely on the excruciating tortures of failure. On the other hand, that account is mediated by the figure of the narrator who, after all, despite the fact that he resembles his creator in certain key regards, is not Toussaint himself. Moreover, the fact that we are holding the novel in our hands serves as the surest guarantor that Toussaint, unlike his narrator, ultimately found a way to overcome his writerly dilemma.

The problem of writer's block is heavily mediated, too, by the fact that Toussaint packages it in a wrapping of comedy. From the beginning, humor has been his signature, a puckish, absurdist sort of humor that leavens even the most dire of the traumas that assail his characters.[10] In *La Télévision,* the comic dimension of Toussaint's discourse is closely organized and framed as a structural principle, because Toussaint stages his novel—and the capital issue of writing itself—very deliberately as a *game.* Like Johan Huizinga before him, Toussaint realizes that literature is fundamentally ludic in nature;[11] and he recognizes, too, the formidable advantages that ludic systems offer, precisely as laboratories of *recherche*. They allow people to test ideas in a circumscribed field of inquiry, according to a set of protocols, in a manner that is both useful and amusing.

Games are meant to be played, of course, and *La Télévision* is no exception. Here, the players are author and reader: they interact in the ludic economy of the text in a dynamic of exchange, sometimes in a collaborative way, sometimes in apparent competition. Like any game, this novel is governed by a set of rules.[12] They might be articulated as follows. First, we shall examine certain phenomena, for instance television and literature, the prolixity of the one medium and the relative muteness of the other, popular culture and elite culture, sloth and work, facility and constraint, aesthetic sterility and creativity. Then we shall turn each of those things inside out and vex them individually and severally against each other. At the end of that process (and here is the leap of faith for any reader who accepts the ludic contract that Toussaint tenders) we will decide who wins. Obviously, Toussaint constructs the rules of this game to his advantage; but many of us (and not least those of us in academe) know that games are often rigged, yet we can take considerable pleasure in them nonetheless. For Toussaint is a most savant gamesman,[13] and he realizes that the stakes are too high in this case to leave the result to mere chance. As we push the various tokens around the board of this novel, it gradually becomes clear that we are being asked to adjudicate an issue that goes well beyond the limits of the game we've been playing so agreeably, the question of whether literature can continue to prosper as a cultural form, or not.

Dominique Fisher sees in Toussaint's early novels a "hyperparodic writing which, not without humor, shows that it's in its end, in its own death, that the novel can exist and continue to be written" (628), and I feel that *La Télévision* contains the same sort of survivalist message. Through the narrator's unequal contest with TV and his fitful endeavors to write a book on Titian, Toussaint plays out a drama that may be read by any writer—and particularly any academic writer—as a cautionary tale. Through the immediate example of his own writing, he adumbrates a ludic parable of literature, speculating upon literature's limits and possibilities on a contemporary cultural horizon where the value of literature is no longer taken as axiomatic, but on the contrary must be demonstrated afresh with each new literary gesture. In the mutual, playful articulation of those examples, what slowly takes shape in *La Télévision,* dimly at first and as if in profile, is a moral lesson that should have been obvious from the start, and which Toussaint offers, with wild surmise and considerable astonishment, both to himself and to us: if you *work* at it long enough and hard enough, any piece of writing will come to an end—even this one.

NOTES

[1] Many of Toussaint's critics have commented on the theme of immobility in his work. See for instance Bertho 19; Caldwell 369 and 373; Delannoi 1198-1200; Fisher 618; Leclerc, "Abstraction" 891 and "Autour" 68; Motte "Toussaint's Small World" 755-56; Prince "L'Appareil récit de Jean-Philippe Toussaint" 110; Taminiaux 91; and Westphal 122. See also Toussaint's remarks about the role of that theme in his first novel, *La Salle de bain* (Ammouche-Kremers 31).

[2] On the use of the photographic image in Toussaint's early novels, see Fauvel 38-39 and Taminiaux 87-93.

[3] See the inaugural words of *La Société du spectacle (The Society of the Spectacle):* "The entire life of societies in which modern consitions of production reign displays itself as an immense accumulation of *spectacles.* Everything that had once been directly lived has now faded into a representation."

[4] On the way the spectacle "inverts" reality, see Debord 11-12.

[5] See Motte "Toussaint's Small World" 750-52 on the representation of banality in *La Salle de bain;* and Fisher, who analyzes the construction of a "daily hyperreal" (621) in Toussaint's first three novels.

[6] Or so I'm told. For my part, I have never seen *Baywatch*—and certainly would not admit it if I had.

[7] Dominique Fisher has commented incisively upon that phenomenon in Toussaint's early novels: "The mediation of reference by the screen or the windowpane leads to an 'atopos of the imaginary' similar to that which Buci-Glucksmann alludes to in *La Folie du voir* (The Madness of Sight). Thus, vision in Toussaint's texts is always obturated by windowpanes. The windowpane works like a screen; it is the double space of the disappearance of the subject and the object" (620).

[8] On the importance of mirror scenes in Toussaint's *La Salle de bain* and *L'Appareil-photo,* see Motte "Toussaint's Small World" 759 and Taminiaux 93, respectively.

[9] See also the intriguing way Harry Mathews puts that dictum into practice in *20 Lines a Day.*

[10] On humor in Toussaint's work, see Leclerc, "Abstraction" 898 and "Autour" 71-72. Toussaint himself has said he was afraid that the comic nature of his writing would prevent him from being accepted at the Editions de Minuit, and that he was relieved to learn that Jérôme Lindon, the head of that publishing house, has a great taste for humor: "Finally, I was lucky that this book [*La Salle de bain*] suited his taste, which was rather surprising. I loved Beckett and some of the Minuit authors, but the reputation of that publishing house seemed to me frankly too intellectual, that is, a little too serious. But in fact Lindon loves humor" (Ammouche-Kremers 27-28).

[11] See Huizinga 119: "The function of the poet still remains fixed in the play-sphere where it was born. *Poiesis,* in fact, is a play-function. It proceeds within the play-ground of the mind, in a world of its own which the mind creates for it. There things have a very different physiognomy from the ones they wear in 'ordinary life', and are bound by ties other than those of logic and causality."

[12] See Roy Caldwell's insightful remark about Toussaint's first four novels: "Even more than Robbe-Grillet's, Toussaint's narratives appear ludic, that is, governed by arbitrary rules, symmetrical, ritualistic" (371). On play in Toussaint, see also Fisher 628; Leclerc, "Abstraction" 896; and Westphal 119.

[13] Yvan Leclerc points out, tantalizingly enough, that Toussaint won the Junior World Championship of *Scrabble* in 1973 ("Abstraction" 896).

X

∾

Lydie Salvayre's Lecture

Among all the writers whom I have considered here, Lydie Salvayre is perhaps the one who is the least well-known, with the possible exception of Eric Laurrent. The daughter of Republican refugees from the Spanish Civil War, Salvayre is a psychiatrist who practices in Toulouse. She has published eight novels thus far, beginning with *La Déclaration* (1990; The Declaration). The stories she tells deal with different sorts of people, each one grappling with a different sort of situation. *La Déclaration,* for instance, focuses on a man whose wife has left him, and who is gradually losing his mind. The heroine of *La Vie commune* (1991; Everyday Life) is a young woman named Suzanne who works as a secretary, and whom office politics threaten to overwhelm.[1] An end-of-year awards ceremony in a factory furnishes the scene for *La Médaille* (1993; *The Award*), as bosses and various corporate sycophants croak the praises of their "best" workers. In *La Puissance des mouches* (1995; The Power of Flies), a convicted murderer reflects upon his life and crime from his prison cell. *La Compagnie des spectres* (1997; The Company of Specters) tells the story of a young woman living with her elderly mother, on the day a process-server arrives to evict them from their apartment for failure to pay the rent; and *Quelques conseils utiles aux élèves huissiers* (1997; Some Useful Advice for Apprentice Process-Servers) returns to that story, telling it this time from the very different point of view of the process-server. In *La Conférence de Cintegabelle* (1999; The Cintegabelle Lecture), a man delivers a lecture on the virtues of conversation to an audience of friends and neighbors in a small town in the provinces. *Les Belles Ames* (2000; Worthy Souls) is a scathing satire about a group of liberal-minded bourgeois who set off on a bus tour to visit the grimmest slums in Europe.

As diverse as their settings may be, Salvayre's novels are strikingly similar in structure and technique, for each one, with the lone exception of *La Médaille,* is narrated monologically and in the first person by its protagonist. (*La Médaille* is "serially monological," as it were, presenting a series of eight award speeches, followed by the laureates' responses.) They are unrelieved discourses, too, starkly univocal narratives where the one voice that speaks is grounded only very tenuously in the broader discursive context of the surrounding world. One might describe them as talking cures, if only there were a prospect of a cure at the end—but that prospect, in every case, seems at best only dim. Irony of the most astringent sort characterizes all of Salvayre's novels from beginning to end, and it is carefully deployed in multiple levels, such that each level questions and vexes the ones that are contiguous to it. In short, Lydie Salvayre's novels are "difficult" texts. Yet they are rich and rewarding ones also, for a variety of reasons, and notably because of the implicit suggestions they offer about the directions that the novel might pursue as the twentieth century stands aside, making way for the twenty-first.

I would like to close my discussion of the French novel since 1990 with a consideration of *La Conférence de Cintegabelle.* I have placed this book in the final position in my own book for a couple of reasons. One is obvious and quite trivially administrative: I have organized my chapters according to the publication date of the novels I have looked at, and *La Conférence de Cintegabelle* is the most recent among them. The other reason is less immediately apparent, and far more subjectivist. More than any other text I have dealt with here, Salvayre's novel seems to me to anticipate the critical act, calling it into question before the fact. It leaves rather little room for the interpretive gesture, and coerces that gesture in interesting ways. The play of irony in the text is so abundant that it becomes hard to say anything reasonably straightforward about it, as if the irony in the novel itself might ineluctably contaminate any reading one might wish to propose. This is a novel that deals centrally with what we choose to say, and how we choose to say it. Moreover, it addresses that issue through counterexample, granted that the lecturer in the text is by no means a master of his art. I am persuaded nonetheless that what *La Conférence de Cintegabelle* has to say about speech, and speeches, however duplicitously it may say it, has intriguing implications for that variety of speech which we call the novel—and also, it seems to me, for the language of literary criticism.

Allow me to describe the setting of *La Conférence de Cintegabelle* in the briefest of terms. The protagonist, who remains anonymous throughout the novel, is a man in his sixties who lives in a small municipality in the Haute Garonne, near the Pyrenees, a town that one can actually find on the map (if one has an excellent map). His wife, we learn, has died two months ago—and we will learn much more about her, too, in the course of the novel, but only gradually, and in bits and pieces. He takes the floor in a common room of the town hall of Cintegabelle in order to deliver a lecture on the topic of "conversation," and begins his remarks in the following manner: "Take a French dinner. In Paris. At the Armand restaurant. A chic dinner. Like I never attend. Pearls, crystal, and all the trimmings," he says. "Look at the guests. Scientifically. They turn to the right and to the left. Nod their heads. Execute with their right arms the repeated gestures known as pronation. Devote themselves to mastication, mouths closed, I hasten to add. And between two mouthfuls of very small volume, I must note, agitate their lips continuously. Like this" (9).

Several things might be observed about this incipit. First, the style of address: the use of the second person plural in the imperative establishes an exhortative tone that will characterize everything that follows. What the lecturer—I call him that for lack of a better name—will offer his audience is nothing less than a *suasoria*. To the reader opening this novel for the first time, however, it is not immediately clear that this man is speaking to an audience; and that reader might well feel, initially at least, that the man's remarks are addressed to him or her. On one level, of course, this is the case, for Salvayre has constructed her text in such a fashion that we readers must "listen" to the man's lecture through the transparent mediation of the audience, reacting to it along with them and sharing their increasing bewilderment. This is one of the most interesting aspects of *La Conférence de Cintegabelle,* and I will have more to say about it later. The choice of a dinner as the inaugural image of his lecture is a considered one: clearly, the lecturer wishes to evoke the Platonic tradition of the symposium, a gathering characterized by food, drink, and the free exchange of potent ideas. In this case, however, those ideas will be exclusively his own. Finally, as the lecturer calls upon his audience to imagine the continual flapping of lips around the dinner table, and obligingly illustrates that same phenomenon himself, he introduces the subject that he will address: conversation.

In his view, conversation is an art, and one which is moreover preeminently French. Yet he fears that such an art is on the decline, and consequently also the country which has given it its most noble expression: "Conversation is going to the dogs, and our country also, together" (11). Unremedied, this tendency will lead to the very gravest of consequences: "The death of conversation announces the death of Man" (32). What the lecturer will propose to those hardy souls of Cintegabelle who have come to hear him is nothing short of a project of conversational—and thus national—revival:

> Herewith, dear citizens of Cintegabelle, is my plan of rescue, conceived in the greatest urgency, and whose national utility I don't hesitate to claim, for, proposing to resuscitate the brilliance of speech in the eyes of a world that has forgotten how to speak, it intends to accomplish nothing less than the civic renewal of our country, and the regilding of its escutcheon, let me catch my breath, such that, armed with reconquered prestige, the France of tomorrow may assure in the entire world the civilizing mission for which, throughout time, it has been responsible. (11-12)

Alas, the task that awaits him is an arduous one, and at times the lecturer feels like a lone voice crying in the desert. He has witnessed the decline of conversation not only on the national level, but also—and perhaps more deplorably still—on the local level. He has carried out a sort of conversational census among his fellow citizens of Cintegabelle, the results of which are very bleak indeed: "After having subtracted jabberers, squawkers, speechifiers, soliloquists, and other cacophonists, we have been able to establish that only 48 persons engage in the art of conversation, of whom 42 do so pleasantly, 5 with talent, 1 with genius, I'll let you guess who" (88). Well there's the rub, obviously: if there exists only one genial conversationalist in all of Cintegabelle, where in the world may he turn? For it takes two to tango, after all, and likewise two to converse.

That consideration is deeply intricated in the first and most pernicious of the ironies that color *La Conférence de Cintegabelle*. What the lecturer is calling for is dialogue; yet he is calling for it in a manner that is unrelentingly monological. Apart from a very few questions from the audience toward the end of his lecture, which the lecturer repeats in his own voice, and dismisses out of hand (effectively preventing any possibility of real dialogue), his words are the only things to be heard in the room. Like Louis-René des Forêt's "Bavard," this is a man who can claim to exist only by virtue of the words he pronounces. Ceasing to speak, he would also cease to be. In that perspective, the actual meaning of his speech is only of secondary importance: what really matters is to keep speaking. Happily enough, the lecturer is equal to that task (if perhaps not to certain others) because his logorrhea knows no bounds. The famous totemic phrase that echoes throughout Raymond Queneau's *Zazie dans le métro (Zazie)* (and uttered by the parrot, Laverdure), "You chat, said Laverdure, you chat, it's all you know how to do,"[2] intended by Queneau to draw his reader's attention to the fundamental emptiness of the kind of language that we habitually use, might well find its ultimate and most felicitous expression in this man. Certainly, his audience is bombarded mercilessly with a flow of increasingly nonsensical language—and, with them, the reader.

To the lecturer's very particular way of thinking, however, words (and most especially his own) constitute a capital, one which must be judiciously husbanded, invested, and made to fructify. Among all of the words in the lexicon, moreover, those which the lecturer prefers are the "big" words: "For I am ridiculous to that extent: I like big words. I like big words when they designate big things" (39). Everywhere he looks, he sees people squandering that capital in irresponsible ways, and notably in the domain of contemporary literature:

> The preceding assertion might seem to be a perfidious attack against certain modern writers whose depth of thought and whose cultural capital, I like that expression, merely uttering it I feel rich, but that feeling never lasts very long, whose cultural—and more particularly syntactic—capital is reduced to mere pocket change. But God forfend that we should despise them! We are friends to all the poor! (20)

Rich man, poor man: blithely oblivious to the howling syntax that he himself inflicts upon his listeners, the lecturer will develop his metaphor in several ways during the course of his remarks, in the hope that it will produce satisfying dividends. Conversation, he argues, reduces the deficit of the National Health System since, making people happier, it renders them less prone to the various illnesses to which unhappy people habitually fall prey; cancer, for instance, strikes mostly those people who are conversationally deficient (23-24).

Yet not all of the capital he possesses is metaphorical in character. He mentions on one occasion that he has recently come into some money, alluding coyly to "a moralist of the seventeenth century whose complete works we recently bought, thanks to our small capital" (29). Further along, the source of his windfall becomes clear: "Moreover, I am in the process of constituting an exceptional library, I say that without false modesty. In two months I bought, at the Ombres Blanches bookstore, 300 works, at least. Thanks to the little legacy which I inherited and to my little widower's pension. Viduity has certain consolations, let's be clear about that" (84-85). As miserable as he may feel after his wife's death, then, he does nevertheless manage to find some modest consolation in his new state, and if he recognizes that life is short, he also believes that art is long. It should be noted, too, that the lecturer's investment strategy is very deliberate and precise. In a gesture that is nothing short of alchemical, he transforms his financial capital into cultural capital. He wastes no time in investing *that* capital in an enterprise where it will produce immediate results, that is, in his own lecture.

He peppers his remarks liberally with allusions to noble figures from the distant (and sometimes less-distant) past, among them Homer, Confucius, Democritus, Diogenes, Seneca, Quintilian, Epictetus, Petronius, Dante, Cervantes, Balthasar Gracián, Fénelon, Jonathan Swift, Laurence Sterne, Kant, Saint-Simon, Herman Melville, and Julien Gracq. "A brief quotation, from time to time, doesn't hurt," he says in his defense. "True or false, it doesn't matter. But antique, if possible" (79-80). The lecturer flits adroitly from one to another of these figures, never alighting on them for very long, pausing just long enough to gather the pollen he needs for his own purposes. One may wonder if his labors are not largely in vain, however, since the only time a member of his audience asks him a question about a literary figure is when a certain Madame Basile asks him if he has met Barbara Cartland (105).[3] From time to time, as if in an access of conscience, the lecturer ponders his own allusional practice, wondering if he is on firm ground: "I'm not quite sure of what I'm telling you, and I'm simply repeating what I've read in some books, like every lecturer does, it fleshes things out" (73).

His lecture is leavened (in his view, at least, if not in that of his audience) with many aphorisms—or "axioms," as he calls them, in order to emphasize the logical character of his argument. "I rather like axioms," he confesses early on in his talk (14); and his audience will have ample opportunity to confirm that assertion. He has found his inspiration in his reading of the classical and neoclassical moralists, and his aphoristic practice, while it falls short of outright plagiary, goes well beyond mere *imitatio*. In the accretion of these utterances, the lecturer intends that his passionate brief for conversation should become limpidly apparent: "Conversation implies the activity of the senses and the stimulation of sex" (30); "In conversation to remain silent and to speak are one and the same thing" (40); "In conversation, politeness ends where maliciousness begins" (52); "Conversation despises purple, the corrupted form of red" (58); "Conversation is insomniac. It forbids the word to fall asleep" (81); "Conversation is a moss that grows between paving stones, to separate them" (81); "Conversation is a fire that can grow and inflame the entire world" (89); "Conversation is a dangerous aphrodisiac for good manners" (98). It's a heady brew that he offers his listeners, however, and they may perhaps be forgiven if they become intoxicated by it.

In the exiguous—but truly welcome—interstices of his jeremiad, the lecturer allows certain personal anecdotes to escape. In that manner, as if unwittingly and despite himself, he tells his audience the story of his life. This is by no means the least interesting narrative thread in *La Conférence de Cintegabelle,* particularly when it is a question of the life the lecturer led until very recently with his wife, Lucienne. He alludes to her throughout his lecture, obliquely at first, mentioning "the day of the funeral" (9) and evoking shortly thereafter "Lucienne's death" without much elaboration (10). He senses that his audience didn't come to hear him speak about his wife, however, and he quickly returns to his subject: "But let us stifle our grief. And let us return to that dinner with which I inaugurated my lecture" (10). Thankfully enough, his resolution will prove to be weak, for a good deal of the hermeneutic code in this novel hinges upon the story of Lucienne, rather than upon anything the lecturer may have to say about the lost art of conversation. That is, the narrative sweetmeats concerning Lucienne which the lecturer scatters here and there serve to pique his listeners' appetites; and they may help to persuade the readers of *La Conférence de Cintegabelle* that what we have here is a novel, rather than a lecture. Apparently interrupting his discourse on conversation, these anecdotes actually serve to make it palatable; and if there is a "story" in this novel, it is most certainly the story of Lucienne.

We learn that Lucienne—"Poor old woman!" (22)—was born in a Spanish village named Fatarella in 1940, and that she died in that same village on the second of January, 1999, just two months before the present time of the narrative.[4] The lecturer won her heart not by virtue of his physical charms, which are by his own admission modest ones, but rather by the irresistible seductiveness of his speech: "Myself, for example, I'm not particularly attractive, with a cowlick on my head that takes hours to comb down, and big ears, yet in Lucienne's eyes, even though she was indifferent to poetry and disinclined toward linguistic acrobatics, I earned an immediate success whenever I began to babble" (15). *Mirabile dictu!* Moreover, that first seduction clearly promises another, for the lecturer will wager on his words, and his words alone, in his efforts to win over his public in Cintegabelle.

As he describes it, his life with Lucienne was an uninterrupted—if tragically abridged—idyll: "Lucienne and I, though very different, were as one" (28). Yet his audience apprehends gradually that certain moments of their life were somewhat less than blissful, and most particularly when it was a question of physical union. Lucienne was morbidly obese, the lecturer mentions, and their sexual gambols consequently necessitated more than a little ingenuity, especially in their early years together:

> Given the difference in our weight and our total lack of experience, penetration, in fact, proved to be very difficult. First, the ascent was arduous. I slipped several times, but each time caught by her magnificent arms. Having attained the central plateau, I held on lopsidedly for a while, before I succeeded in steadying myself, with my feet wedged against her knees. As to the coupling

205 ᠙ Lydie Salvayre's Lecture

itself, we had to try a variety of techniques. Her beneath and me above. Necessarily. In view of our respective bulks. First, in the same direction. Then head to toe. A horror, from the point of view of the scenery. And once again in the same direction. My tact prevents me from saying more. (100)

Thank heavens for tact, without which this confession might have wandered from the poetic register into the merely sordid.

Like many romantic heroines, Lucienne's days were shortened by a wasting disease. Gradually but ineluctably, she became paralyzed. She progressively lost her powers of speech, too, toward the end being capable of uttering merely groans and wails, so that her husband found himself sadly obliged to gag her; Lucienne's gaze was so wild, moreover, that the lecturer saw no other recourse than to blindfold her (30). Having journeyed to Paris to begin negotiations with publishers who might be interested in the text of his lecture, the lecturer returned home to find his wife in a stage-four coma (111). She expired shortly thereafter, and though her husband had ordered a specially-made coffin, Lucienne's imposing body proved as difficult to embier as it was, while she yet lived, to embrace: "We had to try several times before we were able to lift her body, whose cadaverous rigidity resisted our maneuvers. We succeeded on the fifth try. Taking a big breath, one! two! three! alley oop! Just like throwing the shotput! Poor dear!" (106).

Reflecting nostalgically on the life they shared, the lecturer remarks with chagrin on one occasion that Lucienne lived her whole life through without experiencing the joys of conversation, and that even during their halcyon years she was never very loquacious: "For, as considerable as her backside was, so too were her words few" (35). Indeed, her vocabulary was constituted by a mere hundred words or so (which may explain why she was so taken with the lecturer's own eloquence); and among those, the words "stomach" and "lottery" gradually attained preeminence. Lucienne also, sad to say, favored vulgar, crude words; and the lecturer fondly recalls that she used to call his more extravagant philosophical pronouncements "unprickables" (55). From time to time, marshaling her lexical resources efficiently, Lucienne would tell her husband that he was "grotesque," or that he was good for nothing (18, 51). Sometimes, she would urge him to temper his own loquacity:

Shut the hell up, she would yell at me, shoving me in the back whenever I sought to lead her through the meanders of pure abstraction. Shut your yap, she would howl at me, until I gave up and begged her pardon. To such an extent that I stopped submitting my transcendental cogitations to her. In order not to frighten her anymore, my timid dear. Then I stopped speaking to her at all. It was simpler. We would only say essential things to each other. Expressions such as: I'm tired, I'm hungry; or interjections like: I'll get you, you dirty worm. In short, we were beginning to touch upon the subliminal. Like in modern novels. (84)

If there was one thing alone that troubled their union, in the lecturer's view, it was the fact that Lucienne always prevented him from buying books, fearing that it would ruin his health—and, not incidentally, their bank account. That small point of contention gradually assumed larger proportions for the lecturer because, as he puts it, "I place the life of the mind well above everything else, and literature well above my Lucienne. Just like great men do" (48). More than anything else, perhaps, that is what finally led him to dream of "a different life, a venerable custom with poets, a life without Lucienne, to be entirely frank, a refined life where conversation would be an art, and poetry one's daily bread" (116).

Little by little, then, the story of Lucienne emerges. It is a tale of a woman driven to distraction—and ultimately death—by her own husband's speech. It is just possible to wonder, moreover, if a more direct agency was not involved in her demise, and if one were cynical enough to raise the question of *qui bono,* one would have to take a long, hard look at the lecturer himself. Stepping back from that dizzying inferential precipice, one consideration about Lucienne's story seems to me abundantly clear: it offers a particularly edifying example of the effects of the lecturer's maunderings upon those who must listen to them.

Salvayre stages certain other examples of that phenomenon in her novel, but she does so with parsimony, and they are few and far between. Patently, this lecturer is a man who does not easily suffer interruption. Early on in his remarks, he takes part of his audience to task in a stern call to order: "I implore you, children, not to snicker. And not to move your chairs. It's annoying" (12). It is perhaps not so much the noisy chairs that puts him off his feed as the laughter, for he is proposing his comments in a spirit of the utmost sobriety. When despite himself his lecture strikes his listeners as comic, he parries their misplaced hilarity manfully: "I know, that makes you laugh, and it won't be the last time" (28). He is well aware that his is a voice crying in the wilderness, and it becomes apparent that his prophecy of the imminent death of conversation (and thus that of civilization itself) has upon occasion been greeted still less indulgently than in the present circumstance: "This risk of death that I am alone in postulating in such an unvarnished way has prompted certain people to claim that I am merely retarded" (32).

Retarded or not, he is astute enough to realize that from time to time the rapturous attentiveness that he has worked so hard to instill in his listeners threatens to erode, and he takes immediate steps to repair it, appealing suavely to their sense of national pride: "I can see that you're getting restless. You burn with impatience. As if you had come only to hear me speak about love. Well, sirs and madams, that proves simply this: you're truly French" (95-96). At other moments, he senses that his argument has not been met with the sort of unanimous approbation he has hoped for: "What? What's happening? Suddenly I read on your faces an air of skepticism that I find rather unpleasant" (89). At moments like this, when he reads his listeners' response and finds that it verges dangerously on the critical, the lecturer's solution is to forge ahead, cranking up the level of his rhetoric a lusty notch or two, relying on the sheer force of his eloquence to seduce his public, just like he seduced (though admittedly in a past now long behind him) Lucienne. To his credit, the lecturer graciously accepts certain extemporaneous interventions from the audience— but only when they are uncritical, and thus do not threaten his authority. Most welcome of all are the questions that serve to reinforce that authority, like the one posed by the kindly Madame Piche: "Madame Piche raises her hand? Madame Piche wishes to know what an epithalamium is? It's a nuptial poem, my dear lady. A lost tradition. Alas. Alas" (101); though it must be noted, too, that the lecturer is quick to extinguish the possibility of real dialogue each time it threatens to inflame his listeners, reappropriating his right to discursive primacy in a manner that will brook no opposition.

In short, his tactics are those of a terrorist; and though the arms he uses are exclusively verbal in character, they are no less effective for all that. All

things considered—that is, in view of the fact that his subject is relatively re-
condite for the good citizens of Cintegabelle, that his presentation is turgid
and stultifying, and that his personality is by no means a magnetic one—the
lecturer does an admirable job in controlling his audience. Less patient folk,
one imagines, would have stampeded out of the hall after a few minutes of
this nonsense, but the lecturer succeeds in keeping his fellow townspeople in
their seats until the bitter end. This is all the more astonishing because the
lecturer, despite his apparent bravura, is not immune to self-doubt. "I feel that
I'm getting bogged down," he admits, when finding himself caught on the
horns of a dangerously mixed metaphor of his own invention, "Like each
time I try to think" (18). Elsewhere, having lost himself in an immoderately
bitter castigation of certain particularly vile categories of people, among them
professors, bankers, catechists, viragos, and druids of different stripes, he goes
so far as to apologize to his audience: "Excuse me, I'm overstepping the bounds.
For a lecturer of my distinction, that's a bummer" (68). Yet these difficult
moments are fleeting, and in each instance the lecturer rapidly recovers his
sang-froid and, with it, his lofty sense of purpose.

Anyone who has suffered through a truly lousy lecture—and anyone
who has delivered such a lecture, for that matter—will be forced, at the very
least, to admire the lecturer's pluck. Like Lucienne's story, the tale of the
lecturer's perseverance has an exemplary character to it. For it is not every
speaker that can hold an audience spellbound. Even the President of the French
Republic, as accomplished an orator as he may be, might envy such an accom-
plishment. Having listened to many of the President's speeches on television,
the lecturer is forced to admit that the man has a certain style: "He spoke
calmly, as befits a President, but there was something in his face that made
you feel that he was on the verge of swearing, ranting, and throwing the
mircophone out the window" (115). He remarks that though the President is
a man of very little culture, and though his speeches are largely vacuous, he
nonetheless succeeds in rendering himself sympathetic to the French public.
With one notable exception, however, for the lecturer remembers that
Lucienne's reactions, each time she heard the President speak, were somewhat less enthusiastic. She would gloss the President's remarks, the lecturer
recalls, with a running critical commentary, in terms that were staggeringly

coarse: "Go ahead and fart! yelled Lucienne, addressing herself to the President, you'll feel better!" (116). This, too, is an exemplary moment in the narrative economy of *La Conférence de Cintegabelle,* and it performs interesting
maneuvers, both on the intradiegetical and the extradiegetical levels. On the
one hand, as an anecdote that the lecturer recounts to his audience, it offers
them a dangerous example of the way listeners might respond to a speech that
is less than enthralling, particularly to a speech as flatulent as his own. On the
other hand, and by the same sort of gesture, Salvayre is addressing her own
audience here, above and beyond the long-suffering heads of the Cintegabellois:
the readers of her novel. Through the ironic mediation of different kinds of
listeners (Lucienne, Madame Basile, Madame Piche, and so forth) Salvayre is
cannily conditioning the manner in which her readers receive this text.

Each question that Salvayre implicitly raises—What gives the lecturer
the right to speak? Where in the world is he going in his lecture? Why do the
Cintegabellois politely hear him out? Why might one choose to listen to somebody who has nothing to say?—becomes a heated one when it is vexed against
the fabric of her own writerly "speech," whose material result is the book we
hold in our hands. It is in that sense that *La Conférence de Cintegabelle* assumes
shape as a fable of the novel, and never more so than when literature itself is
directly and explicitly at issue in the lecturer's remarks. In the time that remains to me (as the lecturer himself might put it) I would like to examine this
metaliterary discourse further.

The lecturer is animated throughout his talk by a firm sense of his own
vocation; and clearly, he feels that his vocation is literary in character. "To
identify the content and manner of men's conversation," he remarks, "would
be to traverse all of France from top to bottom, and to write its entire history,
neither more nor less" (27). His project is thus a vast one, and the role that he
has cast for himself is arduous and singularly privileged: "Quite alone, I am
reshaping the history of French literature, it's my hobby" (39). It is important
to recognize the solitary nature of his quest, as he conceives it. He suggests to
his audience on many occasions during his lecture, with the elephantine coy-
ness that is his trademark, that he alone sees the horizon of French literature
as it really is—"Me. The unique one. The bard of Cintegabelle" (101)—, and
that his fellow citizens are very lucky indeed to have a glimpse of that perspec-

tive, however brief. Yet it is clear, too, that he is speaking not so much for their benefit as for his own. He is, one will recall, the only conversationalist of genius in all of Cintegabelle; and moreover he alone is capable of appreciating the full pungency of the sort of argument he's putting forward here. In short, he is speaking very largely to himself, and he views his audience, at best, as the stage upon which he performs his soliloquy. Of course, the lecturer is not the only literary figure to claim that he works principally for himself.[5]

This curious occlusion of the audience has consequences on another level as well, for through the mediation of the audience the readers of *La Conférence de Cintegabelle* may come to feel that there is rather little room for them here. For my part, I believe that this phenomenon is yet another move in the game that Lydie Salvayre is playing with her readers, as she asks them, ironically and ludically, to consider certain fundamental issues of literary communication: Who "speaks" in literature these days? To what purpose? Who "listens" to that speech? What are the conditions of possibility that currently govern the literary act, both in the dimension of its production and in that of its reception? In that sense, *La Conférence de Cintegabelle* is a test case for the contemporary novel, one which puts that cultural form directly and uncompromisingly on trial, in a text that continually questions the novel as we have come to expect it to *be*.

Thankfully enough, the lecturer is not utterly solipsistic in his literary vision. If some small part of his vision should perchance become clear to those folk who listen to him, so much the better. He emphasizes moreover that he has more—far more—to say on the subject than he has chosen, and he alludes (harrowingly enough) to other "treatises" that he is even now meditating: "Three of them await me. If the media fallout, national as well as international, of this lecture leaves me any breathing room" (56-57). Moreover, he is not adverse to making his thoughts available to an audience beyond the confines of Cintegabelle; and it is with this goal in mind that he traveled to Paris. Confident of finding there a publisher farsighted enough to recognize the literary merit of his lecture, he encountered only indifference: "Having gone up, as one says, to Paris, to offer the text of this lecture, which you are the very first to hear, to the most eminent publishers, I was met with no less than seventeen rejections" (48). His experience among another species of literati, pro-

fessional writers, was equally disappointing to him, and he evokes his "meeting with those great men, writers" (48) with bitter irony. Having successfully
insinuated himself into a literary cocktail party (thanks to the benevolent in-
tercession of a "regional writer" friend of his), and thinking that he had finally
attained the epicenter of the only cultural world that he esteems, the lecturer
discovered to his chagrin that "A literary cocktail party is an ugly thing" (104).
The writers there gathered, he found, cordially detested each other, avoiding
each other like the plague. In that sea of misanthropy, the lecturer was astonished to see the writers paying shameless court to one young figure, whose
role was described to him by his friend using a term with which the lecturer
was unfamiliar: "He's an aide, he explained to me, whose function is to distribute laurels and rewards to other writers. In other terms, lots of dough"
(105). Yet the lecturer in his ignorance mistakes *aide* ("aide") for *aède* (a "bard"
of antiquity), demonstrating how far removed he is from the more sordid
reaches of the literary circuit; and when one of his listeners in Cintegabelle
asks the meaning of that term, he obliges her suavely: "The definition of an
aède? Well, Homer was one, Madame Piche" (105).

   During the cocktail party, his attempts to engage his fellow writers in
conversation—an art in which he excels, of course—proved, despite his efforts, unfruitful:

> Having flitted from group to group, I entered into conversation with a poet
> who was cruising through the room, suffering from an existential anguish
> that he was trying vainly to sow among the others. I intended thereby, dear
> friends, to enrich and perfect my discursive register, thinking about the lec-
> ture I was about to deliver to you. To whom do I have the honor of speaking?
> asked the poet, with an expression of nobly suppressed pain. I gave him a brief
> resume of my life and works—necessarily brief, as some cruel souls will un-
> doubtedly say. I'm an author myself, I told him, holding out a hand that, like
> any real poet, he failed to notice. Seeking publisher intention long-term rela-
> tionship, I added saucily, putting my disappointed hand back into my pocket.
> (109)

   When that poet turned his back upon him, the lecturer was obliged to
conclude that writers are very poor conversationalists indeed, and constitute

in fact a dreadfully sycophantic, backbiting, narcissistic breed entirely unlike the one he had imagined: "It's very difficult to talk about literature with literary people. For some are trying merely to survive, others trying to flatter, most of them are vilifying the rest, and all of them are so enamored of their own work that nothing can distract them from it" (110).

The lecturer's experience in Paris only confirmed his suspicion that French literature has fallen into the hands of the Philistines; and he reserves his most vituperative criticism for the contemporary novel, in which he finds nothing but prurience and senseless vulgarity. "Don't guffaw in public," he warns his fellow citizens, "when you hear the words 'cunt,' 'prick,' or 'ass,' like my Lucienne used to do, she who knew how to hide neither her pains nor her pleasures, dear innocent one. Wait, rather, until you can find a moment of solitude to read contemporary novels. Those kind of attributes abound in them" (46). He carefully positions his own literary activity (such as it is) *against* the contemporary novel; and it is in that oppositional mode that he will propose his plan for the renovation of French literature. His own prose will be characterized by the neoclassical values of seemliness and decorum which the lecturer holds so dear; and also by a sense of restraint, judiciously exercised. For, chief among all others, those are the values, he feels, that have been abandoned in contemporary literature:

> When applied to writing, the sense of what's right leads inevitably to the suppression of empty phrases, commonplaces, frills, and turgidity of various kinds. The risk for certain books, you'll say, is that there will only remain an empty husk. But the writers thus concerned should be reassured. The reading public of Cintegabelle, like the international reading public, adores empty husks, as long as they are perfectly innocuous. (72)

In other terms, the lecturer will address the lamentable vacuity of French literature unflinchingly, and fill it up with the plenitude that it once enjoyed. It is to that end that he fills his audience's ears to overflowing, touching on this point, then that one, but never stopping.

There is, however, one vexatious problem to be considered: orality and writing are not quite the same thing. The lecturer recognizes that (if only dimly), and his plea for conversation valorizes the oral over the written. His own eloquence, he feels, will surely persuade his audience that the spoken word can compete effectively with the written. It will be recalled, too, that the lecturer has not much success with the written version of his remarks; and that fact may not be indifferent to the brief for the oral which he offers to the citizens of Cintegabelle. He is confident nonetheless that his lecture will carry the day. He argues that it is only in speech that a man truly reveals himself (here and throughout his remarks, the lecturer gives little or no attention to women), and, framing his argument more radically still, he suggests that a man's speech *is* that man himself, in his entirety (27). Moreover, he has remarked in certain men of letters a deplorable inaptitude for speech: "I have, you see, a friend whose name I'll not mention, a regional writer, a specialist of southwestern French craftsmanship, who, whenever he launches himself into society, gets mixed up, stutters, gazes at his shoes—about which there's nothing really remarkable—in stupefaction, and can only utter Ah and Oh and Umm and sometimes Ha-Ha" (17).[6] Yet orality (and more particularly still, conversation), he warns his audience, entails a special sort of risk: "imbecility is very quickly unmasked therein" (25).

One might be tempted to suggest that such a risk is just as great when it is a question of the written word; and in order to illustrate such a hypothesis, one need look no farther than *La Conférence de Cintegabelle* itself. As utterly unreliable a narrator as the lecturer may be elsewhere in this novel, I believe that we can take him confidently and literally at his word in this case. For through his own words, and in very short order, he declares himself an imbecile—not an idiot, like Eric Chevillard's "Crab," nor a schlemiel, like Eric Laurrent's "Chester," nor yet an antihero like the narrator of Jean-Philippe Toussaint's *La Télévision,* but rather simply an imbecile, a half-bright, wet-brained imbecile. Lydie Salvayre allows the lecturer to give full rein to his imbecility, and she exploits that character trait of his to great advantage. She plays with him constantly, in order precisely to play with her readers. While she engages in many, many kinds of play in this novel, it is worth focusing for a moment on the play of the oral and the written. We have seen what the lecturer has to say about that; and we know, too, that his "authority" (itself an interesting notion in this text) is very dubious at best. Within the fiction that Salvayre elaborates here, orality clearly dominates, since everything we "hear"

214 @v FABLES OF THE NOVEL

is the lecturer's speech; yet, stepping outside of that fiction for the moment, the written far overshadows the oral, because, after all, we are reading a novel. The lecture delivered here is an abysmal one; yet the novel (in my view at least) is an intriguing, potent piece of writing. Salvayre constructs an articulative tension between several sets of complementary poles in *La Conférence de Cintegabelle:* the oral and the written, the fiction and the text, character and author, citizens of Cintegabelle and readers of the novel. She does that in order to amuse us, certainly, but also to prompt us—indeed to coerce us—to reflect upon how we read novels, offering us a text that reads like the negative image of a novel, where most of the conventional gestures of the *romanesque* have been inverted.

Thus she "speaks" to us, knowing that she is writing; and thus we "hear" her, knowing that we are reading. Importantly, the lecturer, too, senses that writing may eventually overcome speech in some fashion. In particular, he knows that some of the younger members of his audience may be tempted to write one day, rather than merely to converse. Though he may deplore that temptation, he nonetheless finds it understandable, and he offers them a bit of advice based on his own experience, couched in a finely honed irony that is undoubtedly lost on them: "If you really want to be a writer, don't dump all of your garbage onto the paper, like writers often do. They have made the air of Paris unbreathable. I have seen it for myself" (25). Elsewhere, he suggests to them that their ill-considered thoughts and jejune reflections are quite nicely suited to contemporary literature, granted the abysmal state into which it has fallen:

> If you have an itch, young folks, to express a few inept opinions (that can happen even to the greatest minds), put them down on paper, rather than saying them aloud. Write a novel, for instance. Or a little essay. Suffice it that they should be published by an editor adept at propaganda, and your ineptitudes will be received as thoughts. You'll be successful. The problem of learning how to converse will no longer trouble you. For everything is forgiven to the man who succeeds. Even idiocy? Certainly. And nastiness? Especially. It's fabulous. Don't you think so? (25)

Returning once again to the notion of culture as capital, the lecturer mentions that whereas in the past the bourgeoisie constructed itself on the backs of the poor, now the intellectual class feeds on its own poor; and clearly, for him, those impoverished souls are the people like you and me who actually *read* contemporary literature: "Let me say in passing that it must be hoped that no government will take the poor away from the intellectuals. Because in filling up their spare time (and intellectuals, you know, don't lack for it), the poor prevent these thinkers from doing damage in other areas" (64). In other terms, the lecturer views literature in its current state as a supplementary activity, one that has renounced the possibility of real consequence in the world, an essentially otiose enterprise produced—and consumed—in vain.[7]

In short, the picture of contemporary literature that he paints is an exceedingly grim one. Obviously, if French culture is to be succored, another form of expression must be found. In the lecturer's view, only conversation can breathe new life into an aesthetically moribund France, just as it has breathed new life into his relationship with Lucienne, for he mentions with evident satisfaction that since her death, "our conversation became ideal" (121). Art—and most particularly the sublime art of conversation—scoffs at death, after all. That is not to say that he doesn't envision the possibility of conversation with the living, too. He closes his remarks in Cintegabelle with a broad and impassioned invitation to dialogue:

> As you can see, I'm bringing my lecture to a brilliant close. I say close, not conclusion, because conclusion is for asses, as Gustave, a cousin, put it, I'm kidding. For now the time to leave each other has come. Ferdinand tells me that it's nine-thirty. Closing time. What can I say to you in closing, my dear friends of Cintegabelle? I'll offer you simply the following advice. Put your coats on, because it's cold outside. Leave the Town Hall. Stride smartly into the Rue Fayol. Walk to the Avenue du Général-Leclerc. Turn left. And go into the Café des Ormes. With or without your dead. I'll wait for you there. To converse. It's the only way to resist.
> Until then. (123)

It's a happy pirouette that the lecturer executes as he leaves the stage, one calculated to confirm in his listeners the impression of an evening of lively debate and warm good fellowship, and to whet their appetites for more of the same to come. It is moreover a deft, elegant way for Lydie Salvayre to end her novel; but it is an ending that nonetheless leaves a certain number of problems in the balance, and I believe that Salvayre leaves them there strategically. Where can "meaning" possibly inhere in this text, which seems so exclusively devoted to the trivial? In other terms, if the lecturer's remarks are very largely meaningless, and if moreover those remarks are the only utterances we "hear" in *La Conférence de Cintegabelle,* what is the point of the novel? For my part, I feel that Salvayre wishes us to read her novel *against* the novel, as it were, in order better to call into question the set of traditions, conventions, and protocols which govern that genre as it is practiced today. *La Conférence de Cintegabelle* is an excellent example of what Ross Chambers has termed "loiterature," that is, writing characterized by digression and dilatoriness, that insistently—and deliberately—distracts. Chambers argues persuasively that "the transvaluation of the trivial is what loiterature is about" (*Loiterature* 34).[8] Other texts that I have considered here (I'm thinking especially of Chevillard's *La Nébuleuse du crabe* and Toussaint's *La Télévision*) similarly promote the trivial and ask us to reconsider the categories of value that subtend contemporary literature. In *La Conférence de Cintegabelle,* however, that promotion is more insistent and unrelieved, and it is foregrounded quite explicitly as one of the novel's themes: "What wind! What smoke! What phrases!" (92).

Such a tactic, carried out as uncompromisingly as Salvayre does, runs the risk of leaving her reader as nonplused as the benighted citizens of Cintegabelle. Salvayre is well aware of that risk, it seems to me, and she alludes to it through the ironic mediation of the lecturer on several occasions, most notably perhaps when the lecturer remarks, "We were saying that there exist, exceptionally, among those exceptional people who are exceptional writers, certain individuals who behave in a suicidal manner" (49). Yet professional hara-kiri is not what Salvayre is after here. Rather, she is attempting to reconfigure the terms according to which we read novels. In point of fact, we cannot read *La Conférence de Cintegabelle* in quite the same way that we might read other novels. As Chambers has suggested, "loiterly writing disarms criticism of itself by presenting a moving target, shifting as its own divided attention constantly shifts" (*Loiterature* 9). Striving to follow the lecturer's endless (and apparently meaningless) digressions, we are constantly confronted with the kinds of choices we make as readers, the various maneuvers and strategies we deploy as we attempt to come to terms with a literary text. In short, as much as anything else, *La Conférence de Cintegabelle* is about us.

The readerly recursiveness that Salvayre foists upon us may bring other considerations to mind, as well. Chief among them is the notion that, as Chambers puts it, "criticism is inevitably contaminated by what it criticizes" (*Loiterature* 50). In the most obvious example of that effect, the multilayered ironies of this novel make it impossible to say anything straightforward about it, as I argued early on in this chapter; and I find that my own reading of this text has been very largely "contaminated" by irony. Yet I believe that effect of contamination is vaster still in *La Conférence de Cintegabelle*. The lecturer delivers a speech here, but what he is actually doing is telling a series of fables, fables about himself and his aspirations, fables about his life with Lucienne, fables about the bankruptcy of contemporary literature. In a similar manner, as we read a novel—any novel, but most obviously and inevitably *this* novel— we tell ourselves fables about our reading. We cast ourselves as the heroes of those fables and allow ourselves to be intrigued by our own readerly peripatetics, by our missteps and occasional bewilderments, by our inferences and assumptions, and by our small triumphs, also. If any text may be said to take shape in the articulation of story and discourse, so too does any reading. As the lecturer shuttles dizzyingly between lecture and fable and back again, it may become apparent that his moves approximate—ironically but nonetheless nicely—the kinds of gestures we engage in as we read a literary text.

Lydie Salvayre recognizes those reciprocities clearly, and wagers firmly upon them as she tells her own fable of the novel and attempts to enlist us therein. Constructing her text as she does, relying upon the force of counterexample and what is left unsaid in this unrelenting tissue of speech, she forces us to read against the grain of her novel, oppositionally, that is, critically—in a mode that bears close affinities to the manner in which she herself writes. For the position that Salvayre takes with regard to contemporary literature is similarly critical, elaborated very largely in the negative mode. Reflecting on what the novel is today, and more pertinently still on what it may become, Salvayre the novelist—the fabulist—delivers a lecture which confirms the promise that her lecturer left largely unfulfilled, insofar as *her* lecture is indeed focused squarely upon conversation. She sees that dialogue as an unbounded one, the kind of "infinite conversation" that Maurice Blanchot described as literature's most fundamental discursive mode. Adopting a stance dramatically different from that of her lecturer, Lydie Salvayre has furnished ample space for the other in the conversation she proposes, a space that her readers may occupy and inhabit, should we choose to accept the invitation which she tenders. In that perspective, the question left suspended at the end of this novel—will the good citizens of Cintegabelle choose to accept the lecturer's invitation to continue this conversation in the Café des Ormes?— echoes still more stridently in the metaliterary register, where writer and reader converse. For, like the other texts I have considered here, and like many other contemporary French novels, that is the choice upon which *La Conférence de Cintegabelle* hinges; and it is just that sort of choice, more broadly conceived, which will determine the fate of the novel as a cultural form.

NOTES

[1] *La Déclaration* and *La Vie commune* were both initially published by the Editions Julliard. They were republished by the Editions Verticales in 1997 and 1999, respectively.

[2] See *Zazie* 22; and also 27-30, 36, 40, 41, 68, 71, 135, 136, 140, 144-47, 152, 170, 177, 181, 185, 187.

[3] Since words and the capital they constitute are at issue for the moment, I would be remiss if I neglected to point out that Barbara Cartland (*pacet* Homer et al.) is listed in the *Guinness Book of World Records* as the bestselling author of all time, having written no less than 623 books and sold no less than 650 million copies.

[4] That fictional present time was calculated by Salvayre to coincide with an event in real time: the copyright registration date of *La Conférence de Cintegabelle* is March 1999.

[5] See for instance Clément Rosset's response to a correspondent who has asked him *why* he writes, since his work seems to proclaim the vanity of writing: "First there's the fact that, even though I 'publish' works and present them as such, without really seeking, moreover, other people's appreciation, I have always written first and foremost for myself, in order to enlighten myself about certain questions that interested and intrigued me in the highest degree. All of my works—and even

this text, which I'm purportedly writing for you, but actually for myself—, are answers conceived by me to questions that I asked myself; and in that perspective I would say, to parody Molière in *Les Femmes savantes,* that 'it's always to myself that I speak'" (*Le Choix des mots* [The Choice of Words] 13-14).

⁶ The man of letters Pascal Quignard would agree with the lecturer: "A writer defines himself simply by this kind of linguistic stupor, which leads most of them, moreover, to be banished from orality" (*Le Nom sur le bout de la langue* [The Name on the Tip of the Tongue] 8). Clément Rosset, for his part, addresses the question of orality and writing from another angle: "I mean that it's precisely writing, and it alone, that allows me, like everyone else, to establish a thought" (28).

⁷ See Clément Rosset's discouraging remarks in *Le Choix des mots:* "And I would add this aggravating consideration, regarding writing in general, that writing offers the additional inconvenience of being a job that is both totally useless and totally exhausting [. . .]. That's why writing, like any form of creation, is not only the vainest of tasks, but also, and this is the last straw, the most laborious and the most arduous. [. . .] Given the range of all conceivable jobs, difficult perhaps but more or less necessary and more or less well paid, the job of writing seems like supplementary and unpaid work" (10-11).

⁸ See also *Loiterature* 8-9: "A reason I'm interested in loiterly literature, then, is that it has this characteristic of the trivial: It blurs categories, and in particular it blurs those of innocent pleasure taking and harmless relaxation and not-so-innocent 'intent'—a certain recalcitrance to the laws that maintain 'good order.' In so doing, it carries an implied social criticism. It casts serious doubt on the values good citizens hold dear—values like discipline, method, organization, rationality, productivity, and, above all, work—but it does so in the guise of innocent and, more particularly, insignificant or frivolous entertainment: a mere passing of the time in idle observations or witty remarks, now this, now that, like the philosopher pursuing his ideas as he sits daydreaming on his bench."

BIBLIOGRAPHY

Ammouche-Kremers, Michèle. "Entretien avec Jean-Philippe Toussaint." In *Jeunes Auteurs de Minuit*. Ed. Michèle Ammouche-Kremers and Henk Hillenaar. Amsterdam: Rodopi, 1994. 27-35.

——, and Henk Hillenaar, eds. *Jeunes Auteurs de Minuit*. Amsterdam: Rodopi, 1994.

Atack, Margaret, and Phil Powrie, eds. *Contemporary French Fiction by Women: Feminist Perspectives*. Manchester: Manchester University Press, 1990.

Barth, John. *The Friday Book, or, Book-Titles Should Be Straightforward and Subtitles Avoided*. New York: Putnam, 1984.

Barthes, Roland. "Analyse textuelle d'un conte d'Edgar Poe." In Claude Chabrol, ed. *Sémiotique narrative et textuelle*. Paris: Larousse, 1973. 29-54.

——. *S/Z*. Paris: Seuil, 1970. (*S/Z*. Trans. Richard Miller. New York: Hill and Wang, 1974.)

Bertho, Sophie. "Jean-Philippe Toussaint et la métaphysique." In *Jeunes Auteurs de Minuit*. Ed. Michèle Ammouche-Kremers and Henk Hillenaar. Amsterdam: Rodopi, 1994. 15-25.

Bessard-Banquy, Olivier. "Chevillard écrivain." *Critique* 559 (1993): 893-905.

——. "Eric Chevillard: Un écrivain à découvrir." *Le Français dans le Monde* 282 (1996): 47-50.

——. "Une Littérature du trou noir." *Critique* 571 (1994): 975-81.

Blanchot, Maurice. "L'Interruption." *Nouvelle Revue Française* 137 (1964): 869-81.

Blanckeman, Bruno. "Sans domicile de fiction: Echenoz SDF." *Critique* 607 (1997): 904-16.

Bounoure, Gabriel. *Edmond Jabès: La demeure et le livre*. Montpellier: Fata Morgana, 1984.

Bridgeman, Teresa. *Negotiating the New in the French Novel: Building Contexts for Fictional Worlds*. London and New York: Routledge, 1998.

Caillois, Roger. *Les Jeux et les hommes: Le masque et le vertige*. 1958. Rev. ed. Paris: Gallimard, 1967.

Caldwell, Roy C. "Jean-Philippe Toussaint." In *The Contemporary Novel in France*. Ed. William Thompson. Gainesville: University Press of Florida, 1995. 369-82.

Calvino, Italo. *Six Memos for the Next Millennium*. Trans. Patrick Creagh. Cambridge: Harvard University Press, 1988.

Camus, Albert. *L'Etranger*. 1942. Paris: Gallimard, 1982. (*The Stranger*. Trans. Stuart Gilbert. New York: Knopf, 1946.)

———. *La Peste*. Paris: Gallimard, 1947. (*The Plague*. Trans. Stuart Gilbert. New York: Knopf, 1948.)

Cellard, Jacques, and Alain Rey. *Dictionnaire du français non-conventionnel*. Paris: Hachette, 1980.

Chambers, Ross. *Loiterature*. Lincoln: University of Nebraska Press, 1999.

———. *Room for Maneuver: Reading (the) Oppositional (in) Narrative*. Chicago: University of Chicago Press, 1991.

Chamisso, Adelbert von. *Peter Schlemiel*. 1814. Trans. Peter Wortsman. New York: Fromm, 1993.

Charpentier, Josane. *La Sorcellerie en Pays Basque*. Paris: Librairie Guénégaud, 1977.

Chevillard, Eric. *Les Absences du Capitaine Cook*. Paris: Minuit, 2001.

———. *Au plafond*. Paris: Minuit, 1997. (*On the Ceiling*. Trans. Jordan Stump. Lincoln: University of Nebraska Press, 2000.)

———. *Le Caoutchouc décidément*. Paris: Minuit, 1992.

———. *Le Démarcheur*. Paris: Minuit, 1988.

———. *Du hérisson*. Paris: Minuit, 2002.

———. *Un Fantôme*. Paris: Minuit, 1995.

———. *Mourir m'enrhume*. Paris: Minuit, 1987.

———. *La Nébuleuse du crabe*. Paris: Minuit, 1993. (*The Crab Nebula*. Trans. Jordan Stump and Eleanor Hardin. Lincoln: University of Nebraska Press, 1997.)

———. *L'Oeuvre posthume de Thomas Pilaster*. Paris: Minuit, 1999.

———. *Palafox*. Paris: Minuit, 1990.

———. *Préhistoire*. Paris: Minuit, 1994.

Cloonan, William. "Jean Echenoz." In *The Contemporary Novel in France*. Ed. William Thompson. Gainesville: University Press of Florida, 1995. 200-14.

Dällenbach, Lucien. *Le Récit spéculaire: Essai sur la mise en abyme*. Paris: Seuil, 1977. (*The Mirror in the Text*. Trans. Jeremy Whiteley and Emma Hughes. Chicago: University of Chicago Press, 1989.)

Debord, Guy. *La Société du spectacle*. Paris: Buchet/Chastel, 1967. (*The Society of the Specatcle*. New York: Zone Books, 1994.)

Delannoi, Gil. "Cruel Zénon." *Critique* 463 (1985): 1198-1200.

Derrida, Jacques. *L'Ecriture et la différence*. Paris: Seuil, 1967. (*Writing and Difference*. Trans. Alan Bass. Chicago: University of Chicago Press, 1978.)

———. *Le Monolinguisme de l'autre, ou, La Prothèse d'origine*. Paris: Galilée, 1996. (*The Monolingualism of the Other, or, The Prosthesis of Origin*. Trans. Patrick Mensah. Stanford: Stanford University Press, 1998.)

Dubois, Claude, ed. *Petit Larousse en couleurs*. Paris: Larousse, 1972.

Duras, Marguerite. *L'Amant*. Paris: Minuit, 1984. (*The Lover*. Trans. Barbara Bray. New York: Pantheon, 1985.)

Echenoz, Jean. *Un An*. Paris : Minuit, 1997.

———. *Cherokee*. Paris : Minuit, 1983. (*Cherokee*. Trans. Mark Polizzotti. Lincoln: University of Nebraska Press, 1994.)

———. *L'Equipée malaise*. Paris : Minuit, 1986. (*Double Jeopardy*. Trans. Mark Polizzotti. Lincoln: University of Nebraska Press, 1993.)

———. *Les Grandes Blondes*. Paris : Minuit, 1995. (*Big Blondes*. Trans. Mark Polizzotti. New York: New Press, 1998.)

———. *Je m'en vais*. Paris: Minuit, 1999. (*I'm Gone*. Trans. Mark Polizzotti. New York: New Press, 2001.)

———. *Jérôme Lindon*. Paris: Minuit, 2001.

———. *Lac.* Paris : Minuit, 1989. (*Lake.* Trans. Guido Waldman. London: Harvill, 1998; American translation by Mark Polizzotti forthcoming.)

———. *Le Méridien de Greenwich.* Paris : Minuit, 1979.

———. *Nous trois.* Paris : Minuit, 1992.

———. *L'Occupation des sols.* Paris : Minuit, 1988. (*Plan of Occupancy.* Trans. Mark Polizzotti. Paris and London: Alyscamps Press, 1995.)

Ehrmann, Jacques. "*Homo Ludens* Revisited." Trans. Cathy and Phil Lewis. In Jacques Ehrmann, ed., *Game, Play, Literature.* Boston: Beacon, 1971. 31-57.

Fauvel, Maryse. "Jean-Philippe Toussaint et la photographie: *Exposer* le roman." *Romance Languages Annual* 6 (1994): 38-42.

Fisher, Dominique. "Les Non-lieux de Jean-Philippe Toussaint: Bricol(l)age textuel et rhétorique du neutre." *University of Toronto Quarterly* 65.4 (1996): 618-31.

Fitch, Brian. *The Narcissistic Text: A Reading of Camus' Fiction.* Toronto: University of Toronto Press, 1982.

Forêts, Louis-René des. *Le Bavard.* Paris: Gallimard, 1946.

Foucault, Michel. *Discipline and Punish: The Birth of the Prison.* 1975. Trans. Alan Sheridan. New York: Pantheon, 1977.

Friedman, Melvin. "The Schlemiel: Jew and Non-Jew." *Studies in the Literary Imagination* 9.1 (1976): 139-53.

Gide, André. *Les Faux-monnayeurs.* Paris: Gallimard, 1925. (*The Counterfeiters.* Trans. Dorothy Bussy. New York: Modern Library, 1931.)

Gilman, Sander. *Inscribing the Other.* Lincoln: University of Nebraska Press, 1991.

Goffman, Erving. *Asylums: Essays on the Social Situation of Mental Patients and Other Inmates.* New York: Anchor, 1961.

Guglielmi, Joseph. *La Ressemblance impossible: Edmond Jabès.* Paris: Les Editeurs Français Réunis, 1978.

Hassan, Ihab. *Radical Innocence: Studies in the Contemporary American Novel.* New York: Harper and Row, 1966.

Hippolyte, Jean-Louis. "Chevillard's Aleatory World: Toward a French Postexotic Literature." *Cincinnati Romance Review* 15 (1996): 27-34.

Houppermans, Sjef. "Pleins et trous dans l'oeuvre de Jean Echenoz." In *Jeunes*

Auteurs de Minuit. Ed. Michèle Ammouche-Kremers and Henk Hillenaar. Amsterdam: Rodopi, 1994. 77-94.

Huizinga, Johan. *Homo Ludens: A Study of the Play-Element in Culture.* 1938. Boston: Beacon, 1955.

Hutcheon, Linda. *Narcissistic Narrative: The Metafictional Paradox.* New York and London: Methuen, 1984.

Isle, Walter. "Acts of Willful Play." Gerald Guinness and Andrew Hurley, eds. *Auctor Ludens: Essays on Play in Literature.* Philadelphia and Amsterdam: Benjamins, 1986. 63-74.

Jouet, Jacques. *Actes de la machine ronde.* Paris: Julliard, 1994.

———. *Actes du jésus.* Paris: Editions du Paon-Saint-André, 2001.

———. *Annette et l'Etna.* Paris: Stock, 2001.

———. *Les Annexes de l'oeil.* Antibes: Editions Anna Tanaquilli, 1997.

———. *L'Anse.* Paris: Editions du Limon, 1988.

———. *Un Art simple et tout d'exécution.* Belfort: Circé, 2001. With Marcel Bénabou, Harry Mathews, and Jacques Roubaud.

———. *La Bibliothèque de Poitiers.* Poitiers: La Licorne, 1999. With Michelle Grangaud and Jacques Roubaud.

———. *La Bibliothèque oulipienne.* Vol. 2. Paris: Ramsay, 1987. 4 vols. to date. 1981-. With Oulipo.

———. *La Bibliothèque oulipienne.* Vol. 3. Paris: Seghers, 1990. 4 vols. to date. 1981-. With Oulipo.

———. *La Bibliothèque oulipienne.* Vol. 4. Bordeaux: Le Castor Astral, 1997. 4 vols. to date. 1981-. With Oulipo.

———. *Le Bestiaire inconstant.* Paris: Ramsay, 1983.

———. *Castel del Monte ou l'octagone.* Bari: Mario Adda, 1999. With Nicola Amato.

———. *107 Ames.* Paris: Ramsay, 1991.

———. *Ce que rapporte l'Envoyé.* Illkirch: Le Verger, 1999.

———. *Une Chambre close.* Paris: Bibliothèque Oulipienne 78, 1996.

———. *Le Chant d'amour grand-singe.* Paris: Bibliothèque Oulipienne 62, 1993.

———. *Le Chantier.* Paris: Editions du Limon, 1993.

———. *Des ans et des ânes.* Paris: Ramsay, 1988.

———. *Le Directeur du Musée des Cadeaux des Chefs d'Etat de l'Etranger.* Paris:

Seuil, 1994.

———. *Echelle et papillons: Le pantoum.* Paris: Les Belles Lettres, 1998.

———. *L'Eclipse.* Paris: Bibliothèque Oulipienne 28, 1984.

———. *Espions.* Paris: Bibliothèque Oulipienne 44, 1990.

———. *L'Evasion de Rochefort.* Saint-Quentin: Festival de la Nouvelle, 1997.

———. *Exercices de la mémoire.* Paris: Bibliothèque Oulipienne 82, 1996.

———. *Fins.* Paris: POL, 1999.

———. *Frise du métro parisien.* Paris: Bibliothèque Oulipienne 97, 1998. With Pierre Rosenstiehl.

———. *Glose de la Comtesse de Die et de Didon.* Paris: Bibliothèque Oulipienne 56,1992.

———. *Guerre froide, mère froide.* Villelongue d'Aude: Atelier du Gué, 1978.

———. *Hinterreise et autres histoires retournées.* Paris: Bibliothèque Oulipienne 108, 1999.

———. *Histoire de Paul Gauguin et de son divan.* Paris: Editions Plurielle, 1996.

———. *Kayserberg.* Paris: Editions Plurielle, 1997. With Claudine Capdeville, Pierre Laurent, and Georges Kolebka.

———. *Monostication de La Fontaine.* Paris: Bibliothèque Oulipienne 72,1995.

———. *La Montagne R.* Paris: Seuil, 1996. (*Mountain R.* Trans. Brian Evenson. Normal: Dalkey Archive Press, 2003.)

———. *Morceaux de théêtre.* Paris: Editions du Limon, 1997.

———. *Les Mots du corps dans les expressions de la langue française.* Paris: Larousse, 1990.

———. *Muséification de Notre Dame.* Paris: Editions Plurielle, 1997.

———. *Navet, linge, oeil-de-vieux.* 3 vols. Paris: POL, 1998.

———. *Nos Vaches.* Bordeaux: L'Attente, 2001.

———. *Obernai.* Paris: Chez l'Auteur, 1999.

———. *L'Oulipien démasqué.* Paris: Bibliothèque Oulipienne 38, 1990.

———. *Pauline (polyne).* Paris: Bibliothèque Oulipienne 93, 1997.

———. *Poèmes avec partenaires.* Paris: POL, 2002.

———. *Poèmes de métro.* Paris: POL, 2000.

———. *Le Point de vue de l'escargot.* Strasbourg: L'Alsace and Le Verger, 1994.

———. *14 Réguliers comprenant leur désir.* Paris: Saint-Germain-des-Près, 1978.

———. *Une Réunion pour le nettoiement.* Paris: POL, 2001.

———. *Qui s'endort*. Remoulins-sur-Gardon: Editions Jacques Brémond, 1988.

———. *Raymond Queneau*. Lyon: La Manufacture, 1988.

———. *La Redonde*. Paris: Bibliothèque Oulipienne 107, 1999.

———. *La République de Meq-Ouyes*. Paris: POL, 2001.

———. *La République romaine*. Paris: Collection Afat Voyages, 1997.

———. *Romillats*. Paris: Ramsay, 1986.

———. *Sauvage*. Paris: Autrement, 2001.

———. *La Scène est sur la scène*. Paris: Editions du Limon, 1994.

———. *La Scène usurpée*. Monaco: Editions du Rocher, 1997.

———. *[ə]*. Paris: Bibliothèque Oulipienne 64, 1993. With Jacques Roubaud.

———. *Les Sept Règles de Perec*. Paris: Bibliothèque Oulipienne 52, 1990.

———. *La Voix qui les faisait toutes*. Montreuil, Roubaix, Lille: V.O. Editions, TEC/CRIAC, Sansonnet, 1999.

Jourde, Pierre. "Les Petits Mondes à l'envers d'Eric Chevillard." *Nouvelle Revue Française* 486-487 (1993): 204-17.

Jullien, Dominique. "Jean Echenoz." In *After the Age of Suspicion: The French Novel Today*. Ed. Charles A. Porter. Spec. issue of *Yale French Studies* (1988): 337-41.

Laurent, Eric. *Les Atomiques*. Paris: Minuit, 1996.

———. *Coup de foudre*. Paris: Minuit, 1995.

———. *Dehors*. Paris: Minuit, 2000.

———. *Liquider*. Paris: Minuit, 1997.

———. *Ne pas toucher*. Paris: Minuit, 2002.

———. *Remue-ménage*. Paris: Minuit, 1999.

Lê, Linda. *Les Aubes*. Paris: Bourgois, 2000.

———. *Autres Jeux avec le feu*. Paris: Bourgois, 2002.

———. *Calomnies*. Paris: Bourgois, 1993. (*Slander*. Trans. Esther Allen. Lincoln: University of Nebraska Press, 1996.)

———. *Les Dits d'un idiot*. Paris: Bourgois, 1995.

———. *Les Evangiles du crime*. Paris: Julliard, 1992.

———. *Fuir*. Paris: La Table Ronde, 1988.

———. *Lettre morte*. Paris: Bourgois, 1999.

———. *Marina Tsvétaïeva: Comment ça va la vie?* Paris: Jean-Michel Place, 2002.

——. *Un si tendre vampire.* Paris: La Table Ronde, 1987.

——. *Solo.* Paris: La Table Ronde, 1989.

——. *Les Trois Parques.* Paris: Bourgois, 1997.

——, ed. *Tu écriras sur le bonheur.* Paris: PUF, 1999.

——. *Voix: Une crise.* Paris: Bourgois, 1998.

Leclerc, Yvan. "Abstraction faite." *Critique* 510 (1989): 889-902.

——. "Autour de Minuit." *Dalhousie French Studies* 17 (1989): 63-74.

Le Clézio, J. M. G. *Balaabilou.* Paris: Gallimard, 1985.

——. *Celui qui n'avait jamais vu la mer, suivi de La Montagne du dieu vivant.* Paris: Gallimard, 1984.

——. *Le Chercheur d'or.* Paris: Gallimard, 1985. (*The Prospector.* Trans. Carol Marks. Boston: Godine, 1993.)

——. *Coeur brûle et autres romances.* Paris: Gallimard, 2001.

——. *Le Déluge.* Paris: Gallimard, 1966. (*Flood.* Trans. Peter Green. London: Hamilton, 1967.)

——. *Désert.* Paris: Gallimard, 1980.

——. *Etoile errante.* Paris: Gallimard, 1992.

——. *L'Extase matérielle.* Paris: Gallimard, 1967.

——. *La Fête chantée.* Paris: Gallimard, 1997.

——. *La Fièvre.* Paris: Gallimard, 1965. (*Fever.* Trans. Daphne Woodward. New York: Atheneum, 1966.)

——. *Les Géants.* Paris: Gallimard, 1973. (*The Giants.* Trans. Simon Watson Taylor. New York: Atheneum, 1975.)

——. *Gens des nuages.* With Jemia Le Clézio. Paris: Stock, 1997.

——. *La Grande Vie, suivi de Peuple du ciel.* Paris: Gallimard, 1990.

——. *La Guerre.* Paris: Gallimard, 1970. (*War.* Trans. Simon Watson Taylor. London: Cape, 1973.)

——. *Haï.* Geneva: Skira, 1971.

——. *Hasard, suivi de Angoli Mala.* Paris: Gallimard, 1999.

——. *L'Inconnu de la terre.* Paris: Gallimard, 1978.

——. *Le Jour où Beaumont fit connaissance avec sa douleur.* Paris: Mercure de France, 1964.

——. *Le Livre des fuites, roman d'aventures.* Paris: Gallimard, 1969. (*The Book of Flights: An Adventure Story.* Trans. Simon Watson Taylor. New York:

Atheneum, 1971.)

———. *Lullaby.* Paris: Gallimard, 1980.

———. *Mondo et autres histoires.* Paris: Gallimard, 1978.

———. *Mydriase.* Montpellier: Fata Morgana, 1973.

———. *Onitsha.* Paris: Gallimard, 1991. (*Onitsha.* Trans. Alison Anderson. Lincoln: University of Nebraska Press, 1997.)

———. *Pawana.* Paris: Gallimard, 1992.

———. *Poisson d'or.* Paris: Gallimard, 1997.

———. *Printemps et autres saisons.* Paris: Gallimard, 1989.

———. *Le Procès-verbal.* Paris: Gallimard, 1963. (*The Interrogation.* Trans. Daphne Woodward. New York: Atheneum, 1964.)

———. *La Quarantaine.* Paris: Gallimard, 1995.

———. *Le Rêve mexicain, ou La Pensée interrompue.* Paris: Gallimard, 1988. (*The Mexican Dream, or, The Interrupted Thought of Amerindian Civilizations.* Trans. Teresa Lavender. Chicago: University of Chicago Press, 1993.)

———. *La Ronde et autres faits divers.* Paris: Gallimard, 1982. (*The Round and Other Cold Hard Facts.* Trans. C. Dickson. Lincoln: University of Nebraska Press, 2002.)

———. *Terra amata.* Paris: Gallimard, 1967. (*Terra Amata.* Trans. Barbara Bray. London: Hamilton, 1969.)

———. *Vers les icebergs.* Montpellier: Fata Morgana, 1978.

———. *Villa Aurore, suivi de Orlamonde.* Paris: Gallimard, 1985.

———. *Visages de femmes.* Bourg-en-Bresse: Entailles, 1987.

———. *Voyage à Rodrigues: Journal.* Paris: Gallimard, 1986.

———. *Voyage au pays des arbres.* Paris: Gallimard, 1986.

———. *Voyages de l'autre côté.* Paris: Gallimard, 1975.

Lepape, Pierre. "Pour raconter cette époque." *Le Monde* 24 March 1990: 34.

Mann, Thomas. "The Making of *The Magic Mountain.*" In *The Magic Mountain.* Trans. H. T. Lowe-Porter. New York: Vintage, 1969. 717-27.

Mansion, J. E., ed. *Harrap's New Shorter French and English Dictionary.* Paris: Bordas, 1974.

Marks, Joseph, ed. *Harrap's French-English Dictionary of Slang and Colloquialisms.* Paris: Bordas, 1975.

Martin du Gard, Roger. *Les Thibault.* 11 vols. Paris: Gallimard, 1922-1940. (*The Thibaults.* Trans. Stuart Gilbert. New York: Viking, 1939.)

Mathews, Harry. *20 Lines a Day.* Elmwood Park, Ill.: Dalkey Archive, 1988.

Michelet, Jules. *La Sorcière.* 1862. Paris: Julliard, 1964.

Molia, François-Xavier. *Fourbi.* Paris: Gallimard, 2000.

Motte, Warren. *Playtexts: Ludics in Contemporary Literature.* Lincoln: University of Nebraska Press, 1995.

———. "A Soulful Jouet." *Neophilologus* 78 (1994): 549-59.

———. "Toussaint's Small World." *Romanic Review* 86.4 (1995): 747-60.

Moudileno, Lydie. "Délits, détours et affabulation: L'écriture de l'anathème dans *En famille* de Marie NDiaye." *French Review* 71.3 (1998): 442-53.

NDiaye, Marie. *Comédie classique.* Paris: Minuit, 1987.

———. *La Diablesse et son enfant.* Paris: L'Ecole des Loisirs, 2000.

———. *En famille.* Paris: Minuit, 1990. (*Among Family.* Trans. Heather Dougal. Tunbridge Wells: Angela Royal, 1997.)

———. *La Femme changée en bûche.* Paris: Minuit, 1989.

———. *Hilda.* Paris: Minuit, 1999.

———. *La Naufragée.* Charenton: Flohic, 1999.

———. *Quant au riche avenir.* Paris: Minuit, 1985.

———. *Rosie Carpe.* Paris: Minuit, 2001.

———. *La Sorcière.* Paris: Minuit, 1996.

———. *Un Temps de saison.* Paris: Minuit, 1994.

Nietzsche, Friedrich. *Ecce Homo.* Trans. and ed. Walter Kaufmann. New York: Vintage, 1967.

Oster, Christian. *L'Aventure.* Paris: Minuit, 1993.

———. *Dans le train.* Paris: Minuit, 2002.

———. *Une Femme de ménage.* Paris: Minuit, 2001. (*A Cleaning Woman.* Trans. Mark Polizzotti. New York: Other Press, 2003.)

———. *Loin d'Odile.* Paris: Minuit, 1998.

———. *Mon grand appartement.* Paris: Minuit, 1999. (*My Big Apartment.* Trans. Jordan Stump. Lincoln: University of Nebraska Press, 2002.)

———. *Paul au téléphone.* Paris: Minuit, 1996.

———. *Le Pique-nique.* Paris: Minuit, 1997.

———. *Le Pont d'Arcueil.* Paris: Minuit, 1994.

————. *Volley-ball*. Paris: Minuit, 1989.

Perec, Georges. *La Disparition*. Paris: Denoël, 1969. (*A Void*. Trans. Gilbert Adair. London: Harvill, 1995.)

————. *Un Homme qui dort*. Paris: Denoël, 1967. (*A Man Asleep*. Trans. Andrew Leak. In *Things: A Story of the Sixties and A Man Asleep*. Boston: Godine, 1990.)

————. *Penser / Classer*. Paris: Hachette, 1985.

————. *W ou le souvenir d'enfance*. Paris: Denoël, 1975. (*W or The Memory of Childhood*. Trans. David Bellos. Boston: Godine, 1988.)

Picard, Michel. *La Lecture comme jeu: Essai sur la littérature*. Paris: Minuit, 1986.

Pobel, Didier. "'Un long voyage' dans l'immobilité du regard: Variations autour d'*Onitsha* et de quelques autres livres de J. M. G. Le Clézio." *Nouvelle Revue Française* 464 (1991): 76-80.

Prince, Gerald. "L'Appareil récit de Jean-Philippe Toussaint." In *Discontinuity and Fragmentation*. Ed. Freeman Henry. Amsterdam: Rodopi, 1994. 109-14.

————. *A Dictionary of Narratology*. Lincoln: University of Nebraska Press, 1987.

————. *Narrative as Theme: Studies in French Fiction*. Lincoln: University of Nebraska Press, 1992.

Queneau, Raymond. *Zazie dans le métro*. Paris: Gallimard, 1959. (*Zazie*. Trans. Barbara Wright. New York: Harper, 1960.)

Quignard, Pascal. *Le Nom sur le bout de la langue*. Paris: POL, 1993.

Reid, Martine. "Echenoz en malfaiteur léger." *Critique* 547 (1992): 988-94.

Rey, Alain, ed. *Dictionnaire historique de la langue française*. Paris: Robert, 1992.

Rey, Alain and Josette Rey-Debove, eds. *Le Petit Robert*. Paris: Robert, 1991.

Robbe-Grillet, Alain. *Dans le labyrinthe*. Paris: Minuit, 1959. (*In the Labyrinth*. Trans. Christine Brooke-Rose. London: Calder, 1980.)

Roche, Maurice. *Circus*. Paris: Seuil, 1972.

————. *Codex*. Paris: Seuil, 1974.

————. *Compact*. Paris: Seuil, 1966.

Rosen, Norma. *Joy to Levine!* New York: Curtis Books, 1961.

Rosset, Clément. *Le Choix des mots*. Paris: Minuit, 1995.

Roubaud, Jacques. *La Pluralité des mondes de Lewis*. Paris: Gallimard, 1991. (*The Plurality of Worlds of Lewis*. Trans. Rosmarie Waldrop. Normal: Dalkey Archive Press, 1995.)

Said, Edward W. *Culture and Imperialism*. New York: Knopf, 1993.

———. *Representations of the Intellectual*. New York: Pantheon, 1994.

Salvayre, Lydie. *Les Belles Ames*. Paris: Seuil, 2000.

———. *La Compagnie des spectres*. Paris: Seuil, 1997.

———. *La Conférence de Cintegabelle*. Paris: Seuil/Verticales, 1999.

———. *Contre*. Paris: Verticales, 2002.

———. *La Déclaration*. Paris: Julliard, 1990. Paris: Verticales, 1997.

———. *Et que les vers mangent le boeuf mort*. Paris: Verticales, 2002.

———. *La Médaille*. Paris: Seuil, 1993. (*The Award*. Trans. Jane Davey. New York: Four Walls Eight Windows, 1997.)

———. *La Puissance des mouches*. Paris: Seuil, 1995.

———. *Quelques Conseils utiles aux élèves huissiers*. Paris: Verticales, 1997.

———. *La Vie commune*. Paris: Julliard, 1991. Paris: Verticales, 1999.

———. *Le Vif du vivant: Picasso carnet de 1964*. Paris: Editions Cercle d'Art, 2001.

Saporta, Marc. *Composition no. 1*. Paris: Seuil, 1962.

Sartre, Jean-Paul. *La Nausée*. Paris: Gallimard, 1938. (*Nausea*. Trans. Lloyd Alexander. Norfolk: New Directions, 1949.)

Schoots, Fieke. *Passer en douce à la douane: L'écriture minimaliste de Minuit: Deville, Echenoz, Redonnet et Toussaint*. Amsterdam: Rodopi, 1997.

Spivak, Gayatri Chakravorty. *In Other Worlds: Essays in Cultural Politics*. New York and London: Methuen, 1987.

Taminiaux, Pierre. "Images de la dépossession: Jean-Philippe Toussaint et Christian Boltanski." *Dalhousie French Studies* 32 (1995): 87-100.

Teko-Agbo, K. Ambroise. "*En famille* or the Problem of Alterity." Trans. Ruthmarie H. Mitsch. *Research in African Literatures* 26.2 (1995): 158-68.

Thompson, William, ed. *The Contemporary Novel in France*. Gainesville: University Press of Florida, 1995.

Toussaint, Jean-Philippe. *L'Appareil-photo*. Paris: Minuit, 1988.

———. *Autoportrait (à l'étranger)*. Paris: Minuit, 2000.

———. *Faire l'amour*. Paris: Minuit, 2002.

———. *Monsieur*. Paris: Minuit, 1986. (*Monsieur*. Trans. John Lambert. New York: Marion Boyars, 1991.)

———. *La Réticence*. Paris: Minuit, 1991.

———. *La Salle de bain*. Paris: Minuit, 1985. (*The Bathroom*. Trans. Nancy Amphoux and Paul De Angelis. New York: Dutton, 1990.)

———. *La Télévision*. Paris: Minuit, 1997.

Trinh, Minh-ha T. *Woman, Native, Other: Writing Postcoloniality and Feminism*. Bloomington: University of Indiana Press, 1989.

Unwin, Timothy, ed. *The Cambridge Companion to the French Novel*. Cambridge: Cambridge University Press, 1997.

Westphal, Bertrand. "Le Quadrillage de l'arène: Temps et histoire chez Jean-Philippe Toussaint." *Versants: Revue Suisse des Littératures Romanes* 25 (1994): 117-30.

Yeager, Jack. "Culture, Citizenship, Nation: The Narrative Texts of Linda Lê." Alec Hargreaves and Mark McKinney, eds. *Post-Colonial Cultures in France*. London and New York: Routledge, 1997. 255-67.

∾

INDEX

Warren Motte chairs the Department of French and Italian at the University of Colorado, Boulder, where he specializes in contemporary writing and focuses particularly on experimental works that challenge conventional notions of literary form. He has written *The Poetics of Experiment: A Study of the Work of Georges Perec, Questioning Edmond Jabès, Playtexts: Ludics in Contemporary Literature,* and *Small Worlds: Minimalism in Contemporary French Literature.* Translator and editor of *Oulipo: A Primer of Potential Literature,* he has also edited an issue of the journal *SubStance* dedicated to the work of Jacques Jouet, and is a contributing editor to *CONTEXT* magazine.

SELECTED DALKEY ARCHIVE PAPERBACKS

FOR A FULL LIST OF PUBLICATIONS, VISIT:
www.dalkeyarchive.com

SELECTED DALKEY ARCHIVE PAPERBACKS

CAROLE MASO, *AVA*.
LADISLAV MATEJKA AND KRYSTYNA POMORSKA, EDS.,
  Readings in Russian Poetics: Formalist and Structuralist Views.
HARRY MATHEWS, *Cigarettes*.
  The Conversions.
  The Human Country: New and Collected Stories.
  The Journalist.
  Singular Pleasures.
  The Sinking of the Odradek Stadium.
  Tlooth.
  20 Lines a Day.
ROBERT L. McLAUGHLIN, ED.,
  Innovations: An Anthology of Modern & Contemporary Fiction.
STEVEN MILLHAUSER, *The Barnum Museum.*
  In the Penny Arcade.
OLIVE MOORE, *Spleen*.
NICHOLAS MOSLEY, *Accident*.
  Assassins.
  Catastrophe Practice.
  Children of Darkness and Light.
  The Hesperides Tree.
  Hopeful Monsters.
  Imago Bird.
  Impossible Object.
  Judith.
  Natalie Natalia.
  Serpent.
WARREN F. MOTTE, JR.,
  Oulipo: A Primer of Potential Literature.
YVES NAVARRE, *Our Share of Time.*
WILFRIDO D. NOLLEDO, *But for the Lovers.*
FLANN O'BRIEN, *At Swim-Two-Birds.*
  The Best of Myles.
  The Dalkey Archive.
  Further Cuttings.
  The Hard Life.
  The Poor Mouth.
  The Third Policeman.
CLAUDE OLLIER, *The Mise-en-Scène.*
FERNANDO DEL PASO, *Palinuro of Mexico.*
RAYMOND QUENEAU, *The Last Days.*
  Odile.
  Pierrot Mon Ami.
  Saint Glinglin.
ANN QUIN, *Berg*.
  Passages.
  Three.
  Tripticks.
ISHMAEL REED, *The Free-Lance Pallbearers.*
  The Last Days of Louisiana Red.
  Reckless Eyeballing.
  The Terrible Threes.
  The Terrible Twos.
  Yellow Back Radio Broke-Down.

JULIÁN RÍOS, *Poundemonium*.
AUGUSTO ROA BASTOS, *I the Supreme.*
JACQUES ROUBAUD, *The Great Fire of London.*
  Hortense in Exile.
  Hortense Is Abducted.
  The Plurality of Worlds of Lewis.
  The Princess Hoppy.
  Some Thing Black.
LEON S. ROUDIEZ, *French Fiction Revisited.*
LUIS RAFAEL SÁNCHEZ, *Macho Camacho's Beat.*
SEVERO SARDUY, *Cobra & Maitreya.*
ARNO SCHMIDT, *Collected Stories.*
  Nobodaddy's Children.
CHRISTINE SCHUTT, *Nightwork*.
JUNE AKERS SEESE,
  Is This What Other Women Feel, Too?
  What Waiting Really Means.
AURELIE SHEEHAN, *Jack Kerouac Is Pregnant.*
VIKTOR SHKLOVSKY, *Theory of Prose.*
  Third Factory.
  Zoo, or Letters Not about Love.
JOSEF ŠKVORECKÝ,
  The Engineer of Human Souls.
CLAUDE SIMON, *The Invitation.*
GILBERT SORRENTINO, *Aberration of Starlight.*
  Blue Pastoral.
  Crystal Vision.
  Imaginative Qualities of Actual Things.
  Mulligan Stew.
  Pack of Lies.
  The Sky Changes.
  Something Said.
  Splendide-Hôtel.
  Steelwork.
  Under the Shadow.
W. M. SPACKMAN, *The Complete Fiction.*
GERTRUDE STEIN, *Lucy Church Amiably.*
  The Making of Americans.
  A Novel of Thank You.
PIOTR SZEWC, *Annihilation*.
ESTHER TUSQUETS, *Stranded*.
LUISA VALENZUELA, *He Who Searches.*
PAUL WEST, *Words for a Deaf Daughter* and *Gala*.
CURTIS WHITE, *Memories of My Father Watching TV.*
  Monstrous Possibility.
  Requiem.
DIANE WILLIAMS, *Excitability: Selected Stories.*
  Romancer Erector.
DOUGLAS WOOLF, *Wall to Wall.*
  Ya! & John-Juan.
PHILIP WYLIE, *Generation of Vipers.*
MARGUERITE YOUNG, *Angel in the Forest.*
  Miss MacIntosh, My Darling.
REYOUNG, *Unbabbling*.
LOUIS ZUKOFSKY, *Collected Fiction.*
SCOTT ZWIREN, *God Head.*

FOR A FULL LIST OF PUBLICATIONS, VISIT:
www.dalkeyarchive.com

4446

AEF-7993